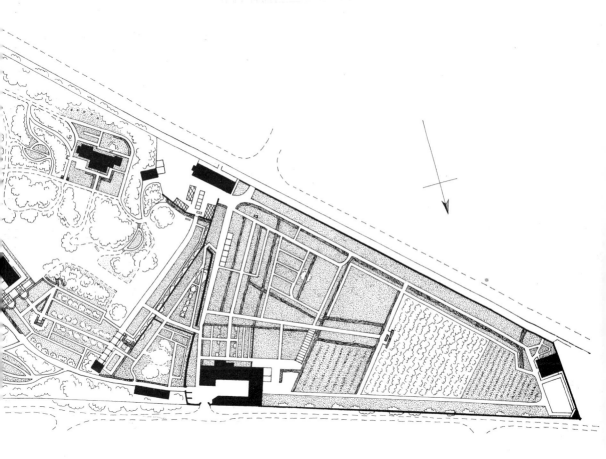

Gertrude
JEKYLL

at

MUNSTEAD WOOD

Writing · Horticulture
Photography · Homebuilding

Lilium auratum *in Tank Garden at Munstead Wood, 1906 (CED–UC Berkeley)*

Gertrude JEKYLL
at
MUNSTEAD WOOD

Writing · *Horticulture*
Photography · *Homebuilding*

JUDITH B. TANKARD
and
MARTIN A. WOOD

Foreword by GRAHAM STUART THOMAS

SUTTON PUBLISHING

SAGAPRESS, INC.

First published in 1996 by
Sutton Publishing Limited · Phoenix Mill
Thrupp · Stroud · Gloucestershire · GL5 2BU

Sagapress, Inc.
PO Box 21 · Sagaponack Road · Sagaponack · New York

British Library Cataloguing in Publication Data
A catalogue record for this book is available from the British Library

ISBN 0-7509-0672-3

Library of Congress Cataloging-in-Publication Data

Tankard, Judith B.
    Gertrude Jekyll at Munstead Wood: writing, horticulture, photography,
homebuilding/Judith B. Tankard and Martin A. Wood.
        p.   cm.
    Includes bibliographical references and index.
    ISBN 0-89831-046-6
    1. Munstead Wood Gardens (England) 2. Jekyll, Gertrude,
1843–1932—Homes and haunts—England—Surrey. I. Wood, Martin A.,
1959–   . II. Title.
SB466.G8M868 1996
712' .092—dc20
                                                                95–49094
                                                                CIP

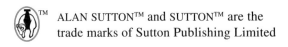 ALAN SUTTON™ and SUTTON™ are the
trade marks of Sutton Publishing Limited

Typeset in 11/12 Ehrhardt.
Typesetting and origination by
Sutton Publishing Limited.
Printed in Great Britain by
Butler & Tanner, Frome, Somerset.

Contents

List of Illustrations		vii
Foreword *by Graham Stuart Thomas*		xi
Acknowledgements		xiv
Introduction		1
1.	*A Walk in the Garden*	4
2.	*The Seed Is Sown*	25
3.	*Picture Perfect*	40
4.	*A Passion for Domestic Architecture*	57
5.	*A Sagacious Client*	75
6.	*At Home*	95
7.	*The Nursery and Kitchen Gardens*	110
8.	*Professional Garden Designer*	125
9.	*An Eloquent Pen*	141
10.	*The Legacy of Munstead Wood*	155
Appendix I: List of Commissions		166
Appendix II: Commissions Listed by Architect		181
Notes		183
Select Bibliography		193
Index		197

List of Illustrations

Colour Plates (between pages 94 and 95)
The Pansy Garden, watercolour by Thomas Hunn
The south front of Munstead Wood, © Judith Tankard
The main hardy flower border, watercolour by Helen Allingham
Michaelmas daisy borders, watercolour by Helen Allingham
The Hut, sketch by Edwin Lutyens
The head gardener's cottage, sketch by Edwin Lutyens
The proposed house from the south-west, sketch by Edwin Lutyens
The south front of the proposed house, sketch by Edwin Lutyens
The main border in the Spring Garden, Country Life autochrome
The red section of the main hardy flower border, Country Life autochrome
The iris and lupin borders framed by The Loft, Country Life autochrome
One of the four beds forming the Grey Garden, Country Life autochrome
The kitchen gardens at Orchards, Country Life autochrome

Black and White Illustrations

Lilium auratum in Tank Garden	frontispiece
The main hardy flower border in 1931	xii
View of the house from a woodland walk	5
The River of Daffodils at the edge of the Green Wood Walk	9
The Fern Walk in August	10
Giant lilies in the woodland	11
Francoa ramosa on the south terrace	12
The half-timbered north court	13
Neapolitan pots above the tank	14
Lilies and cannas reflected in the pool	15
The Cenotaph of Sigismunda	16
October borders of Michaelmas daisies	17
The Primrose Garden	18
Aesculus parviflora and *Olearia* × *haastii* in the main shrub border	19
An *Exochorda racemosa* on the west lawn	20
Spring Garden with Tittlebat	21
The eastern end of the main hardy flower border	23
'A good place for gudgeons' at Bramley House	26
The south front of Munstead House	28

Gertrude Jekyll's workshop at Munstead House   29
Gertrude Jekyll around 1880   30
William Robinson at Gravetye Manor   31
A stone seat at Munstead House   34
The Primrose Garden at Munstead House   35
Revd John Bennett-Poe and Mrs Davidson at Munstead House   36
Michaelmas daisy borders at Munstead House   37
The south border at Munstead House   38
The garden doorway at Munstead House   39
Tabby sleeping in the photo basket   43
Ivy growing in beech along Unstead Lane   44
Climbing roses at Munstead House   45
Bergenia cordifolia and *B. crassifolia*   47
Hollyhocks in a cottage garden   48
Romneya coulteri flowers   49
Munstead glass vases filled with arrangements of flowers   50
The Squirrell public house in Hurtmore   51
Rustic log porch at The Squirrell   51
Holly stems in an old hedgerow   53
Horse chestnuts in Busbridge   54
Scotch firs thrown on to frozen water by a snowstorm   55
Gertrude Jekyll's sketch of a dovecote at Priory Farm   59
A silly gate made of nonsense tools   59
The drawing room at 43 Hyde Park Gate, for the Blumenthals   60
Old and new cottages in Elstead   62
The medieval bridge near Unstead   63
The kitchen yard at Unstead Farm   64
The half-timbered manor house at Unstead Farm   64
Mitchell's tile-hung cottage in Dunsfold   66
Half-timbered cottages in Eashing   67
Renovations at Gravetye Manor   68
The walled moat and tea-house at Loseley House   69
Garden gate at Great Tangley Manor   70
Philip Webb's library addition at Great Tangley Manor   71
Edwin Landseer Lutyens around 1896   72
Crooksbury House, Farnham   73
Renovations at Winkworth Farm in Hascombe   74
The Hut   77
Cottage fireplace and inglenook in The Hut   78
The head gardener's cottage   79
The 'old wall' and The Loft   81
The stable-yard and coach-house   81
Edwin Lutyens's plan for stable renovations   82
Vine and fig at the door to the mushroom house   83
Mrs Cannon outside the potting shed   84
South front of Munstead Wood   85

The porch flanked by tubs of hydrangeas 88
Ground and first floor plans by Edwin Lutyens 89
Gertrude Jekyll's sketch of the sitting room chimney-piece 91
The main staircase, with the book-room on the mezzanine level 91
The long oak-beamed gallery 92
Edwin Lutyens's sketch for the Tank Garden 93
Low steps from the south terrace to the lawn 94
Pewter collection on dining room sideboard 96
Letters to American friends 97
Under-gardener Frank Young 98
Under-gardener Arthur Berry in the pleasure gardens 99
Under-gardener Fred Boxall in the kitchen gardens 99
The workshop fireplace 101
Harold Falkner, a frequent visitor 102
Gertrude Jekyll's sketch of Munstead Wood 103
Gertrude Jekyll seated in the Spring Garden 104
The Revd Edwyn and Alice Arkwright admiring the October aster borders 105
The American garden writer Mrs Francis King 106
'Delicious funny odd luggage' 108
Head gardener Albert Zumbach trimming the cypress hedge 112
The September borders framed by an arch of laburnum 114
Early asters in the September borders 115
The summer flower borders 116
The Grey Garden in front of The Loft 117
Mrs Cannon with hollyhock 'Pink Beauty' outside The Loft 118
Delphinium × belladonna in the Grey Garden 119
Vegetable marrows near the stables 120
Bins for storing leaves in the garden yard 121
The Munstead Wood nursery catalogue 123
The south side of Wangford Hall, Suffolk 129
General layout plan for Wangford Hall 129
Planting plan for forecourt at Wangford Hall 130
Gertrude Jekyll's plan for Folly Farm 132
The north face of the tank garden at Gledstone Hall 133
A page from planting notebook for Gledstone Hall 133
Garden front of Millmead seen from the middle terrace 134
The house at Woodhouse Copse 137
A rough site plan for Woodhouse Copse 138
Plan for the double flower borders at Woodhouse Copse 139
Edward Hudson, proprietor of *Country Life* magazine 143
Barbara Jekyll making a primrose ball 145
Lilies for English Gardens 146
Annuals and Biennials and *Colour Schemes for the Flower Garden* 147
Gertrude Jekyll's sketch for the spine of *Old West Surrey* 151
An original manuscript page for *Old West Surrey* 152
A page proof for *Old West Surrey* 152

Gertrude Jekyll's sketch for *Home and Garden*   153
A manuscript page for an article in the *Bulletin of the Garden Club of America*   154
Gertrude Jekyll in the Spring Garden   156
The south front from the Green Wood Walk   158
Caricature of Gertrude Jekyll by S. Pleydell-Bouverie   159
The garden at Munstead Wood in 1938   161
Beatrix Farrand in her library   162
September borders at Munstead Wood   164

Plans
Main pleasure gardens at Munstead Wood, drawn by Simon Dorrell   6–7
Gardens at Munstead House, drawn by Simon Dorrell   32
Nursery and kitchen gardens at Munstead Wood, drawn by Simon Dorrell   111

Figures in brackets in the text refer to the plan of Munstead Wood and letters to that of Munstead House.

Foreword

Being desirous of taking up horticulture for a living, the fact that I was born in Cambridge, England, led me to the University Botanic Garden to further my education after leaving school. During my years there I came across books written by Gertrude Jekyll. The volume that interested me most was *Colour Schemes for the Flower Garden*, so much so that I read and re-read it, and even gave a talk upon the subject to my fellow students. She lived in Surrey, where the soil was lime-free, and this influenced my steps when I came to seek a job on leaving the Garden. And so, having secured work in a nursery in Surrey in 1931, on Saturday 6 September I cycled from Woking to Munstead, south of Godalming. I had been given an introduction to Miss Jekyll, and very fortunately had been invited by her to visit her garden. I have never ceased to be grateful for this happening, for she was not really receiving strangers at that advanced time of her life. She died fifteen months later.

Her house, which she called Munstead Wood, had been designed in the Surrey vernacular by Edwin Lutyens, later to be knighted for his services to architecture. It had no imposing gateway and drive; a simple hand-gate in the fence led directly to the door. I was shown into her room and I remember her looking almost the same as Sir William Nicholson's portrait of her, sitting in her chair. I was welcomed, bidden to go round the garden, pick a piece of anything I wished to talk about, and come back and have tea with her.

Her garden was almost the first one of any size in private hands which I had seen; moreover it was on sandy acid soil, much of it covered by a thin woodland of Scotch pines, Spanish chestnuts, oak and birch – a totally different assembly from what would have obtained in Cambridge, on its sticky, limy loam. Even the native plants – heathers, vacciniums, *Galium* and *Teucrium* – were different from anything I had previously met.

Wandering through the formal areas around the house exceeded my greatest expectations. There were the colour borders, still full of bloom, with gradations of tints so skilfully managed. Although she was a great lover of flowers and plants, it was her desire to extract the greatest effect from them that exercised her mind more than anything else. The colour, the stance, the form were to her of much greater value in the garden than botanical rarities, and she kept her magnificent and principal border in colourful condition by several expedients. Foremost among these was the expert use of making one plant drape itself over the spent display of another, and the growing in pots, in readiness for popping into gaps, of

The main hardy flower border at Munstead Wood, photographed by Graham Stuart Thomas on 6 September 1931

late-flowering hydrangeas, dahlias and others for augmenting the display. Thus was the main border kept in splendid condition from early July till mid-September. I was spellbound: it was a new world to me, though I had been a little prepared for it by her book. The gradation of tints in the whole two-hundred-foot length by fourteen-foot width testified to the skill of her garden staff, and to her ideas, developed from the deep study of various arts in this country and the countries around the Mediterranean. Thus her appreciation of colours and their grouping were influenced by her studies – and prowess – at embroidery, gilding, carving and others of the arts. I think that though she obviously loved plants they were to her the means to an end, and any plant which would grow well in her sandy soil was as a colour in a paint-box. The form of plants also came to her aid. We all know of her predilection for the solid rounded leaves of her megaseas (*Bergenia*); to these she added the spiky leaves of yuccas and a wide range of shrubs.

But the garden was not only composed of borders. There were two opposite ways of using plants decoratively; one was the grouping of handsome plants – *Francoa*, hostas, begonias were a few – in the courtyards and little garden 'rooms', and the other the gentle grouping of shrubs and plants in the wooded areas. Thus at the time of my visit there were clumps of willow gentian in moist positions; azaleas and rhododendrons were disposed with due regard to colours, to govern the views and to follow on from the drifts of spring flowers. I think it may be added that she first taught us a new use for rambling roses, encouraging them to grow freely through small trees and over hedgerows. There is no doubt that her garden gave her great delight. Fortunately her lucid prose has brought it all freshly to us.

Gertrude Jekyll (to rhyme with 'treacle') was born in London, in 1843, but she was brought up in Bramley, Surrey. I am sure that this part of Surrey, so rich in its wooded, hilly terrain, took a hold on her that never palled. Here she lived until 1863 when the family moved to Wargrave, near Henley-on-Thames, a move on to a chalky hill far removed from the lush, lime-free valley in Surrey. However, after the death of her father the family moved back to Surrey, to Munstead, and she threw herself into studying and practising many and varied arts. She acquired a semi-woodland site on the opposite side of the road to her mother's house, where she eventually developed her own garden and home. Here she lived for forty years; failing eyesight forced her gradually to relinquish her hold upon the numerous arts at which she had excelled, but she found a ready outlet for her talents in the artistic side of gardening. Her advice in garden layout and planting was often sought by garden owners and architects, as the astonishing list at the end of this volume will prove.

To her we owe the use of grey-foliaged plants – a taste acquired from her Mediterranean rambles – which did so well at Munstead. Nor was she averse to using a common plant, such as golden privet, to reinforce her colour schemes. She lived a long and full life, devoting herself to her garden, her friends and her cats. Throughout her garden writings is revealed her deep love of the beauty provided in this world, and a true Christian contentment with each flower, even though perhaps of fleeting duration.

From a contribution to *The World*, published 15 August 1905, comes this quotation from an article by her entitled 'A Definite Purpose in Gardening':

Just as an un-assorted assemblage of mere words, though they may be the best words in our language, will express no thought, or as the purest colours on an artist's palette – so long as they remain on the palette – do not form a picture, so our garden plants, placed without due consideration or definite intention, cannot show what they can best do for us.

GRAHAM STUART THOMAS

Acknowledgements

This book could not have been written without the assistance of numerous individuals and institutions, in particular the College of Environmental Design Documents Collection, University of California, Berkeley, which allowed access to Jekyll's papers and photographs. We are also grateful to the Estate of Gertrude Jekyll for allowing us to reproduce material in this book. The resources of the Royal Horticultural Society Lindley Library, the Bradford Central Library, the Massachusetts Horticultural Society Library, and the Frances Loeb Library (Harvard University) provided access to hundreds of articles written by Gertrude Jekyll for *The Garden* and *Gardening Illustrated*.

We would like to thank the following people for their encouragement and help in creating this book. Diane Kostial McGuire, Fenja Gunn, and John R. Tankard who read early drafts of the manuscript; David Wheeler, editor of *Hortus*, who published early versions of some of this material; and Simon Dorrell, art director of *Hortus*, who drew the new plans for the book. At the College of Environmental Design Documents Collection, we would like to thank Stephen Tobriner, Curator, and Paul Burgin and Travis Culwell, archivists; Dan Johnston, who prepared new prints of Gertrude Jekyll's photographs.

In addition, we would like to thank Primrose Arnander; The Hon. Hugh and Mrs Astor; Mavis Batey; Virginia Lopez Begg; Mary Bland; Jane Brown; Joan Charman, Librarian, Godalming Museum; Sir Robert and Lady Clark; Camilla Costello, Country Life Picture Library; Hilary Creighton, North Shore Garden Club; Brent Elliott, Librarian, Lindley Library; Robert Elwall, Photographs Curator, the British Architectural Library; Penelope Hobhouse; Valerie Kenward; Mary Hope Lewis, Garden Club of America; Mary Lutyens; David McKenna; Duncan Mirylees, Surrey Local Studies Library; Corbett Macadam; Ngaere A. Macray, Sagapress; David Nelson; David Penney; Kate Quarry; Margaret Richardson; Jane Ridley; Monica Saunders; Susan E. Schnare; Alex Starkey; Graham Stuart Thomas; Agnes Wolff, Brooklyn Botanic Garden; Kate Pertwee, Christopher Wood Gallery; Colin Young.

The Graham Foundation for Advanced Studies in the Fine Arts, Chicago, provided financial support in part for Tankard's initial research on Gertrude Jekyll's photography career.

Introduction

Much has been written in recent years about Gertrude Jekyll, the celebrated artist-gardener, who was born more than a hundred and fifty years ago. Using the example of her home and garden at Munstead Wood, she set forth her theories in many books and articles, capturing the imagination of untold admirers worldwide. At the turn of the century her direct prose style and photographs precisely illustrating her points caused a revolution in the ways people thought about decorative gardening. She approached horticulture from the perspective of a painter, as William Kent had nearly two centuries before, but unlike Kent she worked on a modest scale. Although she was not an architect (that was the role of her collaborators, pre-eminently Sir Edwin Lutyens), she had an abiding interest in architecture, and a decided talent for design. Like Kent she was an accomplished decorator; she was also a skilled silversmith and woodworker, an inspired photographer, and an enthusiastic craftswoman – as well as an innovative gardener.

These diverse talents and interests came together in the creation of her own home, Munstead Wood. The architect Sir Herbert Baker once noted that she had 'the power to see, as a poet, the art and creation of home-making as a whole in relation to Life; the best simple English country life of her day, frugal yet rich in beauty and comfort, in the building and its furnishings and their homely craftsmanship, its garden uniting the house with surrounding nature, all in harmony and breathing the spirit of its creator'.

That harmony was largely the result of Gertrude Jekyll's collaboration with Lutyens, whose work in helping her realize her ideas about domestic architecture had a formative effect on one of the most distinguished architectural careers of this century. Lutyens candidly recalled his first meeting with her in 1889, at the tea-table of friends. She was strikingly dressed, appearing to him as 'a bunch of cloaked propriety topped by a black felt hat, turned down in front and up behind', but when he arrived at Munstead the following week, 'on the tick of four', he was met by a very different person, 'genial and communicative, dressed in a short blue skirt, that in no way hid her ankles' – nor the boots later made famous through their portrayal by his friend William Nicholson. The weekends that followed were filled with the excitement of exploring local villages to study buildings, and of discussing the design of the cottages Gertrude Jekyll planned to build.

The home and garden she created at Munstead Wood were the perfect expression of the owner's personal ideals and unusually purposeful life. It embodied her artistic training, the garden planned as a series of 'pictures', the house both inside and out displaying her love of rural building arts and traditions. When she moved into her new home in October 1897, she had just received the prestigious Victoria Medal of Honour from the Royal Horticultural Society, one of the original sixty eminent gardeners honoured to mark the Diamond Jubilee of Queen Victoria's reign.

Munstead Wood became a legend in its time; and as it became more and more familiar through her books and articles, people from around the world were drawn to the living example of her ideas. Although she was shy of personal publicity, for many years she gladly welcomed like-minded gardeners to Munstead Wood, among them the garden writer Mrs Francis King, who so tirelessly promoted Gertrude Jekyll's books in America. When Mrs King saw for herself the famous drift plantings in the Spring Garden, she exclaimed that this was 'one of the compositions by a master hand which, once seen, could never be forgotten . . . a revelation of the artist's hand in gardening'. Russell Page and Mein Ruys were among the many landscape architects whose careers were influenced by their visits to Munstead Wood, but Beatrix Farrand's visit in the 1890s was to prove the most significant, in the sense that later, in the 1940s, she saved Gertrude Jekyll's papers from destruction.

Even though much of the character of Munstead Wood was lost after Gertrude Jekyll's death in 1932, she continues to exercise a particular fascination because of the eloquence of her writing and the examples of her theories; more than her associate William Robinson, whose mind was less open and pen less eloquent. She is sometimes compared to two other Englishwomen of the era: her friend Theresa Earle wrote wonderful books on similar topics, but they are now largely forgotten; Ellen Willmott, who was the only other woman to receive the Victoria Medal of Honour, was responsible for the creation of far more elaborate gardens than those at Munstead Wood, but in the end lost both her gardens and her fortune.

The present book is intended neither as a biography of Gertrude Jekyll nor as a discussion of her important contribution to garden design, both of which have been treated in some detail elsewhere. Using Munstead Wood as a *point d'appui*, the authors have chosen instead to explore some of the many activities and enterprises in which she engaged, in an attempt to paint a fuller picture of a remarkable woman who had 'a passion for doing useful things'. The range and diversity of those 'things' was a clear echo in the ideals of the Arts and Crafts Movement. From the outset of her career she was artist, designer, craftswoman – she designed patterns, carved wood, conserved plants, arranged flowers – all activities and interests her early exercise of which set the stage for their later and more lasting application to the arts of homebuilding, writing and garden design.

In order to look at Gertrude Jekyll's activities and enterprises in their proper context, the authors have sought to recreate Munstead Wood as it was in her time, through her writings and photographs, and the memories of friends and associates. Her own photographs, many of them never reproduced before, are at the heart of this book, and the recollections of visitors and others in memoirs, letters and interviews, provide an insight into the way she lived. As a prelude to the chapters devoted to Munstead Wood – its building, gardens, and domestic life

– a glimpse of her years at Munstead House indicates how her artistic training and horticultural skills came to evolve into a personal style of gardening. A passionate interest in photography which also developed during these early years led her to a thorough study of the local vernacular architecture which eventually inspired the building of Munstead Wood. The relationship between her nursery and garden design enterprises and the intertwining of her photography skills with her writing, studied in some detail, further exemplify the unity of the practical and creative arts which ran through her life's work. New plans have been prepared to show both Munstead House and Munstead Wood as they were in Gertrude Jekyll's time. A list of her garden design commissions records the extent of her work in that arena, and a select bibliography lists not only her major writings but also significant publications devoted to her life and work which have appeared in recent years.

CHAPTER 1

A Walk in the Garden

After climbing the hill towards Hascombe from Godalming and walking up a sandy track, a visitor to Munstead Wood eventually came to a little gate in an oak paling fence. There was no carriage drive sweeping up to the front door, as one might have expected, merely a simple footpath, generously planted with shrubs to allow tantalising glimpses far into the woodland (1). An essential sense of mystery was conjured as the path abruptly disappeared into a tunnel of hollies leading to the porch, with its timber arches framing views across the lawn. All was simplicity and restraint, 'like the overture to an opera' preparing the visitor for the 'restfulness and beauty of the garden'.[1] Such modesty gave the impression that Munstead Wood was merely a cottage set in a wooded clearing. This was, of course, all skilful illusion, but an illusion which had taken more than forty years to create.

In her book *Gardens for Small Country Houses* Gertrude Jekyll described Munstead Wood as 'fifteen acres of the poorest possible soil, sloping a little down towards the north', roughly triangular in shape. The southern portion (the widest point) had once been a plantation of Scots pine which, felled in the early 1870s after some seventy years' growth, had been replaced by a self-sown mixed wood. In the central portion, where the house eventually stood, a chestnut copse had been established, and the remainder, which later became the working gardens, was a poor arable field. Jekyll began developing the woodland almost immediately after acquiring the land in the early 1880s, using what natural advantages she found as inspiration. There was, in fact, 'no definite planning at the beginning': each area was treated on its merits 'and the whole afterwards reconciled as might most suitably be contrived'. This unfortunate piecemeal approach resulted in some 'awkward angles', and the basic structure of the garden was not particularly good, as she readily admitted.[2]

The woodland fell quite naturally into areas devoted to one or two types of trees. These 'natural groupings were accepted' and all others were thinned out so sensitively, and almost imperceptibly, that 'one kind of tree join[ed] hands with the next' leaving no 'harsh frontiers'. An old Scots pine (2), spared the axe because its trunk had forked, became the essence and focal point of two broad woodland avenues, linked by a number of narrower cross paths and minor paths which provided easy access to all parts of the woodland.[3]

The south lawn (3) formed the hub of the woodland garden, and all main paths led from its broad expanse. To the west, the lawn was broader and fringed by five

A view of the house from the third woodland walk, late May 1900. On the right is
Rhododendron 'Multimaculatum' *(CED-UC Berkeley)*

selected birches and a sweet chestnut; their proximity to it strengthened the impression of a house set in a wood. But Jekyll also enjoyed the sounds made by wind playing through their leaves, and she delighted in the 'fragrance almost as sweet [as that of sweetbriars], but infinitely more subtle, from the fresh green of the young birches . . . [which is] like a distant whiff of Lily of the Valley'.[4]

The Green Wood Walk (4), which was nearly four hundred feet long and broad enough for two people to walk comfortably side by side, was the principal woodland avenue. Jekyll described the walk as 'the most precious possession of the place, the bluish distance giving a sense of some extent and the bounding woodland one of repose and security, while in slightly misty weather the illusions of distance and mystery are endless and full of charm'.[5] Although the trees appeared to have been placed quite randomly by nature, they had in fact been carefully selected and arranged, a process which continued for more than fifty years. Before any tree was felled, a white paper collar was tied around the trunk and it was viewed from all angles to see whether it had any 'pictorial value' to merit a change of heart. Near the house Jekyll took great pains to gather the silver birches into groups, observing that individual moorland trees generally bend outward towards the free, open space, and groups take a form that is 'graceful and highly pictorial'.[6]

1. Entrance Footpath
2. Forked Scots Pine
3. South Lawn
4. Green Wood Walk
5. Second Avenue
6. Third Walk
7. Walk to The Hut
8. Azalea Garden
9. River of Daffodils
10. Second Scots pine
11. Fern Walk
12. Lily Walk
13. Heath Garden
14. South Terrace
15. North Court and Tank Garden
16. Cenotaph
17. October Michaelmas Daisy Borders
18. Primrose Garden
19. Nut Walk
20. Brier Rose Bank
21. Shrub Borders
22. Topiary Cat
23. The Hut Garden
24. Early Bulb Border
25. Hidden Garden
26. Sunken Rock Garden
27. Spring Garden
28. Old Peony Garden: Three Corner Garden
29. Main Hardy Flower Border
30. Pergola
44. Main Garden Yard

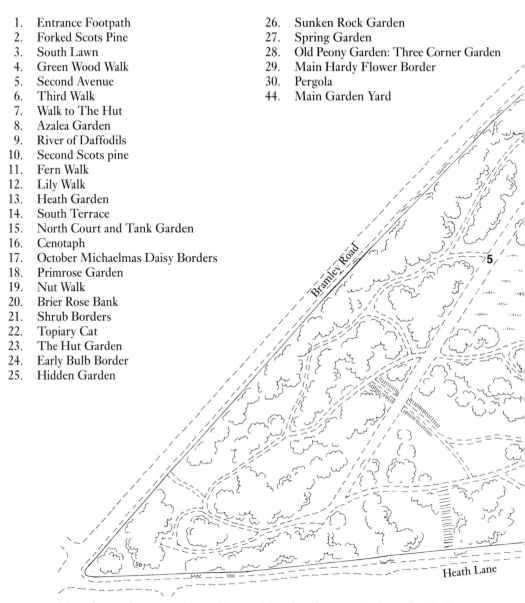

Plan of main pleasure gardens at Munstead Wood as they were in Gertrude Jekyll's day (Simon Dorrell)

Near the house, on either side of the Green Wood Walk, groups of silver birch mingled with large plantings of salmon and pink rhododendrons (including 'Bianchii', still one of the few true-pink-flowered hybrids), which gave way to white-flowered types where the woodland became denser and the shade deepened. Beyond the rhododendrons, beneath the shade of some large sweet

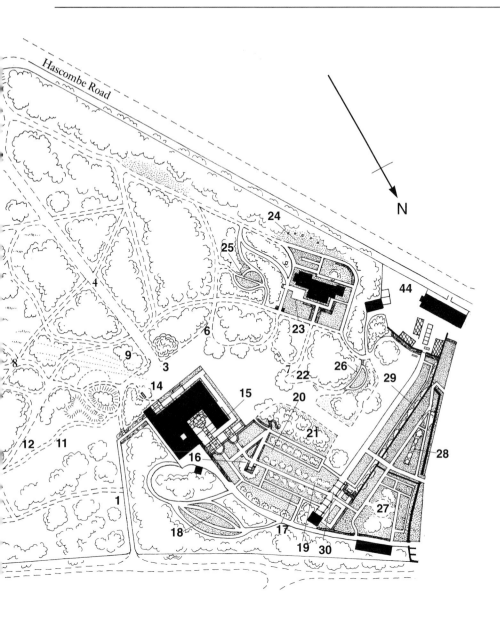

chestnuts, the ground was covered with poet's narcissus and a broad carpet of lily-of-the-valley, with cloudy branches of *Amelanchier lamarckii* above. Later in the year a natural growth of bracken and broad patches of ornamental brambles covered the ground while bold groups of *Lilium auratum*, planted among the rhododendrons, provided further seasonal interest. A second avenue (5), at right-angles to the first, also used the forked Scots pine as a fulcrum. Unusually, it was carpeted in heather, and every August became 'a fourteen-foot wide road of grey-rosy bloom' stretching for more than six hundred feet through the woodland.[7]

A third walk (6), not as broad as the Green Wood Walk, opened off the south lawn further to the west and was lined with crimson, claret and pink rhododendrons, carefully arranged so that their colours blended harmoniously. A very large holly on the lawn prevented the eye from viewing both groups of rhododendrons (the salmon and pinks on one walk, the crimsons and claret on the other) simultaneously, save from a distance. Further to the west another heavily shaded walk, which led to The Hut (7), Jekyll's small cottage, was planted with purple rhododendrons, mostly selected seedlings of *Rhododendron ponticum*. Although there were many fine purple-flowered hybrid rhododendrons available, the smaller flowers and lighter colours of *R. ponticum* seedlings were preferred to the larger flowers and heavier colours of the hybrids, which would not have given the effect she sought. The deep purple colours acquired additional richness in shade, and she added patches of white to give essential touches of light and enliven the sumptuously-coloured tapestry.

Almost in the centre of the woodland a broad clearing was made for an Azalea Garden (8). Most of the azaleas at Munstead Wood were planted in the 1890s, with more bushes possibly added around 1900, but in 1926 the plantings were extended, with a large beech used as a feature. Although azaleas and rhododendrons were closely related, they 'should never be planted among or even within sight' of one another; for, as Jekyll wrote, 'they are incongruous in appearance, and impossible to group together for colour'.[8] The backbone of the plantings was the common yellow Pontic azalea, *R. luteum*, to which were added shades of pink, white and fiery orange, predominantly Ghent hybrids, with some pure yellows, such as 'Nancy Waterer' and the unusual 'Narcissiflora'.[9] A scattering of silver birch among the azaleas provided dappled shade, while groups of cistus continued the seasonal interest.

Scarring much of the woodland were numerous 'shallow, parallel hollows', probably the remains of old pack-horse tracks (9). Still discernible today, they run three or four together, the result of one track becoming worn and another being formed by its side. Where several old tracks running through the birch copse came to within yards of the house, Jekyll planted a few hundred bulbs of *Narcissus* 'Horsfieldii' (an old variety in her time, since probably extinct) and *N.* 'Princeps' (believed to be *N. gayi*) in the depressions; in time, this gave the effect of 'waving rivers of bloom, in many lights and accidents of cloud and sunshine full of pictorial effect'.[10]

Beyond where the river of daffodils emerged on to the lawn, a broad grassy path led to the Fern and Lily Walks, which came together at a second double-stemmed Scots pine (10), the pivot of the eastern part of the wood. The narrow Fern Walk (11) was 'merely an easy way that the eye just perceives and the foot follows', resembling a moorland sheep track. Groups of choice ferns were established in small bays or hollows slightly lower than the path, so that water drained into them.[11] The surrounding natural growth of whortleberry was

The end of the River of Daffodils at the edge of the Green Wood Walk, with the forked Scots pine in the distance, late 1890s (CED–UC Berkeley)

enlivened with trilliums, *Maianthemum bifolium* and drifts of Solomon's seal. The Lily Walk (12), by contrast, was much broader and derived its name from plantings of *Cardiocrinum giganteum* which Jekyll had struggled for years to establish. Since it was not easy to persuade the giant lily to grow in poor sandy soil, she resorted to digging large pits twelve feet across and three feet deep which were filled with garden rubbish. One visitor, seeing the excavations and piles of what appeared to be building sand, asked whether she was 'quarrying stone, or is it for the cellar of a building?'[12] A neighbour attributed the secret of her eventual success to the addition of a freshly-killed rabbit thrown in the hole and covered with leaf-mould; the large bulbs were then planted on top and given a clockwise twist before they were covered with soil.[13]

The paths that meandered through the azaleas emerged into the Heath Garden (13), created on the eve of the First World War. With the natural ground-covering growth of native heaths (*Calluna vulgaris*, *Erica cinerea*, and *E. tetralix*) as a basis,

The Fern Walk in August, late 1890s, was like a moorland track (CED–UC Berkeley)

nursery plants were arranged in 'longish drifts following each other in a quite uneven succession, varied by thicker or thinner patches and here and there entirely broken by projecting promontories of natural heath and whortleberry'. 'Prosperous growths of young plants', regenerated after a heathland fire, were used to fill any spaces between the nursery plants, and she encouraged the young heaths and thyme growing in the natural heathland grass to cover the paths.[14]

The Heath Garden led to the Green Wood Walk, the house in the distance framed by masses of tall rhododendrons and delicate silver birches, a picture enhanced by a subtle tapestry of colour and texture formed by the lawns. So that they would blend with the surrounding woodland, the lawns were made from tufts of wild grass which were 'forked up, . . . pulled into pieces about the size of the palm of one's hand, and . . . [planted] eight inches apart'. Seed collected from the two main grasses used, sheep's fescue (*Festuca ovina*) and crested dog's-tail

*Giant lilies (*Cardiocrinum giganteum*) in the woodland were probably on the Lily Walk, 17 July 1888 (CED–UC Berkeley)*

(*Cynosurus cristatus*), was sown in bare patches, and after two years the patches had joined together to form a lawn. Because of the fine texture of the grasses used, the lawn not only gave a pleasant, 'quiet, low-toned colour', but also had the advantage of requiring mowing only once in three weeks.[15]

The ornamental gardens fell 'naturally into various portions, distinct enough from each other to allow of separate treatment . . . [and the devotion of] one space at a time, sometimes mainly, sometimes entirely, to the flowers of one season of the year'.[16] This interest in seasonal gardens is one of the hallmarks of Gertrude Jekyll's style of gardening, fully explained and illustrated in her book *Colour in the Flower Garden*. The linking of house and garden is always important, but at Munstead Wood the difficulties were exacerbated simply because the house was built long after the garden had been laid out. On the south side of the house, a door opened from the sitting-room on to a long terrace (14), the borders richly planted with China roses (*Rosa × odorata* 'Pallida'), rosemary, hydrangeas and vines, while a broad flight of steps led to the south lawn. On the north side, the lobby adjacent to the sitting room opened on to the north court (15), the only part of the garden to have 'a definite plan'. Paved with a circle of ripple-marked flagstone, the circular shape was enhanced by a dwarf box hedge. In summer, the court was decorated with carefully arranged groups of pots filled with hostas and

Francoa ramosa *on the south terrace, 1906. A grape vine is trained on the wall and beneath the* windows is a Chaenomeles speciosa, *with masses of rosemary and pink China roses (CED–UC Berkeley)*

ferns, with lilies and hydrangeas added later in the season. A *Clematis montana*, which was trained around the workshop window and beneath the gallery, gave garlands of flowers in May and helped to soften the rather 'boxy' appearance of the architecture.

A line of Italian orange pots filled with maiden's wreath (*Francoa ramosa*) edged the terrace, while a lion's mask, nestling among 'a wealth of ferns', spouted the water into the tank below. The square tank, the only formal water feature in the garden, was flanked by two flights of steps – punctuated by topiary spheres of box – which connected with two broad cross-walks, forming a rough triangle. This curious path layout (obviously one of the awkward angles to which Jekyll referred) manipulated the axis of the garden by linking the north court and workshop door with the main flower border. One cross-walk, which linked together the paths running through the shrub borders, the brier rose bank and the Nut Walk, terminated in a massive timber seat beneath the shade of a silver birch, a peaceful retreat for guests and resident cats alike. This pleasant seat in a 'monumental mass of elm, and . . . [the] somewhat funereal environment of

The half-timbered north court was wreathed in Clematis montana *and decorated with pots filled with hostas and male fern, May 1905 (CED–UC Berkeley)*

Neapolitan pots above the tank, with George Leslie's lion mask nestled among the ferns (courtesy Mary Bland)

weeping birch and spire-like mullein' was christened the Cenotaph of Sigismunda (16) by a friend, and later gave its name to the Cenotaph in Whitehall.[17]

The path from the north court, passing at the back of the Cenotaph, led to the October Michaelmas daisy borders (17). These borders, so perfectly portrayed by artists Helen Allingham and George Elgood, are synonymous with the style of planting advocated by Gertrude Jekyll. The seemingly simple cascades of purple, blue and white flowers spilling on to the path belie the care and ingenuity used in staking the plants to create the effect. An edge of grey-leaved pinks provided the perfect foil for later-blooming asters, such as the pale blue 'Climax' (the last to flower) or 'Coombe Fishacre' (a pale lilac aging to cream tinged with rose), which were combined with moon daisies (*Leucanthemella serotina*), whose white flowers follow the sun. In 1927 a gale broke up the surrounding screen of shrubs and trees which provided a backdrop to the rich display of asters, opening out a view to the distant landscape.[18]

Beyond the Michaelmas daisy borders and a short walk across the back drive lay the Primrose Garden (18), which was among the first areas to be laid out and remained the least changed. It was set in a small clearing surrounded by holly and Portuguese laurel, with large oaks and hazel for shade. Masses of white and yellow April-blooming bunch-flowered primroses of the famous Munstead strain were

Lilies and cannas reflected in the pool in the Tank Garden, 28 July 1899 (CED-UC Berkeley)

planted in an ellipse beneath the trees. They were best seen in the early evening when they gave the effect of a magical primrose glow, reflected and enhanced by the evergreen screen.

A shady Nut Walk (19) provided the principal thoroughfare from the workshop door to the main hardy flower border, spring gardens and working gardens beyond. Planted in 1887, it consisted of two double rows of hazel nuts (*Corylus avellana*) arranged zigzag fashion ten feet apart so that they would arch and meet overhead. Beneath the nuts a collection of Lenten hellebores formed the main planting, to which were added 'wide patches of the common dog-tooth violet (*Erythronium dens-canis*)' and the purple fumitory (*Corydalis solida*), succeeded by masses of Munstead primroses and clouds of blue forget-me-nots to form a rich carpet. As spring gave way to summer, columbines and a white form of *Campanula latifolia* with a generous background of Alexandrian laurel (*Danaë racemosa*) added further interest.[19]

Gertrude Jekyll was particularly fond of brier roses, and had collected many from cottage gardens where they had been cherished for years. She grouped together different forms of the same rose, such as semi-double rose-pinks of varying shades and habit, using them to cover a broad bank (20) which backed the

The Cenotaph of Sigismunda was a simple bench set beneath a weeping birch tree, 1899. In late summer tubs of hydrangeas replaced the verbascums (CED–UC Berkeley)

October borders of Michaelmas daisies and groups of moon daisies, edged by white garden pinks,
6 October 1906 (CED–UC Berkeley)

Nut Walk and faced the east side of the shrub walk. They were also used to form
a hedge which separated the south lawn from the terrace, as Miss Jekyll found 'no
bushy thing is better for the capping of a dry wall' and in winter took great
pleasure in the thicket of bronze stems.[20]

Two raised banks were devoted to a collection of shrubs, those she liked best of
all, 'whether new friends or old'. Although she wrote about these borders (21) in
Wood and Garden, her use of shrubs has been overshadowed by her more familiar
work with herbaceous plants. The main shrub border had a central backbone of
magnolias and junipers, some of which grew to a considerable size. A twelve-foot-
high *Magnolia stellata* jostled for space with a *Forsythia suspensa*, itself more than
ten feet high. On the cool east face a double-flowered *Spiraea prunifolia* was used
to extend the season, its neat leaves turning a brilliant red and crimson in autumn
that contrasted well with the cool grey, almost white, foliage of *Artemisia*

*The Primrose Garden featured Gertrude Jekyll's famous 'Munstead bunch' primroses, 1901
(CED-UC Berkeley)*

Aesculus parviflora *and* Olearia × haastii *in the main shrub border, looking east toward the house, late summer 1907 (CED–UC Berkeley)*

stelleriana.[21] A bush horse chestnut (*Aesculus parviflora*), which backed the spiraea, proved very effective underplanted with *Olearia × haastii;* she later regretted that she had not added some of the blue, silvery-foliaged *Perovskia atriplicifolia*, but it was unknown to her when the planting was made. Some plants were grown for the colour of their foliage, such as the grey-leaved Jerusalem sage (*Phlomis fruticosa*), but *Leycesteria formosa*, which she knew in her childhood home, was grown purely for sentimental reasons. On the sunny south-west face a *Styrax japonicus* flowered 'well in hot summers', and a pearl bush (*Exochorda racemosa*) cascaded on to the lawn.

Across the lawn, facing the shrub border, a large topiary cat (22) guarded the entrance to a small sunken rock garden. Gertrude Jekyll rarely used topiary, but this example occurred spontaneously when a group of yews took on a 'cat-like shape', and was then encouraged into the form of a cat resting on its paws.[22] Beyond the cat a path led to The Hut (23), which was surrounded by a quintessential cottage garden, complete with water pump and dovecote, shielded and screened from the road by a bank of firs and hollies at the foot of which was a border devoted to early bulbs (24). The box-edged beds surrounding the cottage were filled with roses, iris, lupins and peonies in June and early July. One bed, too

An Exochorda racemosa *cascades on the west lawn, the main hardy flower border and door in the distance, June 1907 (CED-UC Berkeley)*

deep front-to-back for convenience, had a small service path across it edged by a dwarf hedge of rosemary, while another was divided by a double row of rose arches set in a sea of male fern and sweet cicely. To extend the season, any spare space was planted with pentstemons and snapdragons, but the area was dominated by giant hogweed (*Heracleum mantegazzianum*) whose bold foliage and huge flower-heads Jekyll admired.

On the southern boundary of The Hut's garden, heavily shaded and cut off from the surrounding lawn by a thick planting of yew and holly, lay the Hidden Garden (25), which bridged two seasons. Two important paths passed only yards from it, but the entrance was concealed and obscured by contorted curved tunnels of yew and bamboo. At first the garden was devoted to alpine plants, with a few tree peonies, but as the tree canopy gradually thickened, casting too much shade for the alpines to survive, it was transformed into a fern garden. A new sunken rock garden was then created whose elliptical shape echoed that of the Hidden Garden. The Sunken Rock Garden (26) had raised beds formed by dry stone walls generously planted with ferns and filled with drifts of *Campanula pulla*, *Linnaea borealis* and *Veronica prostrata*.

Perhaps the most remarkable of all was the Spring Garden (27). Laid out in the early 1890s, it is one of the few areas of Munstead Wood documented by early colour photographs, which bring to life the many descriptions of it. Intended to be 'wholly devoted to plants that bloom in April or May', it was deliberately designed not to be 'within the main summer garden scheme, . . . [but just beyond] the boundaries of the more dressed pleasure garden'.[23] The basic design was simplicity itself, with a central circular lawn set with two large oak trees and rocks known as 'Near and Further Rock', and borders along the west and north sides. A high stone wall backing the main, north, border (and also, on its other face, the

Spring Garden with Tittlebat, May 1907. Further rock is on the right and the old peony garden can be seen in the distance (CED–UC Berkeley)

main hardy flower border), was used for espaliered Morello cherries which, together with clumps of sweet cicely and *Veratrum nigrum* in the border, provided a background for the delicate spring flowers.

Harold Falkner, a local architect who was a frequent visitor, recalled that 'Once, soon after the [First World] War, the Spring Garden blossomed out into a fearful and wonderful scheme of purple honesty on a yellow and green background, but I am not sure that I or anyone else was supposed to notice it.'[24] Normally the colour scheme was more muted, beginning with drifts of pale yellow daffodils, primroses, and iris, leading to deeper tones. Pale lilac aubrietias and drifts of white arabis edging the border, with purple wallflowers and a double purple tulip, 'Bleu Celeste', at the back, created the illusion that the border was deeper than was the case. Where the border was backed by a yew hedge, the colours became even stronger, picking up the bronze tints in the new growth of yew. Orange and scarlet tulips, orange crown imperials and a *Euphorbia characias wulfenii* completed the composition.

Adjacent to the Spring Garden was a sheltered area devoted to tree peonies, which proved to be difficult to establish on the light sandy soil, even though it was 'liberally enriched with what one judges to be the most gratifying comfort'. Sometime after 1910 the peony garden was replaced by one devoted to annual or bedding plants. The use of annuals often surprised visitors but, as Gertrude Jekyll remarked, 'a geranium was a geranium long before it was a bedding plant', and it was hardly the plant's fault if it was 'employed in a dull or even stupid way'.[25] Because the triangular plot, known as Three Corner Garden (28), was an awkward shape, the central bed was divided by an elevated backbone of yuccas and two types of euphorbia. A plan for 'A Garden of Summer Flowers', published in later editions of *Colour in the Flower Garden*, shows that it was composed of brilliantly coloured dahlias, cannas, geraniums, African marigolds and deep purple heliotropes, edged with variegated mint and golden feather feverfew.[26]

Gertrude Jekyll's most widely admired creation at Munstead Wood was the main hardy flower border (29), which she made in the early 1890s. Some two hundred feet long and fourteen feet deep, it was backed by an eleven-foot-high bargate stone wall which separated it from the Spring Garden. The border was deliberately broken after about fifty feet by a cross-path and doorway leading to the spring and annual gardens behind the wall. A feature was made of the break by the use of bold groups of yuccas and a deep green edge of bergenia foliage, which appeared almost black in some lights.

The border had a complex and intricate colour scheme based on harmonious colour relationships and the principle that 'blue conveys a sense of distance, while warm colours bring objects closer to the viewer'.[27] The inspiration for the scheme may have come from J.M.W. Turner's paintings, such as 'The Fighting *Téméraire*', which Gertrude Jekyll had copied in her youth.[28] The colour relationships she sought to recreate in the border can be seen in Turner's brilliant sunset where the sun, represented by a dot of white and an edge of fiery red, fades into orange and deeper yellow. In the border the colours continued to fade, through deep yellow to paler yellow, cream and pink, culminating in a ground of grey and glaucous foliage at both ends. Comparing the border with 'The Fighting

The eastern end of the main hardy flower border, late summer 1907. Senecio cineraria, *santolina and elymus provide a foil to pink hydrangeas, tall yellow snapdragons and* Lilium auratum *(CED-UC Berkeley)*

Téméraire' is apt, for both artists used white as a central feature of their compositions, represented in the border by gypsophila.

At the western end of the border, where it was slightly kinked, Gertrude Jekyll placed blue flowers on a ground of grey foliage, while at the eastern end she used flowers of a purple and lilac colouring, again on a ground of grey and glaucous foliage. The whole arrangement was actually an elaborate piece of *trompe-l'oeil*. Visitors who had enjoyed the quiet patterning of greens and diffused light while strolling down the Nut Walk and through the pergola (30) emerged abruptly into bright sunlight to be confronted by a carefully arranged river of colour and texture. The whole picture was clearly seen from the lawn, 'the cool colouring at the ends [enhancing] the brilliant warmth of the middle'. Closer observation revealed that each section of the border was 'a picture in itself, and every one is of such a colouring that it best prepares the eye, in accordance with natural law, for what is to follow'. The eye passed from the greys and blues 'with extraordinary avidity to the succeeding yellows' and, in turn, to scarlets, blood-reds and clarets, before returning to yellows. By this point the eye, saturated by rich colouring, 'by the law of complementary colour, acquired a strong appetite for [the] greys and purples' following, which assumed an 'appearance of brilliancy'.[29]

The wall behind the border was also used as an integral part of the elaborate composition, but where it turned to enclose the garden yard, a yew hedge was planted to obscure it and provide a green backdrop (rather than the yellow of the stone) for views along the border. To reinforce the colours in the red section of the border a pomegranate (*Punica granatum*) with red-tinted foliage was combined with a red-leaved claret vine (*Vitis vinifera* 'Purpurea') to echo the colours of the geraniums, annual salvias, clumps of cannas, and scarlet dahlias 'Fire King', leading to a long drift of crimson dahlias, possibly 'Crimson Beauty' (all of which can be clearly seen in another of the early colour photographs). The crimson dahlias were echoed by a deep crimson hollyhock at the very back of the border, so dark that it appeared almost black. Not all visitors appreciated a composition so careful and subtle. One American, who did not care for 'the red portions of her great border', exclaimed that she had never seen 'such frightful examples of red geranium bedding . . . even in Newport or Bar Harbor'.[30] To Gertrude Jekyll it was always the effect that mattered, and she had 'no dogmatic views about having in the so-called hardy flower-border none but hardy flowers. All flowers are welcome that are right in colour, and that make a brave show where a brave show is wanted'; she also kept an open mind, and was 'always observing and always learning and trying to do better'.[31]

One of the secrets of the border's success lay in the style of the planting. All her borders were habitually planted in 'long rather than block-shaped patches' because, as she observed, 'a thin long planting does not leave an unsightly empty space when the flowers are done', especially if the border were built up in layers, using long narrow-shaped drifts that interlocked and overlapped one another.[32] Nor was the border a static creation, rather a constantly changing tapestry of colour and form that evolved as the season progressed. Central to this evolution were the tricks and devices employed to maintain interest over a long season, from mid-July to early September. Some of these resulted in subtle changes, such as training *Rudbeckia* 'Golden Glow' into a golden cut-leaved elder (*Sambucus nigra* 'Aurea') to produce a mixture of two different shades of yellow. In another part of the border a *Ceanothus* 'Gloire de Versailles' had a *Clematis* 'Jackmanii' trained through its branches, a subtle change of emphasis from pale powder blue to rich purple which cascaded on to a foam of white gypsophila at the border's edge.

Gardening is not for the impatient, nor for the faint-hearted, and Gertrude Jekyll readily admitted that it had taken her 'half a lifetime merely to find out what is best worth doing, and a good slice out of another half to puzzle out the ways [and the means] of doing it'.[33] As she wrote in her first book, 'like everything else, . . . good gardening . . . must be done just right, and the artist-gardener finds that hardly the placing of a single plant can be deputed to any other hand than his own; for though, when it is done, it looks quite simple and easy, he must paint his own picture himself – no one can paint it for him'.[34]

CHAPTER 2

The Seed Is Sown

As with most great gardeners, the seed of Gertrude Jekyll's passion for gardening was sown during childhood. Her Proustian sense of smell, sharp hearing, and capacity for precise observation, familiar themes in her many books, were all early habits and traits. In the art of gardening she happily combined a keen eye for detail and unfailing insight, but gardening was only one of numerous subjects to which this industrious and intelligent woman turned her insatiable curiosity. Lord Riddell captured the essence of Gertrude Jekyll when he observed that she brilliantly represented a noble class of women 'who have a passion for doing useful things as well as can be done and who combine feminine sympathies with a masculine intellect and a sagacious outlook'.[1]

Gertrude Jekyll was not a countrywoman by birth, as is often supposed, but by inclination. She was born in 1843 in the heart of London, in Grafton Street, Mayfair, where her parents owned a fine Georgian house. Her earliest memories were of trees and grass in Green Park where she went for daily walks with her nanny. She delighted in the colours and fragrances, even in dandelions, forbidden in the nursery as 'Nasty Things'. To the end of her life, the smell of mown grass brought back memories of Berkeley Square, where she had learned to make daisy-chains and followed other pleasurable childhood pursuits, later fondly recalled in *Children and Gardens*.

When Gertrude was nearly five years old, the Jekyll family moved to the country, taking a lease on Bramley Park, a Regency mansion in a small Surrey village near Guildford. During these halcyon days when the county was still largely rural her lifelong love of Surrey – its people, architecture, and landscape – took firm hold. Along with her elder sister Carry and younger brothers Herbert and Walter she delighted in the park that surrounded this generous country house.[2] Two ponds and several streams running through the park provided many amusements, such as fishing and boating, and also sparked a fascination with 'the ways of water' and streamside plants.

After her brothers went away to school Gertrude was left very much to her own amusements. Accompanied by her pony Toby and her dog Crim, she would wander 'into the woods and heaths and along all the little lanes and by-paths'. She delighted in the meadows awash with wild flowers, but took an interest, too, in the gardens and shrubberies around the houses. Wide turf paths running through clumps of azaleas, pieris and *Rhododendron ponticum* made this a good place 'in which a child might gain early acquaintance with shrubs', and she knew them all

'A good place for gudgeons' in one of the ponds at Bramley House, 1907 (CED–UC Berkeley)

by sight and touch. The borders were a jumble of daylilies, lilac, phlox, China asters and summer bedding plants, but of more interest to the young gardener were the beds of lily-of-the-valley in the kitchen garden, and a tiny plot with a rose-covered arbour that was her first garden.[3] As she later remembered, 'I have been more or less a gardener all my life'.[4]

These solitary years instilled in Gertrude habits of independence and resourcefulness. From her father, Captain Edward Jekyll, she inherited a curiosity about how things worked which, combined with sharp observation, was to prove invaluable in later life. From her mother, Julia Hammersley, who as a child had taken piano lessons with Mendelssohn, Gertrude inherited a lifelong appreciation of music, and other arts.[5] When she was eighteen Gertrude began to study in London with the intention of becoming a painter. She and her new companions absorbed John Ruskin's theories and were soon sitting in galleries, copying Turner's paintings. In 1863, just nineteen, she discovered the joys of foreign travel on a memorable trip to Greece and Turkey with fellow-artist Mary Newton and her husband Charles, Keeper of Greek Antiquities at the British Museum. There followed visits to Paris, and to Rome, where she took gilding lessons – one of numerous crafts in which she quickly became proficient.

When Gertrude returned from Rome in April 1868 she found her family, who had lived in Bramley for nearly twenty years, on the point of moving to Wargrave Hill, in Berkshire – Captain Jekyll having decided to give up Bramley Park when the lease of his family home reverted to him. It was an unwelcome development for a young lady who had grown to love the Surrey countryside, but in later years Gertrude admitted that she only disliked Berkshire because it wasn't Surrey. For the next eight years (exile years, she called them) she enjoyed an ever-widening circle of artist friends in London, who included George Frederick Watts, Frederic Leighton and William Morris. She went to musical parties, travelled, and nourished her interest in plants. During a winter spent in Algiers with the artist Barbara Bodichon, Gertrude delighted in finding wild *Iris unguicularis* and hedges of prickly pear during her rambles.[6] Beginning in 1873 she spent many happy holidays in Switzerland, collecting alpine plants and enjoying musical diversions at the Chalet de Sonzier at Les Avants above Lake Geneva as a guest of Jacques and Léonie Blumenthal.[7] She was also a frequent guest at their London home, which she later decorated.

It may have been at the Chalet that Gertrude first met Hercules Brabazon, an English watercolour artist who had studied with Turner and who was to have a profound influence on her use of colour in the garden. Brabazon's impressionist studies, quickly executed in watercolour, pencil and pastel on tinted papers, inspired Ruskin to remark to Herbert Jekyll in 1882 that 'Brabazon is the only person since Turner at whose feet I can sit and worship and learn about colour.'[8] Gertrude took lessons with Brabazon, and later acknowledged her debt to him in helping her 'understand and enjoy the beauty of colour'. When she embarked upon gardening in earnest, she wrote enthusiastically to Brabazon, 'I have been doing some vigorous landscape gardening . . . doing living pictures with land and trees and flowers!'[9]

The artist George Leslie, who later designed the lion's mask in the Tank Garden at Munstead Wood, described Gertrude around 1870 as a young lady with many singular and remarkable accomplishments: 'There is hardly any useful handicraft the mysteries of which she has not mastered – carving, modelling, house-painting, carpentry, smith's work, repoussé work, gilding, wood-inlaying, embroidery, gardening, and all manner of herb and flower knowledge and culture.'[10] Throughout the 1870s embroidery and interior design commissions provided an outlet in London for her creative energies, stimulated by her meeting with Morris in 1869.

Little remains today to show the extent of Gertrude's work in these fields. In November 1870 she created a series of embroidery designs intended for cushion covers, based on three fruits – pomegranate, strawberry and mistletoe – and three flowers – dandelion, periwinkle and iris. Of the six designs, only those for periwinkle and iris have survived, published in the *Handbook of Embroidery* compiled by Miss L. Higgin and edited by Lady Marian Alford, chairman of the Council of the Royal School of Needlework. The thorough grasp of the technicalities of textile design and the use of pattern bases revealed in these two designs, together with an almost subconscious understanding of the natural forms of flowers, are also evident in a wallpaper design dated November 1875 which uses ivy imposed on a shallow ogee pattern base.

More unusually, Gertrude also designed jewellery. A workbook or scrapbook acquired in 1993 by the Royal Horticultural Society's Lindley Library gives some indication of the extent of this work; among the most striking examples are a series of necklaces to be fashioned from gold. These very intricate and delicate designs, one of which incorporates the flower, fruit and leaf of the myrtle, were most probably derived from ancient Greek or Roman examples. She followed the fashion for embellishing articles of plain Georgian silver with repoussé swags of flowers, and also designed decorative articles to be fashioned in silver, such as a watch stand with twining honeysuckle incorporating the initials 'CL', which was probably done for Charles Liddell.

This workbook does not neglect gardening subjects: there are a number of patterns for brick pavements and garden seats. Gardening was starting to play an increasingly important part in her life. 'Much interest in garden plants', she wrote in July 1871, and before long she was adding opium poppies and white *Lychnis viscaria* 'Alba' to the borders at Wargrave, and planting broom and furze near a neighbour's spring. George Leslie described her garden as 'a perfect wilderness of sweets . . . old-fashioned flowers bloomed there in greatest profusion [and] there were lavender hedges of marvellous growth'.[11]

After the death of Captain Jekyll in 1876, his widow decided to return to Surrey, and soon found a site for a new house not far from Bramley.[12] Its location on Munstead Heath was considered remote and unsafe, as the heath was still populated by gypsies and even occasional smugglers, making their way to Portsmouth. Gertrude and her brother Herbert, then living in London, had something to say about the choice of the site and the selection of the architect for their mother's house. Munstead House, dismissed by Pevsner as a dull essay in 'Parsonage Gothic', was built in 1878 by the Scottish architect John James Stevenson.[13] Perhaps someone in the Jekyll family had noticed his early Queen Anne-style town houses in Mayfair or Knightsbridge, or the Red House on the

Munstead House, the south front, with Gertrude Jekyll's workshop on the left, photographed in 1934 by Anne Wertsner Wood (courtesy Susan E. Schnare)

Gertrude Jekyll's workshop at Munstead House in 1885, with her paintings, pottery collections, and cabinets filled with artists' supplies (CED–UC Berkeley)

Bayswater Road.[14] Gertrude may well have played a role in planning the house, and certainly designed a Jacobean-style fireplace for the hall; Herbert later added panelling in the style of Grinling Gibbons in the dining room.

At Munstead House Gertrude had a spacious workshop where she could work undisturbed, with a spiral staircase leading to her bedroom above. The workshop was filled with cabinets, cupboards, and shelves. Along one wall were storage drawers for craft-working supplies such as exotic woods and mother-of-pearl for inlay work, and fabric samples for interior design commissions. There were shelves for her books and the pottery collected on her travels, and every available wall space was filled with her paintings. In the autumn of 1877 Gertrude, who was to play a key role in laying out the gardens at Munstead House, was moving fruit trees and plants from Wargrave; by the following summer, the house was ready for occupation. Her diary for September 26th records 'to Munstead for good', and the sigh of relief at returning to Surrey is almost audible.[15]

Gertrude Jekyll's early years at Munstead House saw a rapid growth in her gardening interests, some of which were to bear fruit years later. The famous nursery at Munstead Wood naturally evolved from her preoccupation with the collection, identification and cultivation of plants. Intensive botanical studies in

Gertrude Jekyll around 1880 when she was in her late thirties (from F. Jekyll, Gertrude Jekyll, *1934)*

Surrey and on travels abroad brought her into contact with other like-minded enthusiasts, contact which often ripened into valued friendship, and with professional gardeners who let her 'pick their brains'.[16] As she later recalled, 'I had the good fortune to become acquainted with . . . that wonderful company of amateurs and others who did so much for better gardening in the last half of the nineteenth century'.[17] Her workshop was flooded with specimens sent by collectors from expeditions near and far, and as her horticultural experiments blossomed, people began to seek her out. Some came to compare notes or to admire the layout of her borders; others, like Henry G. Moon, painted the rarer plants. Among those who visited were the Revd John Thomas Bennett-Poe, a well-known amateur grower of prize-winning narcissi and tulips; and two distinguished horticulturists from Ireland, Frederick Burbridge of the Trinity College Botanical Gardens and Frederick Moore, Director of the Glasnevin Botanic Garden.[18]

In the summer of 1880 the influential gardening writer and editor William Robinson and the rosarian Reynolds Hole (later Dean of Rochester) visited Munstead.[19] Gertrude Jekyll first met Robinson in 1875 when she called at the Covent Garden offices of *The Garden*, a weekly magazine he edited. She subsequently sent in a steady stream of plants for identification, and soon queries

William Robinson in his garden at Gravetye Manor, Sussex, around 1900 (courtesy Peter Herbert)

from 'G.J.' began to appear in the magazine. In 1881 a bolder 'G. Jekyll, Munstead, Godalming' was the by-line for a note entitled 'Some Plants from Algeria' detailing a consignment of plants she had received from the botanist M. Durando.[20] From this modest start she progressed to longer articles in *The Garden* and in other publications, laying the foundation for the books she began to write in 1899.

To judge from the maturity of the gardens at Munstead House by the early 1880s Gertrude Jekyll seems to have laid them out at a brisk pace, in comparison with the slow deliberation she brought to the creation of her more famous gardens at Munstead Wood. In 1882 Robinson's assistant editor William Goldring wrote an article on Munstead House for *The Garden*; his description, and Gertrude's photographs, provide most of what is known about this early garden. 'In the midst of wild heath land, diversified with picturesque clusters of Hollies, Scotch Firs, wild Junipers, and a variety of other spontaneous growth,' Goldring wrote, 'is a beautiful garden made by a lady within the past four years, and along the whole range of the Surrey sandstone hills there could scarcely have been found a better position for a house and garden than this'.[21]

The relationship between house, lawn and garden and the surrounding landscape was of primary concern to Robinson, who preached that one should

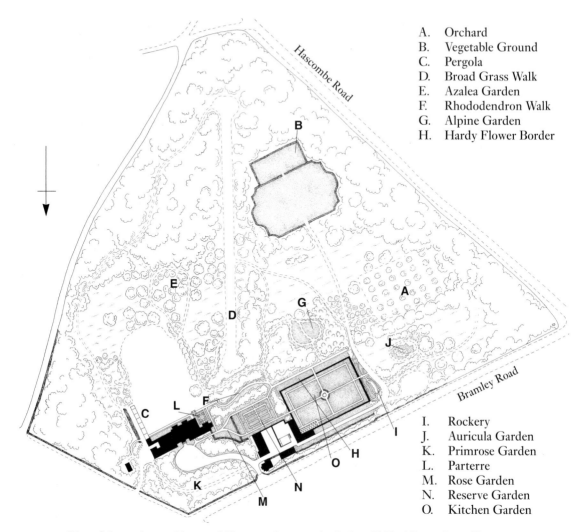

A. Orchard
B. Vegetable Ground
C. Pergola
D. Broad Grass Walk
E. Azalea Garden
F. Rhododendron Walk
G. Alpine Garden
H. Hardy Flower Border

I. Rockery
J. Auricula Garden
K. Primrose Garden
L. Parterre
M. Rose Garden
N. Reserve Garden
O. Kitchen Garden

Plan of the gardens at Munstead House as they were in the late 1880s (Simon Dorrell)

'take a higher view of the garden than as a receptacle for everything crowded into it'. The garden at Munstead House, which he frequently visited and may have had a part in designing, excellently exemplified this 'higher' view. Following one of his visits in 1883, a plan appeared in *The Garden* which clearly shows a panoply of specialized areas incorporated with varying degrees of success into traditional Victorian country-house grounds. The accompanying article praises the discretion of the plantings, as well as 'capital use' of 'carefree' hardy plants, and the ease of access to the various parts of the garden, 'within a minute's walk', where one could enjoy the flowers – as opposed to the obvious device of spreading them all out for viewing from the window.[22] Birch woods surrounded the house along the north-east boundary, and a large kitchen garden, orchard (A), and vegetable ground (B), lay to the west and south. Adjacent to the house, but carefully separated from it by informal plantings, was an unusually large reserve garden, and farther afield lay a medley of garden 'departments'. Many features of the garden – azalea and rhododendron banks, an alpine garden, rockery, primrose garden, ornamental orchard, hardy flower border, pergola (C), bank of brier roses, and wide grass walks – were used again at Munstead Wood, where Gertrude perfected her earlier experiments, most notably the integral relationship between house and garden.

To give 'a sense of some extent', the south terrace opened on to a large lawn of loose but narrowing shape, leading directly on to the natural heath. To the east, a yew hedge and a pergola covered with vines and climbing roses and backed by a bank of brier roses created a boundary, and a narrow path through the heath linked it with a broad grass walk (D), precursor of the Green Wood Walk at Munstead Wood. Another path led to the azalea garden (E), beneath Scotch fir and birch and backed by junipers, and nearer to the house rhododendrons and clumps of lilies were planted along a path leading to the flower border (F).

The retention within the garden of rough ground with heather and gorse, unconventional at the time, may reflect the influence of Robinson's book *The Wild Garden*, published in 1870. In this he promoted the use of hardy plants in informal settings, and in particular the idea of using native plants in naturalistic groups along the outer perimeter of the garden, where the lawn should melt imperceptibly into the woodland garden. At Munstead House the wild heathland came to within a hundred and fifty feet of the house, and wild foxgloves and verbascums grew in the bracken at the edge of the pine wood. A broad grass walk running almost north-south gave access to the woodland and heath; curiously, it did not lead directly on to the lawn, as later at Munstead Wood, but ended awkwardly, near the rhododendrons. A second avenue running more to the west, towards the vegetable ground, and terminated with a pine tree brought back from Ravenna, was laid out after 1895 when Herbert Jekyll inherited Munstead House.

The alpine garden (G) was considered slightly unorthodox in 1880. It was on slightly rising ground and composed of half-buried blocks of sandstone put in when the ground was trenched. Solid masses of *Gentiana acaulis* covering several yards, and an equally bold group of *Campanula pulla* more than a yard square, were noted by Goldring. This was by no means the only area devoted to alpines. Opposite the hardy flower border (H), a 'rocky bank, about four feet high', entirely of stone, was built to serve as a retaining wall for the higher ground beyond. Although the wall was nearly perpendicular colonies of houseleeks, stonecrops, harebells and dianthus were established with great success. A more conventional rockery (I) outside the west wall of the kitchen garden, with undulating rocky mounds and pockets of sandy and peaty soil, provided a picturesque setting for a variety of shade-tolerant and sun-loving rare and uncommon plants; a rough stone seat 'with back cushions of thyme', was tucked into one of the mounds. Goldring remarked on *Haberlea rhodopensis* growing in a shady crevice and *Ourisia coccinea* clinging to the face of the rock, and reckoned that he had never seen 'such fine tufts' of *Arnebia pulchra* as there were growing

A stone seat 'with back cushions of thyme' in the rock garden at Munstead House, 1886 (CED-UC Berkeley)

on the ledge facing the sun, nor of *Onosma taurica*, which grew to 'an unusual size, sheltered and shady'.[23]

In 1882 a small clearing was made for an auricula garden (J); although Gertrude Jekyll mentions the use of border auriculas in *Wood and Garden*, this was not an idea she repeated at Munstead Wood. One she did repeat was a primrose garden, but she later wrote that the earlier garden at Munstead House (K) was in 'a prettier place, a more natural bit of woodland'.[24] A narrow, sweeping path leading from the kitchen side of the house ran through birch woods to link with the main drive. In a space approximately seventy yards long by ten to fifteen yards wide were masses of the primroses she made famous, flowing between the birches in wide streams and sparkling against their silver-grey trunks.

Most of the flower gardens at Munstead House were to the west of the house, and they included a brilliantly-coloured small parterre (L) at the south-west corner filled with scarlet zonal pelargoniums and masses of tuberous begonias. This little parterre, which she could see from her clematis-festooned workshop window, effectively terminated the south terrace; groups of flowering shrubs and

The Primrose Garden under birches at Munstead House, May 1886 (CED-UC Berkeley)

rhododendrons hid the hardy flower border from view. Another path beside the house led to a small rose garden (M), and on to the reserve and kitchen gardens beyond.

The reserve garden (N) was unusual and its design was both practical and attractive; Robinson included a plan of it in most editions of his book *The English Flower Garden*. It served as an embryonic nursery garden for stock and also as an experimental garden for ideas and theories before their use in the wider garden. This outdoor 'workshop' was the precursor of the numerous ornamental borders in the working gardens at Munstead Wood, where Gertrude Jekyll worked with grey foliage and unusual plant combinations. The outer beds were filled with spring-flowering plants – scillas, crocuses and double primroses – but the central beds were reserved for taller perennials such as alstromerias, double sweet rocket, pyrethrums and phlox. All these beds were neatly edged with stones that soon became overgrown with moss, giving a simple and natural effect.

The large, high-walled kitchen garden (O) (190 ft by 100 ft) was a familiar feature of country-house gardens of the period. Each of the four paths

The Revd John Bennett-Poe, a narcissus fancier, and Mrs Davidson, author of The Unheated Greenhouse, *met in the garden at Munstead House, 1886 (CED–UC Berkeley)*

converging on a central, circular well-head were flanked by double borders – a typical arrangement. Along one of the shorter cross-paths were double Michaelmas daisy borders, similar to those later so famous at Munstead Wood.

The single most memorable feature for most garden visitors at Munstead House, as later at Munstead Wood, was the long hardy flower border (H), at the foot of the south wall of the kitchen garden. 'Never before have we seen hardy plants set out so well or cultivated in such a systematic way,' Goldring wrote.[25] Much of the practical and design experience that went into the later border was first experimented with here. The two borders were almost the same size, approximately two hundred feet long and fourteen feet wide, but the plan that the Munstead House border should give 'a continuous tide of bloom from daffodil-time till frosts destroyed the scanty blooms late in autumn' proved to be a mistake; the celebrated Munstead Wood border, created ten years later, made no attempt to sustain floral interest for such a long season. Nor was the position of the Munstead House border ideal: it was difficult to view the whole picture from a distance, other than obliquely. The border was split by a central cross-path from the kitchen garden, whereas at Munstead Wood the cross-path was positioned off-centre. The wall at the back of the border was cloaked in vines to enhance the plantings in front, and where the doorway arch was cut in the stone was tile-capped for added interest. Handsome German hinges decorated the wooden door, and the stone above the doorway bore the inscription 'Audiverunt vocem Domini Dei deambulantis in horto' ('They heard the voice of the Lord God walking in the garden').[26] The

Michaelmas daisy borders in the kitchen garden at Munstead House, September 1885. The Scots pines in the background are in Munstead Wood, along the boundary edge (CED–UC Berkeley)

The lower end of the south border at Munstead House, 9 July 1886. A Rosa arvensis *covers the arbour (CED–UC Berkeley)*

path in front of the border led to a rustic arbour, covered with *Rosa arvensis* and framed by weeping birch in the background, which afforded a view along the whole border.

The Garden declared this 'the richest and most effective border of hardy flowers that we know of near London'.[27] Gertrude Jekyll looked to nature for inspiration in creating her border, but cautioned that 'purely natural forms of flower groupings must not be looked for in fields and hedges', because of the activities of the farmer and landowner: natural groupings – 'beds of bulrushes, a pool of white water lily, a copse carpet of primroses . . . [or] a stretch of grey and purple heather' – were to be found in 'old woods, riversides, and moorland'. These lessons were not to be copied or transcribed, but 'interpreted in such a way as may best suit our space and means'.[28] Her own interpretation was both innovative and highly successful, praised by Goldring for the skilful blending of plants to produce a harmonious whole: 'It is the soft and insensible transition from one mass of colour to another which is so

The garden doorway that leads to the kitchen garden at Munstead House, 1885. The hinges are German and above the door is a Latin inscription (CED–UC Berkeley)

effective.' He extolled an artist's sense of colour-mixing, extended to the arrangement of hardy flowers: 'Looked at from a distance, nothing in particular catches the eye in this border; everything is in harmony.' He continued, 'No bare earth is seen; the whole is carpeted with plants, those of taller growth rising from a carpet of dwarf ones.'[29] It was an exceptional accomplishment for an amateur.

CHAPTER 3

Picture Perfect

The 1880s found Gertrude Jekyll settled into a life centred around gardening and writing. After studying painting and then trying her hand at gilding, wood-working and silversmithing (to name but a few crafts), she discovered an interest that was to have a profound effect on her artistic development, and one that helped to preserve the evidence of her gardening talent for posterity. Once she had mastered the technical aspects of her new pursuit of photography, she was quick to appreciate its creative and practical possibilities; her exploration of both has left solid visual evidence of both her gardening accomplishments and her other interests. While her many garden plans provide the details of her theories, long after the living examples have disappeared, her photographs are a glorious and intimate revelation of her skill in both design and composition.

Gertrude Jekyll became a competent photographer with the same ease she brought to the mastery of other skills. In some ways the artistic side of photography was a natural extension of her early art training. It demanded all her perceptiveness, and gave her an opportunity of improving her compositional skills. Just as she was not the only artistic and musical member of her family, so Gertrude was not the only Jekyll to be interested in photography.[1] Her brother Herbert was probably the instructor who scrawled on the back of one of Gertrude's first prints, ' . . . little over exposed. Not quite in focus.' Another photograph bears more specific advice: 'Keep the camera level – use rising front - expose less – more pyro more bromide.'[2] With her artistic talent and technical dexterity Gertrude was soon able to make productive use of her photography in illustrating articles and books, and also as a personal note-taking device, much like a sketch-book.

If it was not Herbert who initially sparked Gertrude's interest in photography, it may have been the result of visits to gallery exhibitions in London. Technical information was readily available, in the *British Journal of Photography* and the *Photographic Almanac*, or Henry Peach Robinson's book *Picture Making by Photography*, aimed at enlightened amateurs such as herself. It is highly unlikely that she belonged to any of the numerous amateur societies that proliferated at the time; one such, the West Surrey Photographic Society, hotly debated the suitability of women exhibiting their work. Their *Photographic Gazette* (aimed at an all-male bastion of tradesmen) once reported, 'We are not acquainted with a great number of lady photographers, but some of those we do know could put the work of many medal-hunters to shame'.[3]

One amateur photographer who may well have inspired Gertrude Jekyll (but whose subject-matter was quite different) was Charles Dodgson, who took up both photography and his familiar pen-name, Lewis Carroll, in 1856. They undoubtedly knew one another through friends such as Alice Liddell, who was nine years younger than Gertrude. She was the original inspiration, of course, for *Alice's Adventures in Wonderland* and one of Carroll's child models. Among several mutual acquaintances were Ruskin, with whom Alice studied, and Mary Newton, who was a friend of Alice's mother.[4] Alice's cousins, Lady Victoria Liddell, married to Edward Rowe Fisher-Rowe and living at Thorncombe Park, near Munstead, and The Hon. Charles Liddell, a librarian at the British Museum, were both close friends of Gertrude Jekyll.

As Gertrude had spent holidays on the Isle of Wight since childhood, there is the intriguing possibility that she knew Julia Margaret Cameron, the famous art photographer who lived in Freshwater.[5] Their way of life, their personalities and their photographic interests could not have been more different, yet Mrs Cameron's example may have been an inspiration. The two had several acquaintances in common, including Alice Liddell, G.F. Watts, and Jacques Blumenthal, all of whom Julia Cameron had photographed. Helen Allingham, the well-known artist who later lived in Witley, Surrey and painted the borders at Munstead Wood, also spent holidays in Freshwater and may have provided another link.

Unlike Julia Cameron, however, Gertrude practised photography not for profit, but for her own pleasure and gratification. In her books she refers to herself as a 'working amateur', but notes that she may have taken 'more trouble in working out certain problems . . . than amateurs in general'. Little is known about how she learned the technicalities, or of the details of her equipment. Francis Jekyll's comment that she began in 1885 tallies with notations in her personal photo albums; photography soon became an absorbing interest, 'and, as usual, the entire process was mastered from start to finish; sinks and dark-rooms were fitted up at home, and the long series of tree and flower studies, farm buildings, and old Surrey types which were to figure in her books began to issue from the "shop"'.[6]

Although this was a period as exciting for photography as it was for garden design, the complexity of the process, from the preparation of plates to the printing from glass negatives, seems daunting today. Nevertheless, by the early 1880s the relative ease of use of the gelatin dry plates which had replaced the messy and cumbersome wet plates, and the reduction in exposure times needed, had opened up photography to a wider range of people. The development of hand-held cameras around 1900, including George Eastman's Brownie camera with roll film ('You press the button, we do the rest'), popularized photography among amateurs from royalty downwards, and many hours were spent posing for pictures and assembling family albums.[7] Paul Martin, a contemporary of Gertrude Jekyll who was learning about photography at the same time, has described buying his first camera, a quarter-plate model, complete with a double dark slide, a chromatic lens, and a folding tripod, for a guinea: 'At last I had a camera with a shutter, . . . but there were always the plates to change, either under the bedcovers or in a temporarily fixed-up dark room. Local dealers were still unreliable and seldom had what you wanted.'[8]

No snapshot has come to light of Gertrude Jekyll in the field, or of her camera, though the Collins camera with a Dallmeyer lens and tripod offered at the Munstead Wood sale in September 1948 may have been hers.[9] She probably began with a folding field camera, such as a Collins, rather than a larger studio camera. The Collins Patent Camera was a field model with a short life on the market. Patented in 1884, its revolutionary design featured a simplified mechanism for folding the lens into the base-board, giving greater portability.[10] The camera also improved the rising front referred to in Herbert's comment, allowing the photographer to adjust architectural views. Field cameras folded up very compactly to a size of 5 by 7 or 7 by 9 inches, depending on their format, and were designed for double plates, one on either side.

Gertrude Jekyll undoubtedly used more than one camera during her thirty years of active photography; the quality of her work, especially the depth of field, improved substantially after 1900, probably indicating the purchase of new equipment. Except for photographs taken in 1885, most examples of her original prints are approximately full-plate size (6½ in by 8½ ins), so she may have had a full-plate camera for studio work, using a lighter-weight half-plate model for outdoor work.

Probably a photographer would not normally use more than a dozen plates at one time (in Gertrude Jekyll's albums, a day's shoot is easily discernible), since the actual set-up time was still almost an hour, even though boxes of factory-coated dry plates could be obtained from local suppliers. The comments which accompany her portrait of her cat Tabby in a basket give some scarce detail of her professional paraphernalia: as she wrote in *Children and Gardens*, 'I was doing photographs down the garden with spare plates in a palm-leaf basket. When I wanted more plates [Tabby] had made himself so comfortable that I could not bear to disturb him, so I went indoors and got more plates and made his picture.'[11]

At the time Gertrude Jekyll was learning the rudiments of photography albumenized paper, which the photographer cut to the size needed, was in general use for making prints, and bromide developing-out paper, which broadened the range of artistic potential, was newly introduced.[12] Since the different papers produced a varying range of results, it is no wonder that she should have been captivated by the technical possibilities of photography. The printing process she used for most prints in her albums in the first year or so was platinotype, characterized by a low contrast, with limited tonal range. By 1886 she had switched to gelatin silver or collodion silver printing-out paper, toned with gold toner. The variations in paper thickness and image colour indicate the use of a wide range of materials and toning procedures.[13]

In *Wood and Garden* Gertrude Jekyll refers modestly to her abilities: 'owing to my want of technical ability as a photographer, [my photographs are] very weak, and have only been rendered available by the skill of the reproducer'; in reality, she was a skilled technician. Examination of the original prints in her personal photograph albums provides a wealth of information, not only as regards her technical expertise, but also concerning the evolution of her design philosophy. The albums, now at the University of California at Berkeley, contain proof prints of most of her known photographs together with many unpublished supplemental

Tabby sleeping in the photo basket in the Hidden Garden, from Children and Gardens, *1907 (CED–UC Berkeley)*

views.[14] Their value is enhanced by the handwritten notations about locations, or observations about design. Few are dated, but most bear the negative number that was etched into the lower right-hand corner of the (now lost) original plates. Some prints, less clean than others, show the photographer's tiny fingerprints, transferred from the glass negatives. These photographs mark Gertrude Jekyll's progress from the enthusiastic amateur of early spring 1885, turning out dozens of plant studies, to the assured professional of the 1890s, with a decided purpose to her work. Ever-practical, she established a system of layering prints one on top of the other in the pages, for ready reference. Multiple prints of the same image, made on various papers and with several tonal variations, as well as adjustments made by sensitive cropping, all indicate her pleasure in experimentation and delight in refining the camera-bound composition.

It is probable that the use of Gertrude Jekyll's photographs to illustrate her books has pre-empted their consideration as works of art. When *Wood and Garden* appeared, Mrs C.W. Earle, herself a garden writer, thought that the photographs, 'good as they were', could never compare with woodcuts – a quibble which may in part reflect the poor quality of the reproductions in the book.[15] Certainly, her photographs have rarely been considered outside the context of book illustration. The quality of the original prints, however, and the range of subjects are compelling. Studies of traditional 'genre' subjects such as rural buildings and scenes of country life abound, but they are highly individual.

Layered prints of ivy growing in beech along Unstead Lane, as arranged in one of Gertrude Jekyll's photo albums, 1885 (CED–UC Berkeley)

Like her own life, Gertrude Jekyll's photographic subjects are devoid of artifice or banality, even when they echo photographic themes popular in earlier decades, such as picturesque bridges, old mills, and vanishing country customs – many of the photographs used in *Old West Surrey* for example, are somewhat anachronistic in mood, without the elegant artistry apparent in her other books. Gertrude Jekyll's inspiration was the naturalistic school of photography typified by Peter Henry Emerson's book *Pictures from East Anglian Life* (1888), rather than the contrived pictorialism promoted by Henry Peach Robinson.[16] Making the rounds of photographic exhibitions in London would have shown her the broad range of aesthetic possibilities.

Not surprisingly, the earliest examples of Jekyll's work are views, taken in spring 1885, of Munstead House gardens – primulas in the rock garden, bergenias along a rocky path, and vases filled with helleborus blossoms – the first dated one is 25 March. The photographer's enthusiasm for her new-found interest is captured in an early-morning shot of profusely-blooming roses taken in June 1885, and its accompanying inscription: '4 in the morning – could have been good but for a leak in the camera'. As her technical competence quickly improved, she learned to co-ordinate sophisticated developing techniques with correct

An unpublished study of climbing roses bears the caption, '4 in the morning – could have been good but for a leak in the camera', 1885 (CED–UC Berkeley)

exposures, and the quality of her prints improved immensely. Blurry, out-of-focus, badly exposed too-dark prints fill the opening pages of her first album, but by 1888 she had taken more than nine hundred photographs and mastered problems of technique and composition. By the second year her photographic excursions were taking her farther afield, to Sussex and Kent, later to Yorkshire. In 1887 her camera went with her to Switzerland, where she took informal portraits of fellow guests such as Theodore Waterhouse (younger brother of the architect Alfred Waterhouse), and views of the house, interiors, and garden; she also took remarkable studies of mountains and clouds, using her camera as an artist would his sketch-book.

Her enthusiasm for photography seems to have begun to dwindle by the early 1890s, a time when she was preoccupied with other pursuits, notably garden-making and the building of Munstead Wood. Certainly her increasingly troublesome eyesight, the specific nature of which remains unclear (although she herself described it as myopia), precluded a number of activities.[17] Acting on the advice of an eye specialist in 1891, Gertrude reluctantly curtailed her embroidery, painting, and other pursuits requiring close vision, in the hope that her condition might improve. To give her eyes a rest, she channelled most of her energies into gardening, as a natural therapy.

In the late 1890s, however, she returned to photography with renewed energy when she began in earnest to write books, books that would benefit from exacting photographs to explain the text fully. By 1900 her photographic pursuits were purposeful rather than exploratory, and rarely led her beyond her immediate neighbourhood. She already had nearly 1500 photographs to choose from to illustrate points, although some were at least fifteen years old and a little outdated. Nearly all the 600 album prints made after 1900 were taken with a specific book or project in mind, and most were of Munstead Wood.

Gertrude Jekyll's very short eyesight, which made anything other than a close scrutiny of plants or an intimate application to such practical skills as embroidery impossible, also had its advantages: 'I often find that I have observed things that have escaped strong and long-sighted people,' she wrote.[18] The mastery of textural depth in her later photographs probably derived from her minute visual investigation of such details as stonework and foliage. Clumps of yuccas, bergenias, and iris growing beside stone paths near the reserve garden at Munstead House reveal a preoccupation with contrasting foliage and an ability to create pleasing compositions with plants. Her notes on the value of bergenia foliage, which appeared in February 1885, reveal that ever-observant eye: 'how valuable the broad-leaved Saxifrages are now! S. cordifolia rather better than S. crassifolia; the latter seems to feel the cold more; in severe weather the leaves lie down limp, while cordifolia holds them stiff and strong through any winter'.[19] Four months later a striking photograph, her first in print, appeared in *The Garden* to illustrate another point: 'Group of Broad-leaved Saxifrages on bank, showing effect of unity as compared with "dotty" planting of borders.'[20] (The caption may have been written by *The Garden*'s editor William Robinson, who waged a campaign against 'dotty' plantings in his own books, particularly *The English Flower Garden*.)

This image of Bergenia cordifolia *and* B. crassifolia, *which appeared in* The Garden *in June 1885, was Gertrude Jekyll's first published photograph (CED-UC Berkeley)*

By spring 1886, after little over a year of practical photography experience, many of the simple plant portraits in the albums bear the notation 'E.F.G.' (for *The English Flower Garden*) or 'G' (for *The Garden*), indicating that a major photographic assignment was under way. Whether the idea was her own or Robinson's is unclear, but it opened up a practical avenue for her photography. For these studies, sprays or stems of the desired plants were arranged in a makeshift outdoor setting sometimes with a clumsy drape strung up to provide a background. Once the photograph had been delivered, the engraver removed such extraneous props as flower pots, glass vases, books, chairs, and children from the final illustration.

A number of 'E.F.G.' studies transcend the merely documentary. The group of *Romneya coulteri* flowers simply arranged on burlap brings to life Gertrude Jekyll's observation that 'The bold centre of strong yellow stamens gives the utmost colour-value to the dainty-milk-white of the petals, with which the pale glaucous, deeply-cut leaves are in quiet harmony.'[21] So successful was the assignment that by the third (1889) and fourth (1893) editions of *The English Flower Garden*, almost every engraving in the plant encyclopedia was derived from a Jekyll photograph.[22] She praised Robinson's book – 'the best and most

Hollyhocks growing in a cottage garden, 1886, was included in Robinson's book The English Flower Garden, *but the children were cropped out (CED-UC Berkeley)*

helpful book of all for those who want to know about hardy plants' – but why her role as photographer was rarely credited in Robinson's publications or whether she was remunerated for her work is unknown.[23]

Only rarely did studies of floral arrangements find a place in Robinson's publications. No doubt he dismissed the subject as ladies' work; for Gertrude Jekyll it was one more element in her conception of the unity of arts and home-making. As with her other deliberate studies, her observation of colour, form, and texture led to an exploration of composition, using cut flowers and foliage, all arranged in the proper vessels. After collecting forays in neighbouring cottage gardens or in her own cutting gardens, she would quickly repair to the workshop and select appropriate containers. The resulting arrangements, sometimes five in a row, were usually photographed on a Jacobean oak linen-hutch. For many she used the clear Munstead glass vases which she had specially made in London when she failed to locate simple ones to suit her taste. In one example, a lavish early-summer gleaning of peonies, roses, iris, campanula, alstroemeria and eryngium reflects the photographer's props in the clear glass vases. Gertrude took several hundred photographs of her arrangements, following the seasons, from a handful of daffodils in an earthenware jug to festoons of Christmas holly in St John's Church, Busbridge. Album pages sometimes include photographs of the

A still-life of Romneya coulteri *flowers, taken expressly for* The Garden *in 1885 (CED-UC Berkeley)*

borders from which she had gathered her material alongside the end results. In 1907, after twenty years of photographing her arrangements, she selected nearly sixty to illustrate *Flower Decoration in the House*.

Photographs of the cottage gardens that sparked her horticultural imagination proliferate in the album pages. In her search for interesting locations, she went to neighbouring farms and villages, occasionally to a public house: James Edgeler's The Squirrell in Hurtmore was the setting for dozens of studies, although she took care that the published pictures were cropped to obliterate the precise nature of the establishment. Mrs Edgeler's lush cottage garden, with cascading roses and a tumble of old-fashioned plants, frequently figured in books and articles. The *Rosa arvensis* growing on the rough arbour at Munstead House may have come originally from Mrs Edgeler's garden – prints of each appear together in the album.

With the exception of cottagers such as the Edgelers, Gertrude Jekyll seems to have been less interested in photographing people. Occasional stiffly-posed portraits of family members and visitors contrast sharply with candid shots of gardeners, children and household cats. To demonstrate childhood pleasures and pursuits she illustrated *Children and Gardens* with numerous examples of children

The Munstead glass vases, filled with arrangements of early summer flowers, were Gertrude Jekyll's own design, 1887 (CED–UC Berkeley)

(her nieces, Lutyens's children, and neighbours such as the Pleydell-Bouverie children at High Barn, Hascombe), but some were unwilling models.

Rural landscapes in all seasons, particularly tree studies, were the subject of her most artistic photographs, and were much praised: in 1885 *The Garden* singled out her photographs of trees at Peper Harow as being the 'best' in their competition.[24] A particular fascination with tree roots – their intrinsic form accentuated by their tenacious grip along steep Surrey embankments – inspired annual visits to selected sites. Her study of fir roots, bearing the inscription 'making natural steps', was one of several taken in the wooded areas along a country lane leading to Unstead Farm. Another more poignant inscription reads, 'the last scene in the life of an old beech tree'.

The Squirrell, James Edgeler's public house in Hurtmore, was the setting for many photographic studies, 1885 (CED–UC Berkeley)

The rustic log porch of The Squirrell was covered with white roses, 1886 (CED–UC Berkeley)

Photographs of tree trunks and their branching limbs record the minute changes Gertrude Jekyll observed from year to year. A late spring view of a row of ancient holly trees, their smooth, silvery bark highlighted in the foreground, is one of several dozen studies taken in 1885 that must be considered art photography. Nearly fifteen years later she selected the holly illustration for *Wood and Garden*.[25] In autumn 1885, after at least six months' experience, she took ten views (possibly a day's shoot) at nearby Busbridge Hall. The setting was stately, with a pond and a canopy of mature larch, plane and beech trees, as well as Scotch and silver fir, the most captivating image a noble group of horse chestnuts. For her composition she chose to focus on a low horizontal tree branch in the foreground, with the pond and a bridge in the distance. Her own comments – that the trees stand on a natural mound surrounded on three sides by unencumbered level lawn 'so that nothing hinders either a distant view of the whole group or a nearer observation of grand trunk and massive limb and delicate branch' – illustrate her artist's training.[26]

During the winter, when most gardeners put their cameras away because of lack of subject-matter and dimming light levels, Gertrude Jekyll was quick to record an unusual event. An intense snowstorm the day after Christmas in 1886 inspired several studies of Scotch firs that had blown over on to a frozen pond in Busbridge; she selected the best for *Wood and Garden*.[27] In the album pages one can sense her excitement as she moved quickly from the recumbent firs to the detail of rime-covered flowering ivy on the bridge over the pond, and frost-nipped holly in the surrounding woodland. Only a week later, on 3 January 1887, she was photographing the patterns of the mounds of snow piled up outside her workshop door at Munstead House.

Landscapes were also an enduring interest. In January 1913 a series devoted to Hydon Heath was among the last photographs she had published. In earlier years she had written about the smugglers' lanes that ran through the sandy heath about two miles from Munstead, and in 1914, as part of an appeal for the National Trust to acquire the property, she described how its wild forest character served as an excellent example for ornamental plantings. She marvelled at the colours and effects of light on the tree bark in the winter, which she considered the best time to appreciate the area: 'All painters know the loveliness of colour of winter woodland in middle distance, while the low sunlight, glancing on the rusty warmth of the dead bracken, on the bright green of the leafless whortleberry and the still more brilliant verdure of the mossy ground cover, give pictures of colour beauty unequalled by the more even green tones of the summer months'.[28]

The strongest sense of intimacy with her subject matter, however, is felt in the photographs of Munstead Wood that are familiar from her books. For more than twenty-five years she captured both the obvious and the extraordinary; of the several hundred photographs she took of the garden, many were never published in her lifetime. Part of their charm is not so much that they convey a vanished era, but that they encapsulate well-executed ideals. The English author E.V. Lucas recalled the stir her photographs made. *Wood and Garden*, he said, served 'the double effect of sending its readers out instantly to buy both a spade . . . and a camera'.[29]

Holly stems in an old hedgerow, 1885, appeared in Wood and Garden *(CED-UC Berkeley)*

Gertrude Jekyll received credit for her photograph of horse chestnuts in Busbridge, 1886, when it was published in The Garden *in April 1887 (CED–UC Berkeley)*

From early views taken when the woodland paths were being laid out to the final shots of the main flower border, taken in August 1914, Gertrude Jekyll created a matchless record of Munstead Wood in images which vividly portray the parallel progress of designer and photographer. The solid information they provide about the development of the garden and her theory of design is unequalled for any other early twentieth-century garden. There is an unfortunate gap in the record for the early 1890s; photographs taken at the end of the decade show a full, maturing garden, rather than one with sparse, underdeveloped areas.

No book better describes and illustrates Munstead Wood than *Colour in the Flower Garden*. The familiar photographs were mostly taken during the spring and summer of 1907, the improved focus and composition suggesting a new surge of energy, possibly a new camera. The Spring Garden and other areas not fully

This striking composition of Scotch firs thrown on to frozen water by a snowstorm was photographed on 26 December 1886 (CED–UC Berkeley)

covered in earlier books receive the lion's share of attention, while the garden surrounding The Hut and the woodland gardens, detailed earlier, play lesser roles. After the publication of *Colour in the Flower Garden*, Gertrude Jekyll's enthusiasm for photography apparently began to wane, as a result of worsening eyesight, at a time when her burgeoning writing commissions increased her need for illustrations.

It is ironic that at the time she was taking photographs for *Colour in the Flower Garden*, a new colour process was being introduced in England by the Lumière brothers: in the summer of 1907 they marketed a workable single-plate colour process, using autochrome plates.[30] The results were somewhat disappointing, characterized by a lack of definition resulting in flat, dense and grainy pictures, very different from the texture and tonality Gertrude Jekyll captured in her black-and-white photographs. As she commented about an autochrome reproduction of one of her borders, 'Colour photography from Nature has not yet reached such a degree of precision and accuracy as can do justice to a careful scheme of colour groupings', but can only serve as a 'suggestion'.[31] Her enquiring mind would have delighted in the complex technique for colour photography, in which green, violet, and orange-coloured starch grains were spread over the plate which was then covered with a panchromatic emulsion. But plates were expensive, exposure times long, processing complex, and good eyesight mandatory, so she evidently concluded that black-and-white photography was better.[32]

Beginning about the time of the First World War, most of the new illustrations for Gertrude Jekyll's articles were taken by Herbert Cowley, the gardening editor for Country Life publications. Her annotation in the albums she kept of tearsheets from the magazines in which they appeared acknowledges that 'with few exceptions' these photographs were his work.[33] Although Cowley's photographs of Munstead Wood are more perfunctory than her own, they serve to continue the record of the garden through the late 1920s, long after she had ceased to photograph it herself.

Gertrude Jekyll's legacy of two thousand black-and-white photographs reveal an artist's curiosity, provide a record of one of the most significant gardens of the era, and admirably illustrate her ideas.

CHAPTER 4

A Passion for Domestic Architecture

Gertrude Jekyll wrote to her friend Herbert Baker, an architect for whom she designed several gardens, that she had 'a passion (though an ignorant one) for matters concerning domestic architecture that almost equals my interest in plants and trees'.[1] The extent of her long-standing appreciation of architecture and the building arts, which played such a pivotal role in the design of Munstead Wood, is not represented in her writings as thoroughly as her theories on gardening. In *Old West Surrey* and *Home and Garden* she offered glimpses of her fascination with rural cottages and regional building methods, but she wrote little on the subject elsewhere. However, her photographic rambles through local villages during the 1880s vividly betray her passionate interest. Whether capturing the ornate Jacobean interiors of local manor houses or paving details in rural farmsteads, her nostalgic photographs, most of which were never published in her lifetime, record her dual interest in both historical interiors richly embellished with wood panelling and intricate carvings, and the humble cottages and furnishings that inspired Munstead Wood.

Gertrude Jekyll's fascination with domestic architecture and country traditions was deeply rooted in her love of Surrey. Later in life she recalled that as a child she harboured 'some appreciative perception' of the value of the 'fine old country buildings' which she discovered along country lanes near Bramley.[2] As a young woman her interest in architecture deepened to include decoration, especially the rich patterns of paving tiles, tapestries and wood carvings that she saw on her travels abroad. In Italy she sketched ornamental plasterwork and made pencil rubbings of carvings; closer to home, she sketched the interiors at Berkeley Castle in Gloucestershire, where she was a house-guest in 1868.[3] The pleasure she took in making these tracings and rubbings soon evolved into a passion for collecting textiles and trying her hand at designing wallpapers and fabrics. Had vision problems not precluded such exacting work, she might have had a remarkable career as a pattern designer or decorator.

Throughout her life Gertrude Jekyll habitually sketched details of the buildings as well as the landscapes and plants that she observed in her travels. Only two of her sketch-books survive, an early one devoted to the Chalet in

Switzerland where she spent holidays with her artist friends, and another she prepared during a visit to Priory Farm, on the Isle of Wight. Her delightful sketches of a stone barn with rough steps and a dovecote, and a whimsical garden gate fashioned from gardener's tools, indicates her consuming interest in all the details of building.[4] Before she took up photography, which she often used in much the same way as sketching, to record vernacular building details, she no doubt filled numerous other sketch-books.

During the 1870s Gertrude Jekyll's taste and discrimination in interior design and her practical experience of various crafts and skills were realized in several important design commissions. Not only did she design and execute embroidery for Edward Burne-Jones and other artists; she even devised some of the furnishings at Eaton Hall for the Duke of Westminster. Possibly the grandest scheme she carried out during these years were the elegant Aesthetic Movement-style interiors she created for the Blumenthals' house at 43 Hyde Park Gate, London. She had met William Morris in 1869, and from the fitted woodwork to the hand-quilted curtains and the peacocks stencilled on walls and ceiling, her work for the Blumenthals reflected ideas similar to his own innovative work at the time. She probably visited several of Morris and Company's commissions and was undoubtedly familiar with the decorations at the home of the *Punch* artist Linley Sambourne, 18 Stafford Terrace, Kensington, which were under way by 1874. Gertrude Jekyll also provided a scheme for her friend Barbara Bodichon's cottage at Scalands, Robertsbridge, Sussex in 1877, its cosy fireside inglenook and simple country furnishings reflecting her appreciation of rustic cottage interiors.

At this time ideas were already percolating in her mind concerning the house she hoped to build and the style of interior furnishings it would have. In an era when large homes like Munstead House were commonplace, her own architectural leanings were more in sympathy with Ruskin's call for truth to nature and sincerity in building. The development of her ideas along these lines may, like her interior design work, have been inspired by William Morris. Certainly her own leanings seem to have been in sympathy with his ideals of artistic reform (which laid the foundation for the Arts and Crafts Movement in the 1880s), and to have extended to his views on the building arts. Red House, Morris's home in Bexleyheath built for him in 1859 by his friend and associate Philip Webb, admirably expressed his personal credo of honesty, tradition, and invention in building. Red House reflects both Webb's training as a Gothic Revivalist and the romantic medieval imagery that ruled Morris's life's work. Based on the ideal of the smaller English manor house – as opposed to the grandiose but soulless houses that proliferated among Victorian industrialists – Red House paved the way for an appreciation of an innovative architectural style solidly grounded in Old English principles. Its white interiors with plain oak trim and a comfortable blend of traditional and custom-designed furnishings signalled a new direction in architecture to which Gertrude Jekyll's artistic proclivities responded.

What other ideas relating to architectural style and the building arts she may have been exploring in the 1870s is not clear, but her search became more purposeful when she acquired the land for Munstead Wood. Exactly when she

*Gertrude Jekyll sketched the dovecote at Priory Farm, Isle of Wight, in September 1903
(Godalming Museum)*

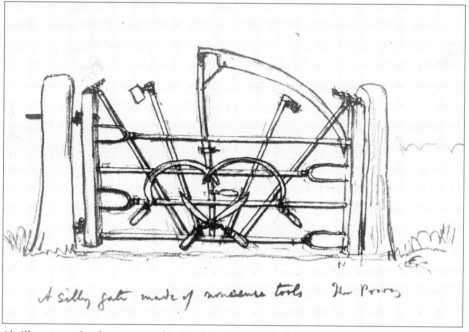

*'A silly gate made of nonsense tools', sketched by Gertrude Jekyll at Priory Farm, Isle of Wight,
September 1903 (Godalming Museum)*

Gertrude Jekyll's stencils of peacocks and orange trees decorate the drawing room she designed for Jacques and Léonie Blumenthal, at 43 Hyde Park Gate, London, 1886 (CED-UC Berkeley)

bought the land, or from whom, is not known. A survey plan marking trees and existing paths and dated November 1883 would seem to indicate that she had acquired the land earlier the same year, or possibly in 1882, perhaps to prevent the building of a school across from Munstead House.[5] It is likely that the parcel – 'a flat-iron of fifteen acres' – was purchased from Edward Rowe Fisher-Rowe, a family friend and squire of Thorncombe Park, who had originally sold Mrs Jekyll the land for Munstead House.[6] Whatever the reason for the purchase, the property was Gertrude Jekyll's to develop at will.

Although her house was not to be built for another dozen years, she was soon absorbed in all the many details. In 1884, for instance, preoccupied with the choice of materials, she asked Ruskin's advice about using English marble. His response was that he could not 'conceive any form of Purgatory more unpleasant than living in England in a house with a marble lining'. Better to use 'good whitewashed timber, and tapestry [which are] proper walls of rooms in cold climates'.[7]

Photographs taken between 1885, when she began, and 1889, the year she found her ideal architect, indicate an assiduous study of architecture and interior design, no doubt in preparation for the building of her own home; from them her appreciation of Surrey architecture and vernacular traditions is clear. She shared this appreciation with her brother Herbert, whose own photographs, very much like hers, and devoted to Surrey and Sussex buildings, are collected in a family album. Studying the yeoman's cottages of Surrey, Sussex and Kent was a popular pastime of the period and inspired many books dealing with their place in building history.[8] These picturesque abodes from a bygone era were romanticized by such late nineteenth-century artists as Miles Birket Foster, John Sylvestre Stannard and, particularly, Gertrude Jekyll's neighbour Helen Allingham, who painted many of the cottages she photographed.

Jekyll discovered many picturesque rural cottages on her visits to out-of-the-way villages in search of cottage garden plants to collect or photograph. On the back of a photograph of Bowbrick's cottage in Bramley, the village she knew well from her childhood, she noted that it was 'an old square cottage with one room on plan. Probably the only one in existence in the country'.[9] Along these almost forgotten by-roads she discovered old cottages that seemed 'to grow out of the ground' because they were built in local materials 'by men who knew no other ways of working'.[10]

In her book *Old West Surrey*, illustrated with some of these photographs, she extolled the attributes and idiosyncrasies of these cottages in the hope that their simplicity and honesty would inspire modern builders to create equally good work. She also applauded the 'stay-at-home sort', as opposed to the more common-place itinerant craftsmen, lavishing praise in particular on a local stonemason named Thomas Bowler: 'For many years I had to do with him on garden and other building work,' she wrote. 'He was nearly stone deaf, left-handed, and had lost one eye, but his work was some of the truest and best I have ever seen. His whole heart was in it.'[11] Her poignant photograph of him at work, his tools inscribed 'T.B.' ready to hand, appears several times in her album pages – once adjacent to a print of a tiny cottage in Elstead where he had repointed the chimney, and again next to a new cottage, appropriately modelled after the old example.

She revelled in local stoneworking customs as she observed them in the building and repair of country cottages and at farms in Bramley, Tuesley and Unstead (all just a pony and trap's ride away from Munstead), where she photographed great kitchens, outbuildings and their adjuncts, such as brick ovens and bacon lofts. Several pages in her albums recapture a day spent at Unstead Farm late in 1885. The day's shoot (seven plates in all) begins with the approach, over a medieval five-arched stone bridge, and ends with a halt at a tile-hung cottage on the road back to Munstead. 'I am happy in having within easy driving reach six good old bridges, built of the rough sandstone quarried in the neighbouring hilly ground,' she wrote, and she photographed them all.[12] Her wry comment on the back of a photograph of the stone bridge at Unstead – 'spoilt by iron railing' – reveals the ever-critical eye at work.

A mélange of prints from an album page shows Gertrude Jekyll's portrait of Thomas Bowler layered over images of old and new cottages in Elstead, early 1890s (CED–UC Berkeley)

Gertrude Jekyll thought that the medieval bridge over the Wey near Unstead was 'spoilt by iron railing', 1885 (CED–UC Berkeley)

The Unstead photographs in particular reveal specific details which interested her, such as paving fashioned with stone flags and ironstone roof slates in the dairy yard, or a traditional hand-pump. In some instances a direct correlation may be made between a detail photographed at Unstead and its later application at Munstead Wood. In her stable-yard at Munstead, for example, she used ironstone pitching (paving of stones set on edge) and bargate kerbing similar to that she had found at Unstead. It was a mixture of sandstone slab laid flat, brick, and sandstone with black ironstone pitching collected from the heath.

Gertrude Jekyll rarely missed a detail, however small. In the dairy yard at Unstead her curiosity was aroused by two perforated lead ventilators, 'of which [she noted] very few now remain', near the side of the window lights.[13] Of more interest, however, was the ancient half-timbered house itself, which would appear to have been one of many local examples she drew on for the Tudor-inspired detailing in her Munstead Wood cottages. Half-timbering was commonly used for decorative effect in such expansive Victorian country mansions as Cragside in

*A traditional Surrey kitchen
yard with paving and pump at
Unstead Farm, autumn 1885
(CED–UC Berkeley)*

*The old half-timbered manor
house at Unstead Farm, which
was illustrated in* Old West
Surrey, *served in part as a model
for the gardener's cottage at
Munstead Wood, 1885 (CED–
UC Berkeley)*

Northumberland, built for Lord Armstrong to designs by Richard Norman Shaw, one of the foremost architects of the latter half of the nineteenth century, at about the same time as Morris's Red House.

She photographed a number of traditional timber and plaster cottages, some with thatched roofs; a decade later, her gardener's cottage at Munstead Wood sported a half-timbered plaster face, and her small potting shed had a thatched roof. She was also interested in tile-hanging, a traditional element of local building that came into play in the design of The Hut, the tiny cottage where she lived in 1895 while her house was being built. There were numerous examples of tile-hung cottages in Bramley and other villages surrounding Godalming, while her photograph of one in Dunsfold admirably illustrates the simple way in which the rooflines join, and the regional variation of tile patterning she so admired on the dormer face. The deep overhang of the tiled roof, sweeping down to the main reception rooms, provides a picturesque setting for vines as well as a sensible channel for rainwater.

She frequently visited the village of Eashing, where she had designed a garden for Mr Turnbell in 1884. Her photographs of Mrs Sweetapple's quintessential cottage garden there, with its cascading roses, appeared in her books and articles.[14] Along the river, near the medieval bridge, she noted a striking group of ancient half-timbered cottages replete with deep-hipped roofs, stepped chimneys, and small dormers. Such details as these, seen on her photographic forays, served her as prototypes when she was designing in her mind's eye the various cottages she planned to build at Munstead.

Running parallel to her expansive interest in vernacular architecture was Gertrude Jekyll's appreciation of old manor houses. She was drawn to the traditional layout and function of the rooms, the handsome interior decorations and furnishings, and the architectural components of the old walled gardens. Although she photographed and no doubt studied a number of such houses, and applied the overall design concepts at Munstead Wood, she ultimately rejected the vocabulary, in particular the ornate interiors, in favour of a vernacular approach to building. In 1886 and 1887 she photographed a number of historic interiors, such as Old House in Shalford and Kippax Park in Yorkshire, focusing in particular on fireplaces and chimney-pieces. It is not known whether these photographs related to interior design commissions, or to details she had in mind for Munstead Wood; only a few of these photographs of buildings, and none of their interiors, were ever used in her books and articles.

It is entirely possible that at one time Gertrude Jekyll was even considering buying and restoring an older manor house. In 1885 her close friend William Robinson bought Gravetye Manor, a large, rambling, neglected late Tudor house in West Sussex, where for a number of years she was a regular guest. She closely followed the progress of the restoration work, and took some of her most interesting photographs there. Those dated 1887 were of the new garden Robinson was busy laying out, the manor house itself, and interior views which include a candid shot of one of his many recalcitrant fireplaces being repointed. She fully shared Robinson's enthusiasm for wood fires over coal, and looked to the day when 'our dirty fuel' would be abolished. If only houses could be built

Old tile-hung cottages, such as Mitchell's cottage in Dunsfold, inspired Jekyll's cottages at Munstead Wood, 1888 (CED-UC Berkeley)

The dormers and the deep roofline of these half-timbered cottages in Eashing inspired The Hut at Munstead Wood (CED–UC Berkeley)

with ample firebrick spaces for wood fires, she mused to Robinson, then people could burn their own wood and banish the miseries of coal-soot.[15]

Gertrude Jekyll was also a guest at Loseley House, an important Elizabethan house in an attractive park setting near Guildford, built in 1562 with stone taken from the ruins of Waverley Abbey. Loseley, famous for its breathtaking Jacobean interiors, with a chimney-piece in the drawing room carved from a single piece of chalk, and wood panelling said to come from Henry VIII's Nonsuch Palace, had been in the More-Molyneux family for generations, and familiar to Gertrude Jekyll since her youth. However, with the exception of two views of the garden that were used in Robinson's publications, her numerous photographs of the house, the interiors and the garden were never published.[16] No doubt she admired the remarkable collection of bamboos, palm trees, yuccas and other Victorian plant passions assembled in the garden, but her outdoor photographs taken in 1886 concentrate rather on the Tudor walled garden, with its steep-roofed tea-house, brick terraces, picturesque canal, wide-bowling green, and long yew hedges.

Gertrude Jekyll's appreciation of historic interiors is shown in her image of the panelled drawing room at Robinson's Gravetye Manor during renovations in 1887 (CED-UC Berkeley)

Gertrude Jekyll's sympathy with architectural features such as those she photographed at Loseley House is of a piece with the Arts and Crafts approach to garden-making that she and Lawrence Weaver postulated in their book *Gardens for Small Country Houses*, while canals, bowling greens edged with hardy borders, and Tudor-inspired garden houses figured prominently in the gardens she designed with Lutyens. The simple openwork design of the brick parapet wall above the canal at Loseley, with curved tiles in quarter-circles, was one of many features that Lutyens reinterpreted in his houses and gardens, notably Deanery Garden in Berkshire (1899).

Great Tangley Manor, hidden along a lane near Wonersh, north of Godalming, was another ancient local house Gertrude Jekyll knew well. She first discovered Great Tangley on her childhood pony rides from Bramley (only three miles away), when she delighted in roaming the thickly overgrown grounds surrounding the then-derelict manor house. Her photographs of the grounds, taken in April 1887, include a memorable view of a line of pollarded willow trees. At the time of her visit Great Tangley's new owner, Wickham Flower, was shaping a garden to complement the house. He had recently planted yew and beech hedges, and had excavated the ancient moat. Like the wall above the canal at Loseley, the tile-capped stone wall in the garden court at Great Tangley, with its simple Tudor gate and brick-dressed oval loopholes, was a feature that Lutyens and Jekyll later adapted for use in the gardens they designed.

In 1892 Gertrude Jekyll returned to Great Tangley again, to admire a handsome addition to the half-timbered front, itself an addition of 1582. The new work, Philip Webb's bargate stone library, had much to offer a connoisseur of architecture such as herself, not least the singular discretion with which it replicated the spirit of, but did not copy, the earlier hall, in respectful subordination. It was certainly no 'shame-faced patch boggled on to a garment', as she mercilessly categorized the work of a less adept architect.[17] Webb's new garden architecture, from the timber-roofed bridge over the moat and the rustic pergolas to the subtly reworked ancient stone enclosure walls, was all that Ruskin could have wished. Webb eschewed notoriety even more than Gertrude Jekyll did;

The walled moat and tea-house at Loseley House, Surrey, 1886, provided design inspiration for the partnership gardens designed by Lutyens and Jekyll (CED-UC Berkeley)

Garden gate and loophole in garden wall at Great Tangley Manor, Surrey, 1887 (CED-UC Berkeley)

he was a master of understatement in his architectural work, and profoundly influenced the coming generation of architects, including Lutyens.

When Edwin Lutyens entered Gertrude Jekyll's life in May 1889, neither could have guessed the enormity of the influence they were to have on one another. Years later he recalled how 'My first visit [to Munstead] led to many more, and the week-end at Munstead became a habit, and gave the opportunity for many a voyage of discovery throughout Surrey and Sussex . . . old houses, farm-houses and cottages were searched for and their modest methods of construction discussed.'[18] Thus began a legendary friendship and partnership that seldom wavered and ended only with Miss Jekyll's death in 1932.

Lutyens hailed from the village of Thursley, within easy bicycling distance of Munstead. After studying at the South Kensington School of Art and working briefly in Sir Ernest George's architectural office, he had just, aged twenty, set himself up as an architect when he met Gertrude Jekyll. He had lately received from Arthur Chapman his all-important first commission, for Crooksbury House in Farnham, and his first invitation to Munstead came about after Harry Mangles, a rhododendron enthusiast and brother-in-law of Arthur Chapman arranged for the young architect to meet the remarkable lady who was already

Philip Webb's library addition, at right, complements the old front at Great Tangley Manor, early 1890s (CED–UC Berkeley)

well known in gardening circles. They met 'at the tea-table, the silver kettle and the conversation reflecting rhododendrons', but she spoke not a word to him.[19] Almost as an afterthought, just as she was taking her leave, with one foot already on the pony trap and the reins in her hand, she asked Lutyens to Munstead the very next Saturday. It was not long before he began to take his new friend with him to see work in progress, and to ask her advice on garden design for his clients. One can only guess that her reaction to his youthful work was to suggest that he make a close study of older buildings in the neighbourhood.

Together they ambled through the Surrey countryside in the pony-trap in search of old cottages and traditional building methods to discuss and debate; no doubt they referred to *Old Cottage and Domestic Architecture in South West Surrey*, a book published the year they met, for which Herbert Jekyll was one of the original subscribers.[20] The author was Ralph Nevill, a local architect who had renovated many buildings in the Godalming area, and the text of his book had been serialized in *The Builder* for several years before publication. It included descriptions and sketches of many old buildings Gertrude Jekyll had already photographed, and to which she now returned with Lutyens.

Edwin Landseer Lutyens, around 1896, while the design of Munstead Wood was under discussion (courtesy Mary Lutyens)

Few will dispute Jekyll's influence on the impressionable young architect, but her photo albums provide evidence of the precise nature of that influence. The time of their meeting and the quickening of their friendship can be pinpointed with some accuracy in the pages of the albums, as photographs of architectural subjects suddenly interrupt her series of annual spring plant studies. These photographs record a panoply of youthful work carried out by Lutyens during the time when his interests and hers were dovetailing, and vividly portray his early grappling with form and experimentation with vernacular idioms, long before his architecture solidified into the well-known Surrey style. At Crooksbury House, for instance, two clapboard dormers above the brick-based dining room and den wing and the exaggerated Tudor-style chimneys show Lutyens's attempts to shuffle elements taken directly from cottages illustrated in Nevill's book. These photographs also show Gertrude Jekyll's newly planted borders: the earliest instance of garden design work carried out by her for one of Lutyens's clients.

On their excursions together the two went to Great Tangley Manor, which made a vivid impression on Lutyens. 'It must have been in 1891 that I first saw an example of Philip Webb's work,' he recalled, 'and I remember exclaiming "That's good; I wonder who the young man is?" . . . the freshness and originality which he maintained in all his work I, in my ignorance, attributed to youth. Not then did

Crooksbury House, Farnham, was Lutyens's first major commission and his first garden collaboration with Gertrude Jekyll, early 1890s (CED-UC Berkeley)

I recognize it to be the eternal youth of genius . . . In [his] work every detail was carefully and equally thought out and fitted to meet its special requirements'. Webb's work was never ostentatious; nothing was superfluous, and while his 'right use of material was masterly', he always respected its integrity.[21] Lutyens adopted details from Great Tangley Manor, such as the brick-dressed loopholes in the garden wall, and made them part of his own architectural vocabulary – the loopholes emerged in walls and façades at Le Bois des Moutiers (1898), Tigbourne Court (1899), and The Hoo (1902); and in 1905, a 'ghost' of the Great Tangley garden doorway took shape at Millmead in Bramley.

Lutyens rapidly acquired new clients through introductions, and at one point Gertrude Jekyll provided him with space in her workshop where, a colleague recalled, he used up yards of tracing paper.[22] A more tangible indication of her pivotal role at this stage in his career is the way photographs of his early work are pasted in the album pages alongside prints of old cottages she had made years earlier. Her juxtaposition of a picture of a tile-hung cottage in Elstead and an example of Lutyens's fledgling work seems to say 'Well done!' By this comparative method, details of rooflines, dormers, gables, tiling and half-

Lutyens's renovations at Winkworth Farm, Hascombe, early 1890s (CED–UC Berkeley)

timbering are shown in the albums – the half-timbered gables of Lutyens's twin lodges at Park Hatch, Hascombe (1890) seem to be derived (again) from Great Tangley Manor, just pages away. Among her pictures of new cottages and lodges, a number of which remain unidentified, is one of George and Owen Barker's newly-built shop in Shere village. Lutyens had designed the building for Sir Reginald Bray, and the photograph shows that it was built in 1892; Jekyll was obviously closely monitoring the progress of his career.

Lutyens's renovations at Winkworth Farm, Hascombe, not far from Munstead, are shown to great effect in one album. Thanks to the positioning of the prints on the pages, where 'before' and 'after' views are glued one on top of the other, Lutyens's initial remodelling can be seen to have been done slightly earlier than 1895, the date previously ascribed to this work.[23] Before his remodelling, Winkworth Farm was a plain and undistinguished working farm, not notable for its 'rambling romance and the oddness of the place', as Lutyens later described it.[24] Part of that romance was attributable to Gertrude Jekyll's newly laid-out courtyard garden, designed in 1893 and clearly in evidence in one of the 'after' views. At Winkworth Lutyens attempted to marry the several old farm buildings; he did not yet possess Webb's assurance, or his restraint, but efforts such as these soon landed him one of his most renowned commissions: Lutyens's formative ideas about architecture, in particular the passion for vernacular buildings he shared with Miss Jekyll, were to be expressed in the building of Munstead Wood.

CHAPTER 5

A Sagacious Client

There are few houses which better express the character and personality of their owner than Munstead Wood, the result of a happy combination of a skilful architect, a determined client, and good fortune. While it offered the client both serviceability and permanence, for the architect it was to open many doors. Munstead Wood combines Gertrude Jekyll's sentimentality and deep appreciation of architecture with Edwin Lutyens's idiosyncratic interpretation of West Surrey building tradition. It is now considered a landmark of his early 'Surrey picturesque' style, but the house would not have been built as it was had it not been for Gertrude Jekyll's vernacular sensibilities and her esteem for the ideals of the Arts and Crafts Movement. Her love of simple materials and excellence in craftsmanship extended to the planning and building of all aspects of Munstead Wood, not only the house.

It took years to achieve this perfect reflection of her personal values. Thoroughly grounded in the Surrey building arts as she was, and inclined after years of careful deliberation to a vernacular approach to architecture, it took the ideal architect to give form to her poetic conception of home-building. Lutyens's weekend tutorials with his mentor in the Surrey countryside were soon followed by 'the excitement of building her future home, Munstead Wood, wherein the business of building became a witty and exciting sport, with full discussions and great disputations'.[1] That sport was enjoyed for several years before they resolved the design of the house.

The house as eventually built was substantial, if not overly large for a single woman, and admirably accommodated its owner's exacting requirements and wide-ranging activities. From a large workshop and copious cupboards for cherished collections to the long, low ranges of windows to keep the glaring light at bay and the simple whitewashed walls that showed her furnishings to best advantage, the house seemed to fulfil its function effortlessly. The process of achieving this effortless perfection, however, had been slightly unusual. As the architect Robert Lorimer commented when he visited in 1897, just six days after she moved into her new home, she had laid out all the gardens first and 'left a hole in the centre of the ground for the house'.[2] Not only had she laid out her woodland gardens long before she met Lutyens, but all the ancillary buildings including the head gardener's cottage, all the garden structures and the walls, were built before she settled on the design for the house. The house would be the jewel in the crown.

In the early 1890s, while the woodland gardens were maturing, Gertrude Jekyll was busy defining the various divisions of her working gardens with hedging and stone walls. High walls, built from bargate stone as the house was to be, enclosed the parallelogram-shaped Kitchen Garden on the Heath Lane side, and a network of low walls and hedging outlined the internal garden divisions. A site plan prepared by Lutyens in 1893 (one of only a handful of documents relating to the development of Munstead Wood) confirms that the pergola, the Nut Walk, and the Spring Garden, as well as several buildings, were already in place.[3] A year or two later, an eleven-foot-high stone wall was added, to provide a background for the south-facing hardy flower border which was being laid out. Picking up a detail from the Munstead House garden wall, she had the south doorway in the wall opening capped, for emphasis. It may be that she built a portion of these walls herself, but Thomas Bowler, the stonemason lauded in *Old West Surrey*, certainly carried out the lion's share of the work. 'What a treat it was to see the foreman building a bit of wall!' she wrote. She was thrilled by his absolute precision, by his command of his tools and material.[4] Bowler probably also built the rustic brick pergola with rough oak beams.[5] The Munstead Wood pergola is quite plain, compared with some of the superb examples found in Lutyens and Jekyll gardens, but admirably served its purpose, that of encouraging a multitude of climbers which spilled over to the adjacent summer-house.

In 1892 Lutyens produced his first proposal for the house, a whitewashed, roughcast villa quite unsuited to a discerning client whose main requirement, as she informed him, was 'serenity of mind'. She had stipulated that the house should have 'the feeling of a convent'. Lutyens's large, rambling house with a picturesque jumble of gables and an odd mixture of components bore a striking resemblance to his recent work at Crooksbury. Quickly dubbed a 'false start', it was referred to as the 'Plazzoh' (for 'Palazzo Pergola'), for its cumbersome battlemented studio annexed to one angle. The interiors were of the typical Tudor-inspired, heavy-timbered sort generally favoured at the time. Like its successor, the proposed house had a formal garden tucked into the shady north side, while the principal front faced the woodland. The architect's wit and charm emerged in his various attempts to meet the exacting requirements of his wise client: several leaves in the sketch-book that he prepared during weekend visits are embellished with such notes of domesticity as a pot of coffee brewing outside a door, or his client quietly knitting. But across one design Lutyens has scrawled 'bad', and the final leaf, a view to the cherished woodland, bears his notation 'to the Egress', an allusion to his being shown The Way Out. He had some distance to go before his client gave her approval.

At the same time as he was preparing numerous sketches for the 'false start' house, he was also working on the design of a tiny cottage known as The Hut. Amiable discussions between architect and client about this cottage clearly ground to an abrupt halt at one point – Lutyens scribbled on the sketch, 'Abandoned Oct. 9th 1892. . . . [but] restored to favour July 16th 93'.[6] The Hut was one of several small cottages built at Munstead Wood that were steeped in the regional vocabulary Lutyens and Gertrude Jekyll cherished. It also served as a prelude to her house, which was in effect the largest of these cottages. Not only

The Hut, with Gertrude Jekyll's studio to the left and Rose 'The Garland' in the foreground, 1901 (CED-UC Berkeley)

were they expressive of client and architect's shared interest in rural buildings; they also embodied Gertrude Jekyll's theories about home-building: 'There is no reason why new cottages of the old pattern should not be made sound and wholesome and delightful to live in,' she later wrote, 'for I have built three cottages that I am not ashamed of.'[7]

The Hut, the first to be built, served as a workshop and a quiet retreat where Gertrude Jekyll could entertain her friends without disturbing her mother at Munstead House. This nostalgic cottage, in some ways a grown-up's version of a child's play-house, took its inspiration from the many tile-hung cottages she had studied with Lutyens on their rambles through the Surrey countryside. The dormers and deeply-hipped roof closely follow the lines of the half-timbered cottage in Eashing she had photographed years before, but the exaggerated, oversized stepped chimney is a piece of Lutyens's own whimsy. The centre-piece of The Hut is a large well-lit studio, its bare brick walls painted white rather than plastered. The fireplace and cosy inglenook at one end are similar to those Gertrude Jekyll herself had designed for Barbara Bodichon fifteen years before. At the fireside were examples from her collection of West Surrey implements, and the mantle above was decorated with pottery, pewter, and a cowrie shell necklace, just as she had observed in rural cottages. Traditional black-stained, rush-seated

Cottage fireplace and inglenook in The Hut, around 1903 (CED-UC Berkeley)

chairs (as popularized by Morris and Company) and other cottage furnishings completed the picture. Two bedrooms above offered storage space and accommodation for Mrs Cannon, an elderly village woman to whom the cottage was lent.

After the death of Mrs Jekyll in 1895 and Herbert Jekyll's subsequent removal to Munstead House, Gertrude formally established herself in The Hut, where she lived for two years before moving into Munstead Wood itself in October 1897. During these years she revelled in her simple way of life and the 'happy absence of all complications'.[8] At night she could hear the rain falling on the tiled roof above her bedroom, and in the morning her bare feet met a floor of bare brick, just like a convent's.

In 1894 another vernacular-style cottage was built at Munstead Wood, for the head gardener. The tiny cottage, which Lutyens had sketched in 1893 while The Hut was under discussion, was located in the narrow end of the triangular-shaped

The head gardener's cottage, photographed around 1903, was one of three exemplar cottages that Gertrude Jekyll built. It was illustrated in Old West Surrey *(CED–UC Berkeley)*

site, built literally on a boundary wall. It had Lutyens's characteristic deep-hipped roof in the front and was tile-hung on three sides, with a striking half-timber and plaster face. Construction details noticed on their outings were used, such as mortar galleted (decorated) with pebbles. When in *Old West Surrey* Gertrude Jekyll described her success in building 'wholesome' cottages, she offered her readers the example of her gardener's cottage, glimpsed through the mature cypress hedge that came within feet of the entry.

The following year a curious little stone building was erected only yards away from the head gardener's cottage, at the junction of the north and east garden walls. Perched on the corner, this was a thunder-house, where Jekyll could sit and watch thunderstorms as they rolled along the Wey valley below.[9] By climbing a short flight of steps in the stone belvedere she could also look out over the surrounding fields on three sides, and survey the garden from above. The simple building, whose only embellishment is a steep, pointed roof, served as a focus of interest for the plain garden walls.

Except for a reference in *Children and Gardens* Gertrude Jekyll wrote little about the barn, sheds and stables (now known as the Quadrangle) at Munstead Wood which appeared on Lutyens's plan of 1893.[10] On Lorimer's visit in 1897 he noted that she had bought an old barn on the point of demolition, and reassembled it at Munstead Wood.[11] The barn may possibly have been there before Lutyens's involvement, but it is more than likely that he supervised its installation. He certainly came to have a knack for the seamless knitting-together of old and new buildings; perhaps this was a more successful early effort than his work at Winkworth Farm.[12]

The focal point of the barn buildings was a clapboard loft over the stables with great stone steps on the garden side leading up to it, similar to examples Gertrude had sketched years before. The Loft was used as a bulb and onion store, and had a room for seed storage, matchboarded to keep out insects. When work was being done on the stables in 1909, The Loft was enlarged to include two bedrooms, with a range of windows overlooking the garden; these additions enable various photographs of the Grey Garden to be roughly dated.

Most carts entered the stable-yard, in the centre of the grouping of sheds and the old stables, from the broad entrance on Heath Lane; the paving of the yard was derived from the kitchen yard at Unstead Farm, photographed by Jekyll in 1885. During the course of building at Munstead Wood, the stable-yard underwent much modification; in 1909, for instance, Lutyens was asked to assist with the design of some new stables along Heath Lane and the conversion of the old stables on the garden side into a coach house. In response to Gertrude Jekyll's preliminary sketch-plan of her ideas, 'Nedi' asked 'Toute Suite' (as he called her) whether she might like a 'little wee door betwixt harness and horse pits'; the finished drawings, showing the 'wee door' were sent in June.[13]

Among the buildings in the stable-yard and barn complex was a curious structure – a mushroom house, beneath a rainwater tank at the end of The Loft. Gertrude Jekyll delighted in collecting wild chanterelles in the woods and morels in the orchards, and may have been inspired to want a mushroom house for cultivating Agaricus, using William Robinson's instructions for building one,

A view of the 'old wall', with The Loft in the distance, early 1890s. The yews on either side of the path eventually formed a tall arch over the opening (CED–UC Berkeley)

The stable-yard, with the coach-house at left and the Thunder-house visible through the opening in the barn, around 1903. The ironstone pitching and the bargate kerb were traditional (CED–UC Berkeley)

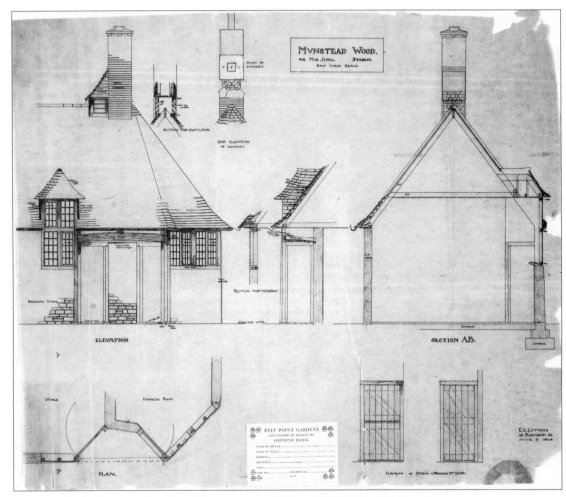

Edwin Lutyens's plan for stable renovations, 3 June 1909 (CED–UC Berkeley)

published more than twenty years earlier.[14] Mushrooms never grew in this building, however – only stalactites, which formed on the ceiling from the slow drip from the tank above – and in the end the cool underground room was used for storing apples and root vegetables.[15]

Near the glasshouses and cold frames in the service yard by the Hascombe Road was a potting shed – at first glance an ordinary clapboard building, but with a vernacular twist: a roof thatched with hoop-chip. Ever curious and resourceful, Gertrude Jekyll hired a 'clever old thatcher' to exercise a vanishing craft in the creation of a twelve-inch deep thatch from the wood chips that were a by-product of making wooden staves for barrels, a declining local industry. The thatcher's work was his pride and he took his time, she recalled (even though he was paid at

Vine and fig at door to the underground mushroom house, located near one end of The Loft, 1899 (CED–UC Berkeley)

Mrs Cannon, the village woman who briefly lived at The Hut, outside the potting shed in the late 1890s. The shed was thatched with hoop-chip shavings, the by-product of a local industry (CED-UC Berkeley)

piece rate), 'preparing and placing each handful of chips as carefully as if he was making a wedding bouquet'.[16] Whether it was the roof of the potting shed or the alignment of the windows in the house, every detail was carefully considered by this client, as part of the greater picture.

The death of Mrs Jekyll in 1895 left Gertrude with no home of her own apart from The Hut. By that date most of the gardens had been laid out and the cottages and other structures had been built, so the time was ripe for her to turn her attention again to the design of her house. Between 1892, when he was 'dismissed' from the job, until 1896 or thereabouts, when he was invited to try again, Lutyens's architectural expertise ripened significantly. The house he eventually created at Munstead Wood is the result of the collaboration of two complimentary minds, those of a rarefied and sagacious client and an uncommon architect. Gertrude Jekyll had been thinking about her house for so long, and it was so familiar to her mind's eye, that when it was finally built she felt as though it had always existed. 'It does not stare with newness', she commented, nor was it in any way a copy of an old building, either, although it embodied the characteristics of old buildings. As she wrote in *Home and Garden*, the 'new-built house [is] so restful, so satisfying, [and] so kindly sympathetic . . . in some ways it is not exactly a new house, although no building ever before stood upon its site'. Lorimer, one of many architects who came to admire the house, observed that it

South front of Munstead Wood with Scotch brier roses and Patty on lawn, around 1900 (from A Gardener's Testament, *1934)*

'looks so reasonable, so kindly, so perfectly beautiful that you feel that people might have been making love and living and dying there [for nearly a] thousand years'.[17]

Lutyens's design married a small Tudor-style manor house with a highly personal interpretation of local vernacular style. The house is at once quirky and contrived but simple, elegant, and eminently comfortable. A number of its features became standards in Lutyens's picturesque early work – exaggerated chimneys, steep-hipped roofs, and an oblique entrance. If Deanery Garden (1900) for his client Edward Hudson was 'the perfect architectural sonnet', as one critic remarked, then its predecessor, Munstead Wood, was a melodious duet.

The house embodied the principles espoused by the Arts and Crafts Movement, notably honesty in building and simplicity of design, but was far more nostalgic than houses designed by other architects more firmly rooted in the Movement, such as M.H. Baillie Scott or Lutyens's slightly older contemporary, C.F.A. Voysey. Voysey, an early supporter of the Art Workers' Guild which formed the nucleus of the Arts and Crafts Movement, had a reputation at this time for imaginative roughcast houses with exaggerated projecting eaves and green slate roofs. In 1897 he had two houses under way in Surrey, Greyfriars in Puttenham, and Norney in Shackleford (not five miles from Munstead), where Lutyens consulted with Voysey's client on the selection of the site for the house.[18] But Voysey was not especially concerned with construction details or regional building materials, and the story-book charm of his whitewashed houses bore no relation to Gertrude Jekyll's passionate interest in vernacular building techniques and materials. Although she later designed gardens for clients of both Voysey and Baillie Scott, for herself she clearly required an architect who was as deeply committed as she was to Surrey traditions.

In *Home and Garden* Gertrude Jekyll credits Lutyens for the success of the design for the house. She wisely counselled that while any resourceful amateur might plan a building after a fashion, it was sure to be wanting in simplicity, 'higher knowledge', and 'wider expression' – counsel which remains pertinent today. Her book relates how the building was done 'in the happiest way possible, a perfect understanding existing between the architect, the builder, and the proprietor'. She had given her architect the job of designing 'a small house with plenty of room', with nothing 'poky or screwy or ill-lighted'. While most discussions were amiable, the 'fur flew' on at least one occasion when he proposed something very much not to her taste. 'My house is to be built for me to live in and to love; it is not to be built as an exposition of architectonic inutility!' she said 'with some warmth'.[19]

Lutyens placed the house on an east-west axis, with a long south-facing terrace overlooking a lawn at the woodland's edge and a shady north court nestled between the two wings of the house. He designed the principal façade to face the woodland gardens to the south, with the entrance to the house on the southeast corner, and the service wing to the north. It was built of golden-buff bargate stone, from a nearby quarry, which a hundred years later has mellowed to a deep honey colour. Old tiles were used on the roof, to give it a weathered appearance, while the chimneys, which give so much character to the house, are of traditional red brick. Except for the half-timbering used on the north façade for the gallery connecting the two north wings, the house is of plain stone, which was unusual for the region. The half-timber and plaster exterior wall construction of the north gallery was a natural choice for a wall supported on cantilevered beams, complementing the serenity of the stone house. The beams and other joinery were of 'good English oak grown in the neighbourhood', and everything in the house was specifically designed for it – 'no random choosings from the ironmonger's pattern-book' and 'no moral slothfulness' in the fittings. Rustic wooden latches were one of Lutyens's trademarks – he did not design fancy metal door and cabinet fittings like Voysey's, so representative of the Arts and Crafts period.

Gertrude Jekyll paid dearly for her house, almost £4,000, but the extra time and trouble taken to get the details just right were richly rewarding in the end.[20] The work was carried out, in 1896, by Thomas and William Underwood, country builders from Dunsfold who were widely employed in the neighbourhood; they renovated Winkworth Farm, and built Orchards (which Lutyens designed the year after Munstead Wood) and High Barn in Hascombe (by Lorimer). The stonemason was William Herbert, from Witley, and there was a 'fine old carpenter who worked to [Lutyens's] drawings in an entirely sympathetic manner' – drawings which no longer exist.[21] Living in The Hut, just eighty yards away, Gertrude enjoyed watching the building of her home – and listening to it. She delighted in all sounds, the 'dull slither' of the moist mortar as it was laid on the brick, the 'melodious scream' of plane against board, the 'beating of the cow-hair' as it was mixed with the wall plaster.[22]

This was also a happy time for the architect, who was courting his future wife, Lady Emily Lytton. There were many outings to Bumpstead to see Aunt Bumps, or Woozal (Oozal and Swoozle), as she was fondly referred to; Gertrude Jekyll, however, became impatient when work ground to a halt during courting interludes. In a poem addressed to her errant architect, Bumps, Poet Galoreate, complained that 'brick-layers playing', 'carpenters smoking' and 'plumbers carousing' ensued during his absence. Lutyens had to spend much time soothing the rough places for his exacting client, doing 'all those things necessary for my salvation – in Bumps's eyes'.[23] Only occasionally did Jekyll over-ride her architect's judgement, and she was quick to acknowledge her error when he was proved right. In one case she determined upon a modification of the placing of the casement window-openings, demanding that the end lights, rather than those next to the end, be made to open. When she discovered that rain dampened and spoiled the curtains and wind caused the thin linen blinds to flap, she had the windows altered – within the year – to Lutyens's original specifications.

A dozen years before Munstead Wood was built, Gertrude Jekyll had written to Robinson that she thought a house should grow up between the ground on one side and its master on the other, it 'must marry both'. A house 'planned in the air', without reference to a particular site, would be as 'soulless as an Aldershot hut'.[24] At Munstead Wood, the house settled comfortably into the site, just like old cottages that 'grew out of the ground'. It was approached quietly from a shady footpath on the east and most visitors who came were surprised by the quiet woodland setting. One recalled arriving 'through a woodsey lane at the entrance gate'; as the party lingered a moment, waiting for an answer to the bell, they could glimpse the gardens in the distance.[25]

Jekyll thought that a house, however small, should not have 'a mean or poky place to come into', but should have an enclosed porch.[26] The front door, at a ninety degree turn, was set at the end of the stone corridor in a 'covered projection of lean-to shape', as she described this oddly annexed porch.[27] Since Lutyens originally proposed a summer-house at the end of the south terrace, the discussions that married these ideas with those of Lutyens must have been lively.

From the entrance hall, with a fireplace set at an angle and a store-room off to the left, visitors had to turn again to reach the main corridor of the house – an early example of Lutyens's play with a deliberately offset entry. Harold Falkner, a local architect and young admirer of Lutyens's work, observed that 'Munstead Wood had one considerable peculiarity. The entrance was through an arched

The porch, flanked by tubs of hydrangeas, from the south terrace looking east, 1899. A footpath from the lane led to the arched opening at left, while the timber arches framed views across the south lawn (CED-UC Berkeley)

opening in a wall . . . with a view of the pantry or larder on the left'. In the uninitiated, it raised some doubt as to whether they had come to the front or the back door. 'After an agonizing wait in utter stillness, one was eventually ushered in through a stone hall and corridor'.[28]

While Lutyens's sketches of 1892 for the exterior bear little resemblance to the house as it was built, his suggestions for the interiors were closer to the mark. Low timber-lined corridors, whitewashed walls and oak doors with heavily wrought hardware were refined to the point where nothing was overbearing or extraneous. 'The whole house [was] redolent of wood burning, pot-pourri and furniture polish', remembered Lutyens's daughter Elisabeth when she visited in 1933. It was 'dark and cool, specially so designed for [Miss Jekyll's] dimming sight, with long galleries overlooking the wonderful garden, large rooms and quiet corners'.[29] Large oak doors with beautiful escutcheons and hinges lined the corridors and preserved the tranquillity. Lorimer was intrigued by all the interior details, especially the oak, of 'the most beautiful sort of silvery grey colour'. When he asked where she had acquired the old timber, he was told it was all new, but had been treated with hot lime. 'One man coats it over, his "mate" follows on [a] quarter of an hour later and cleans it off, and *voilà*! you have oak that looks as if it had been there since the beginning'.[30]

Unlike those of Lutyens's later houses, the layout of the rooms at Munstead Wood is fairly conventional. Passing a small dining room on the left overlooking

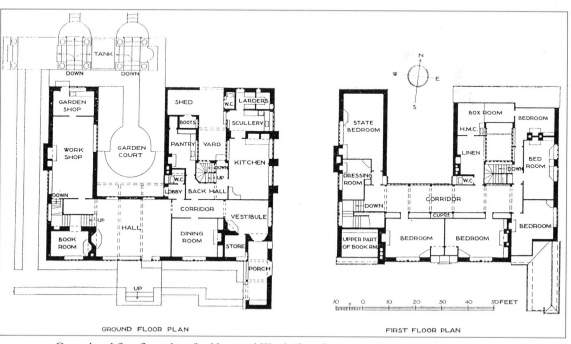

Ground and first floor plans for Munstead Wood (from Lawrence Weaver, Houses and Gardens by E.L. Lutyens, *1913)*

the lawn, a broad corridor led from the entrance hall to a well-proportioned hall. Gertrude Jekyll's ideal house, which she had described to Robinson years earlier, had a good-sized hall that could be used as an extra sitting room and a place to dine in, with stairs rising from it.[31] The generously-sized sitting room at Munstead Wood, with a low range of oak-mullioned windows flush with the outer wall, was designed to overlook the woodland and the Green Wood Walk. This room, measuring 27 feet by 21 feet, has low 8-foot ceilings framed by three massive beams of English oak. It faces south, but, to keep strong light to a minimum it was lit by a long, low range of windows; in the afternoon, it was flooded with western light from a window on the adjacent stairs.[32]

At one end of the room is a deeply-hooded bargate stone fireplace, designed by Gertrude Jekyll herself, its simplicity and massing more appropriate to the house than were the many ornate historical examples she had photographed in the 1880s. Her sketch for the chimney-piece shows the exact placement of stones and the desired profiles, no doubt adapted from something she had seen. Next to the fireplace low, broad oak steps lead up to a small book-room on the south-west corner, off the first half-landing, and then to the upstairs corridor. Beneath the book-room were the photographic dark-room, fitted out with sinks and other appropriate paraphernalia, and the wine-cellar, with a door-head she had carved, herself.

The west wing of the house was devoted to 'business', and the workshop was the hub of Gertrude Jekyll's activities. Storage cabinets and working tables lined the room, but the centre-piece was a fireplace with large niches on either side of the hood which held country pottery and teapots. In the place of honour (a niche in the centre of the fireplace) was Bellatrice, a casting from a Greek terracotta, and quietly sitting on one shelf was Pigot, the deity of the workshop, who kept a sharp eye on the quality of his mistress's work. The hearth below had the requisite Old West Surrey fireside implements, and wood was neatly stacked to one side in a carrier designed by Lutyens. Beyond the far end of the room, a small room with a door directly into the garden was used for flower-arranging.

The dining room was next to the entrance hall, with the kitchens and store rooms on the opposite side of the main corridor; its location was not very practical, as everything had to be carried across the corridor and through the back hall. The kitchen, scullery, larders and pantry had a back entrance from the stone-paved kitchen yard, served by a back drive, wide enough for a pony and cart; in the early years, before the hedges grew up, the kitchen court looked across to the October aster borders. A back staircase led to the servants' bedrooms above. Upstairs, a central light-well had corridors and storerooms on three sides, and the staircase on the fourth.

Although she rarely had overnight guests, there were three guest rooms at Munstead Wood, in addition to two bedrooms for servants and Gertrude Jekyll's own room.[33] The most important guest bedroom (over the workshop) had no windows overlooking the north court and service wing to the right, and only one window, too high-placed to look out of, on the garden side, where one would have expected to find a low range: no doubt this would have spoilt the composition of the exterior façade. The other guest rooms were in the twin gables on the south side, overlooking the lawn and woodland. The great chimney for the sitting room fireplace, above the left gable, dominated the long, low roofline. Gertrude Jekyll's

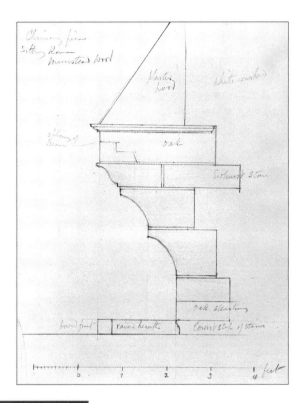

Gertrude Jekyll's undated sketch of the sitting room chimney-piece (RHS Lindley Library)

The main staircase, 1899. The book-room is on the mezzanine level at the back of the fireplace (CED-UC Berkeley)

modest bedroom was tucked away in the south-east corner over the entry, not far from the back stairs. It may seem a curious position, but she deliberately chose a room at the further end of the gallery so that she might 'enjoy a walk down its length': every morning as she came out of her room she was thankful that her home had 'on its upper floor so roomy and pleasant a highway'.[34] It was also the bedroom nearest the woodland, so she could hear the sounds of the trees and birds – she claimed to have very acute hearing, in compensation perhaps for her poor sight.

The principal feature upstairs was the oak gallery, sixty feet long and ten wide. In order to provide this comfortably wide corridor where the ground-floor plan beneath allowed only a modest one, without sacrificing the comfort of the two south-facing guest rooms, Lutyens 'hung' it over the north court below ('a foretaste of later naughtiness', as Pevsner has quipped.)[35] The timbered gallery was lit by a

The long, low, oak-beamed gallery, lined with tables and cabinets, cantilevers over the north court below, 1899 (CED–UC Berkeley)

long range of north-facing windows overlooking the garden court below and lined with deep cupboards and linen hutches (chests) which held her 'little treasures . . . such as are almost unconsciously gathered together by a person of an accumulative proclivity' – the fruits of decades of collecting.[36] The cupboards later held a secret, too: in 1902 a tension rod was added (but not by Lutyens), hung from the roof structure and hidden behind the cupboards, to give additional support to the ceiling beams in the hall below. Either Lutyens had miscalculated the weight the long span of beams could carry, or the 'home-grown' oak was of inferior quality.

Lutyens's role in the planning of the gardens at Munstead Wood was minimal, but he did have to contend with those gardens in his siting of the house and terraces, and part of his problem was to smooth out some of the transitional areas between house and garden. A rare sketch by him, found among Gertrude Jekyll's

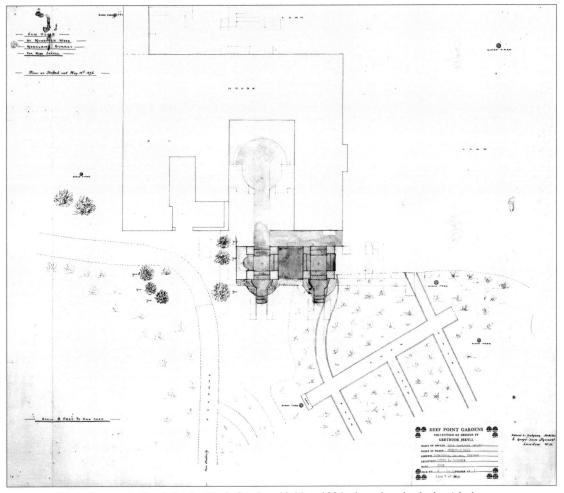

Edwin Lutyens's sketch for the Tank Garden, 12 May 1896, shows how he dealt with the existing paths (CED-UC Berkeley)

Low steps lead from the south terrace to the lawn, with the third woodland walk in the distance, 1901 (CED–UC Berkeley)

papers, shows how he worried away at the placement of the steps in the Tank Garden vis-à-vis the existing paths. His design for the paved courtyard between the two wings of the house, one of the few areas of the garden with 'a definite plan', served to link the house to the Nut Walk and the shrub plantings which brushed the environs of the house. The stone Tank Garden at the foot of the Paved Court is flanked at each corner by twin sets of steps and stone planters. While the courtyard works well with the house, the Tank Garden seems to strike an oddly forced note with the informal garden at its foot.

By contrast, all that was needed for the elegant south front of the house was a terrace with gentle steps leading up to the lawn; a low stone retaining wall accommodated the slight change in level, but the handsome double-gabled façade itself, with its deeply-hipped low roof and enormous chimneys, was the important message. With its quiet, leafy approach and woodland lapping up to its south terrace, it is no wonder the house looked as though it had always been there.

Thomas Hunn's watercolour, The Pansy Garden, Munstead Wood, Surrey, *depicts a garden which Gertrude Jekyll never wrote about. It was probably used to supply flowers for the house (Bridgeman Art Library)*

The south front of Munstead Wood. The bargate stone house was built in 1896 (© Judith B. Tankard)

Helen Allingham's watercolour In Munstead Wood Garden *shows the break in the main hardy flower border, which was emphasized by masses of yuccas and bergenia (Christopher Wood Gallery)*

Michaelmas Daisies at Munstead Wood *by Helen Allingham captures the essence of Gertrude Jekyll's planting style (Leger Galleries)*

In his Munstead Wood sketchbook, Edwin Lutyens inscribed his drawing for The Hut, 'abandoned Oct 9th/1892/ Restored to favour July 16th 93' (BAL-RIBA)

The head gardener's cottage, which was built in 1894, was tile–hung and half-timbered (BAL-RIBA)

Lutyens's early proposal for the house at Munstead Wood, shown from the south-west, was named 'Plazzoh', for the curious 'plazzoh pergola' at left (BAL-RIBA)

The south front of the proposed house bears a striking resemblance to the more modest house that was built (BAL-RIBA)

The main border in the Spring Garden, autochrome, c. 1912. Morello cherries cover the wall and a Euphorbia characias wulfenii *creates an effective focal point (Country Life Picture Library)*

The red section of the main hardy flower border, autochrome, c. 1912. Gertrude Jekyll's use of red geraniums and salvias shocked some visitors (Country Life Picture Library)

One of the most famous areas of Munstead Wood was the iris and lupin border, with the Loft building in the distance, autochrome, c. 1912 (Country Life Picture Library)

One of the four beds forming the Grey Garden, autochrome, c. 1912. Gertrude Jekyll delighted in the subtle tapestry of colour, highlighted by masses of white flowers (Country Life Picture Library)

The kitchen gardens at Orchards, designed by Gertrude Jekyll in 1898 (Country Life Picture Library)

CHAPTER 6

At Home

For Gertrude Jekyll the day began at eight o'clock, when she was called by her maid. She had probably been awake for hours enjoying 'the glad song of many birds' and the thin mist, just sufficient to give 'a background of tender blue mystery' far into the woodland, which came to within yards of her bedroom window. 'Hungry for breakfast and ready for the day's work', she passed cupboards lining the gallery filled by 'a person of an accumulative proclivity', with trinkets as diverse as pieces of delicate Venetian glass, to examples of English patchwork. Gertrude Jekyll was an assiduous collector of textiles and a family friend never forgot the sight of her emerging from a Venetian sacristy laden with yards of lace and vestments 'hot from the priest's back'.[1]

Breakfast was served at nine o'clock in the dining room, small but surprisingly classical in feeling, that opened off the main corridor. This room was not ideally positioned and had no servery, so everything had to be carried from the kitchen, through the back hall and across the corridor to a refectory table, laid with a sideboard cloth, from which meals were served. A deep cornice gave the dining room a formal air absent from other rooms in the house, which were not so finely finished. Simple ebonized oak ladderback chairs and an oblong oak table set the style, and the room was dominated by an oak sideboard, its shelves groaning with a fine collection of pewter. As was the custom in Edwardian households, breakfast was a substantial meal; Lutyens, when he stayed in August 1909, was served sausages, eggs, coffee and, rather unusually, cold bacon.

Directly after breakfast Gertrude Jekyll would go to her workshop and begin the task of answering her daily correspondence, which she had probably opened and sifted through during breakfast. She liked to complete the task before noon, when the youngest gardener collected the outgoing post from the workshop door and took it to the Bramley crossroad post box for the lunchtime collection. Her correspondence was considerable but, as one would expect, she replied to all who wrote. She was a prodigious letter-writer, partly out of necessity; all her garden design work was conducted by correspondence, most of her articles for publication were dispatched by post, and she arranged her financial affairs with Coutts and Company in London, the private bank which managed her investments, by letter. To her many friends she would send postcards asking them to call on certain days; these were regarded by most recipients as a kind of passport of admission, and few would come without such an invitation.

After the publication and huge success of *Wood and Garden* Gertrude Jekyll was so besieged with requests from unknown people asking to visit her garden

Gertrude Jekyll's pewter collection on her dining room sideboard, designed by Lutyens, 1899 (CED-UC Berkeley)

that she felt compelled in her next book to request privacy. As she confided to Alice Morse Earle, author of *Old Time Gardens*, 'It seems to be a general idea that if one has written a book one becomes in a way the public property of all idle and curious people'.[2] To another friend she confessed, 'If I could only know what were the genuine applicants I would still make exceptions'. Worst still, she said, 'you can have no idea what I have suffered (actually in health) from the pertinacity of Americans and Germans and of journalists.'[3] All attempts by her family to persuade her to employ a secretary were to no avail, and in the end she resorted to dispatching pre-printed letters, which spared her the task of writing long excuses: as one such memo cautioned, 'Miss Jekyll suffers from her eyes, and the oculist forbids letter-writing.'[4]

The major event of the morning, however, was at ten o'clock, when the head gardener came to the workshop to receive his 'orders'. She did not concern herself with the minute detail of the garden's management, nor indeed of the household's, for these were the responsibility of the head gardener and the housekeeper. The gardens were so well run that the gardeners knew what tasks required doing, and her daily instructions were to do with special tasks, such as

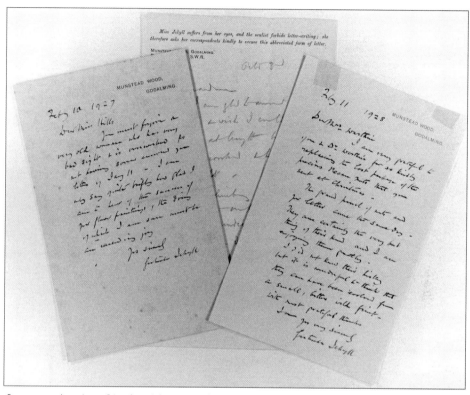

Letters to American friends, with a printed memo cautioning, 'Miss Jekyll suffers from her eyes, and the oculist forbids letter-writing'

moving plants which, on her walks around the garden, she had noticed needed it, or, during the season, giving out the collecting sheets for plant orders. If she intended to work in the gardens in the afternoon and would require a gardener to assist her, this would also be arranged at the morning conference. On Thursdays the head gardener would go to the Godalming branch of Martin's Bank, where a general account was maintained for all household expenses and for the nursery business, to collect the wages for the staff.

The garden staff were managed by the head gardener, Albert Zumbach, originally a retainer of Jacques and Léonie Blumenthal at the Chalet in Switzerland, where his father had been the gardener.[5] During Gertrude Jekyll's many visits to the Chalet Albert Zumbach had 'attached himself' to her, and it proved an easy task to entice him away to the leafy lanes of Surrey. He came to work at Munstead in November 1893 and became, in time, a highly competent head gardener. Since Zumbach was at Munstead Wood during most of the years Jekyll lived there, he must have been entirely familiar with, and probably had some influence upon, the many ideas that were experimented with in the garden. In later life he was crippled by arthritis; he retired in 1928 and was replaced by Arthur Gibbins.[6]

Over the years stories have proliferated as to how many gardeners Gertrude Jekyll employed. Much of the confusion seems to stem from a witty comment made by Lutyens following his last visit to Munstead Wood in 1933. 'It is sad to see', he wrote to his wife Lady Emily, 'how the garden at Munstead W. has collapsed, but it can't be helped, no Bumps and no longer the 11 essential gardeners.'[7] There were, in fact, but four gardeners; it is possible that the staff was slightly larger before the First World War, but Gertrude Jekyll never employed the numbers often claimed, nor would she have had either the resources to maintain them or the work to keep them busy. Although it is often said that a Jekyll garden requires a veritable army of gardeners, this is not the case. Munstead Wood had some four to five acres of 'dressed ground', ornamental gardens and kitchen gardens, and the traditional rough calculation of one gardener per acre of dressed ground was as valid then as it is today.

From the reminiscences of one under-gardener, Frank Young, much is now known about who the gardeners were and what their duties were in the late 1920s. The ornamental gardens, which extended to two acres of 'dressed ground' and comprised all the decorative borders, were worked by just two men, Arthur Berry and Frank Young. The working gardens, which comprised the kitchen garden and nursery and extended to about two acres, were worked by Fred Boxall and William Hawkes, who both died before Gertrude Jekyll and were replaced by Arthur Berry's

Frank Young, an under-gardener at Munstead Wood, shown at Bowyers Court, West Sussex, in 1934 (courtesy Valerie Kenward and Colin Young, copyright © estate of Frank Young)

Arthur Berry, an under-gardener in the pleasure gardens (from Gardening Illustrated, *13 October 1928)*

Fred Boxall, an under-gardener in the kitchen gardens, posed near the potting shed as a mower for Old West Surrey, *1903 (CED–UC Berkeley)*

son William and an old man from Busbridge, named Bailey.[8] The gardeners were always addressed by their surnames with the exception of the youngest (in the late 1920s it happened to be Frank Young), who was always addressed by his Christian name. There was little cross-over in the work patterns, and as Frank Young was employed in the ornamental gardens he seldom went to the kitchen gardens.

Jarot, the groom, looked after the pony used for transport and to pull the old-fashioned lawnmower which was used in preference to a 'newfangled' motor-mower. Gertrude Jekyll kept a 'stout cob' or a 'shelty' (a Shetland pony) to pull 'a rough kind of dog-cart' (or a 'high dog cart'), giving a range of about thirty miles with a 'shelty' and nearer fifty with a 'stout cob'. Lady Chance, for whom Lutyens built Orchards, not far from Munstead Wood, became a good friend; as she was new to the neighbourhood, Gertrude Jekyll would often drive her out to admire some beauty spot. Years later Lady Chance recalled these drives as 'a perilous proceeding as her [Miss Jekyll's] sight was even then very defective and extremely short. But we never came to grief, and with that astonishing power of quick perception which is often lacking in people with good sight, she never missed the smallest flower or object of interest on the wayside.'[9] Sometimes they would stop for a picnic tea, when Lady Chance was shown the correct way to make a fire and boil a kettle (a square flat-shaped kettle of Gertrude Jekyll's own design); it was considered a 'point of honour to have the kettle boiling within five minutes of lighting the fire.'[10]

After The Hut was built Gertrude Jekyll lent it to an 'old cottager friend', a Mrs Cannon. She had hoped, when the time came for her to live in The Hut herself, to retain this simple cottager as her housekeeper, she soon realized, however, that Mrs Cannon was not physically up to keeping house for them both, and as 'her knowledge of cooking was less than rudimentary' a home was found for her in the village and a 'more able-bodied' servant engaged.[11] Munstead Wood was, of course, considerably larger than The Hut, and required an indoor staff of three to run it efficiently. Most of her servants, both indoors and out, remained for years. Her lady's maid Florence Hayter, who also acted as housekeeper, worked for her from 1906, and her cook, Mary Irons, joined the household in 1911, replacing a 'melancholy cook'. Finding suitable servants, never easy, was probably more difficult when the other servants had been employed for such a long time, but Mary Platt, an 'oldish house-parlour maid' who was engaged in July 1930, came with such a glowing recommendation that Gertrude Jekyll wrote to her previous employer merely for the sake of the 'usual form'.[12]

Like the gardeners, the indoor servants had probably been at work since seven o'clock. They began the day by rekindling the kitchen range and laying fires, if necessary, in the main rooms. There was also a small range in the butler's pantry (across the back hall) which was probably used to heat the domestic hot water (as the housemaids' closet was directly above) and to provide hot water for washing all the glass, silver and china returning from the dining room, while the saucepans and kitchen implements would have been washed in the scullery beyond the kitchen. The butler's pantry may also have been intended for use as a servants' hall, something not included in the house design, but the servants most likely used the kitchen as their sitting room as its windows looked out across to the entrance path. Curiously, the house was not over-endowed with bathrooms; as late as the 1920s,

Lutyens often found even his wealthiest clients reluctant to install a bathroom for every bedroom. Hip baths in front of the bedroom fire were still widely used, with all the water required being carried back and forth from the housemaids' closet.

Luncheon was served at the traditional hour of one o'clock, and would today be considered a substantial meal. Lutyens, who was served vegetarian food at home, was aghast to be confronted with 'beef steak pudding, beer and stuffed tomatoes' on a blistering hot August day when, as he remarked, it was '365 degrees in the shade'.[13] This seems indeed an odd menu for a hot day, with a guest to lunch, and the hostess who would offer it has to be admired for a degree of eccentricity, if nothing else. House-guests seem rarely to have been entertained at Munstead Wood, but the few that were welcomed were reminded that they were 'coming to a cottage with the very simplest ways – no evening clothes are allowed; only your barest necessities in a small bag'.[14] Lutyens was, of course, always welcome, and in the 1920s Herbert Cowley, the editor of *Gardening Illustrated*, sometimes stayed so that he could photograph the garden in the early morning light.

After lunch Gertrude Jekyll read the newspaper, and in later years, on the advice of her doctor, rested in her bedroom. Around three o'clock she would emerge to work in the garden, sometimes with the assistance of a gardener whose attendance had been arranged with the head gardener in the morning. Alternatively, if the weather was inclement or she was especially busy, she wrote or worked in her workshop. Neatly stored in the cupboards there were dozens of tools, 'for carving, for etching, for inlaying; paints, chalks, brushes, easels,

The workshop fireplace, with Bellatrice in the central niche and Pigot on the top left shelf (from Lawrence Weaver, Houses and Gardens of E.L. Lutyens, *1913)*

palettes, tripods, and all the cumbrous paraphernalia of the photographer.' Drawers 'labelled in neat block letters' contained shells and pieces of coral graded as to size and colour, all used in making shell pictures on winter evenings; many of them she sold to American visitors.[15]

Visitors summoned by post-card were requested to come on a particular day, any time after half-past three; a select few were told, 'come when you will, you are always welcome.'[16] Old friends were the most welcome callers, of course, but she had the curious habit of staggering their visits, even such regulars as Harold Falkner, who came once a month for twenty years, and Herbert Cowley.[17] Munstead Wood was, as she explained to the American Nellie B. Allen, 'rather hidden away in a back lane', the taxi driver should be told that 'my entrance, a hand gate only, is at the 5th telephone post up the lane'.[18] Miss Jekyll would be either in the garden or her workshop, but would soon appear to greet her guest.

The Edwardian age, frequently described, with some justification, as a 'golden afternoon', is often regarded as perhaps the very apotheosis of gracious living. Munstead Wood was every inch an Edwardian house, but it was also the very embodiment of William Morris's dictum that 'we should have nothing in our houses which we do not either know to be useful or believe to be beautiful'. The simple country furniture used throughout the house reflected Gertrude Jekyll's

Harold Falkner, a frequent visitor to Munstead Wood, in a photograph taken shortly before he died in 1963 (Farnham Museum)

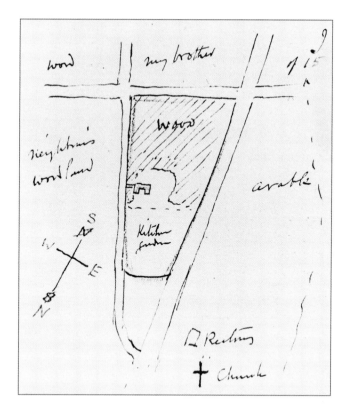

In her sketch of Munstead Wood, sent in a letter to Alice Morse Earle on 27 June 1904, Gertrude Jekyll wrote that she lived in 'a flat-iron of 15 acres, with walking entrance only from a shady back lane' (Brooklyn Botanic Garden)

collecting instincts as well as her unpretentious way of life, and one American visitor remarked how her interest in 'color, needlecraft, furniture and flower arrangement is expressed by the house into which she fits perfectly and which betrays her in a way her quiet talk and reticence do not'.[19]

Time seemed to have stood still, as Mrs Francis King recalled when describing her last visit in 1925: 'Though I had not seen Munstead Wood for twenty years the same gravely-smiling white-haired serving woman answered my pull of the interesting bell at the door, ushered me into the same beautiful room with its fine furniture and porcelains all about, the windows giving upon the wide grass walk through the woodland. In a moment came swiftly toward me dear Miss Jekyll herself, both hands held forth in welcome. We sat in talk for a little, then she sent me to the garden.'[20] As she grew older, she seldom escorted visitors around the garden. In 1926 Anna Gilman Hill, who owned a remarkable garden on Long Island, recalled carrying 'her stool, and when we came to any particularly fine combination in her glorious borders we would sit down and quietly discuss it' – a scene memorably captured in a candid photograph taken by Professor John Harshberger of Philadelphia a few years earlier.[21]

After a walk in the garden, the visitor was usually entertained to tea, which was normally served at half-past four. There would be thin slices of bread and butter, some form of cake, perhaps an unusual preserve such as crab-apple jelly or quince

Gertrude Jekyll seated on her camp-stool in the Spring Garden, 6 September 1923, was photographed by Professor John Harshberger from Philadelphia

jam; occasionally, for regular visitors, some greater oddity was produced, such as radishes grown in leaf-mould. All this consideration was, however, for the benefit of the guest, 'for G.J. was always on saccharined tea and one biscuit'.[22] The sitting room, with its long range of windows overlooking the Green Wood Walk, was quite simply furnished, with comfortable sofas and armchairs upholstered in beige and fawn striped fabric, a brown Axminster carpet and apricot satin curtains. An oak revolving bookcase, its contents overflowing on to an oak refectory table, and a small table near Gertrude Jekyll's chair, were in marked contrast to the ornate cabinet with inlaid marquetry panels opposite the fireplace. All around were examples of her craftsmanship. A corner cupboard inlaid with a classical frieze in mother-of-pearl and a large silver repoussé dish bespoke her skills in cabinetmaking and silversmithing, while the walls were adorned with watercolours by her friends Barbara Bodichon and Hercules Brabazon, together with her own sketches and paintings.

Long before such pursuits became fashionable, Gertrude Jekyll had been in the habit of visiting old cottages in the district and had become interested in their furnishings, the objects in every day use, and the way such simple country people lived. Over the years she collected chimney-cranes, (from which a kettle was suspended), rush-light holders and other obsolete objects, which she described in *Old West Surrey* and later donated to the Surrey Archaeological Society. Much of the furniture at Munstead Wood, such as the linen hutches, the chests, and the oak refectory tables in the gallery, were once common in farmhouses; she collected simple painted furniture, long before it became fashionable in the 1920s. The fashion for 'humble elegance' in interior decoration that developed in the inter-war years owed much to this interest in simple country life.

For the visitor, however, the room posed one slight problem, that of finding somewhere to sit down – for the house was literally overrun with cats, who naturally purloined all the best chairs. At first there were four or five cats, but soon they were to be numbered in double figures. The visitor was forced to play musical chairs, and if he was 'lucky enough to find a chair unoccupied, he was soon to discover that Gertrude's attention . . . was divided into three parts, one for himself, one for the tea-things, and one for Pinkieboy or Tittlebat, whose desire for company was not to be satisfied by a perfunctory caress.'[23]

Although Gertrude Jekyll was generous with her hospitality, she could not entertain all those who might have wished to visit her, and no doubt many people

The Revd Edwyn and Alice Arkwright admiring the October aster borders during their visit in the late 1890s. Revd Arkwright, a resident of Algiers, discovered a white-flowered Iris unguicularis *(CED-UC Berkeley)*

were turned away. Sometimes those who did get beyond the gate left with an unfortunate impression, but she had more manners and charm than some accounts of her would indicate. Years later the novelist Edith Wharton recalled her own visit: 'I had a hundred questions to ask, a thousand things to learn. I went with a party of fashionable and indifferent people, all totally ignorant of gardens and gardening. I put one timid question to Miss Jekyll, who answered curtly, and turned her back on me to point out a hybrid iris to an eminent statesman who knew neither what a hybrid nor an iris was.'[24] Perhaps if Mrs Wharton had been able to go on her own, her reception would have been different. Vita Sackville-West, not herself widely noted for gracious hospitality, recalled 'Miss Jekyll rather fat, and rather grumbly; garden not at its best, but can see it must be lovely'. As the year was 1917, at the height of the war, her comment on the garden is hardly surprising.[25] Vita may also have been an unwilling visitor; she had been taken by Lutyens, who was anxious for her mother, Lady Sackville, to meet 'Aunt Bumps'. According to Lutyens the two ladies were 'funny together', and the visit was such a great success that it was to be followed by 'an exchange of foie gras and pot pourri'.[26]

Gertrude Jekyll corresponded with and welcomed many Americans, especially those who were affiliated with garden clubs.[27] Aldred Scott Warthin, from the Garden Club of Michigan, recalled spending 'one of the most delightful afternoons' of her life at Munstead Wood, and at the end of the day Miss Jekyll sent cuttings of scented geraniums to her steamer.[28] One of her most lasting American friendships was with the garden writer Mrs Francis King, who did much to promote Jekyll's

The American garden writer Mrs Francis King,
who was a friend and frequent correspondent
(from House Beautiful, *April 1922; courtesy*
Virginia Lopez Begg)

books in America. Their friendship began when Mrs King wrote, enclosing a photograph of *Delphinium grandiflorum* of a remarkable shade of blue, and was asked for some seed, almost by return. Although Mrs King's visits to Munstead were infrequent, the two ladies maintained a warm correspondence for more than twenty years and often exchanged small gifts and plants.[29]

Some of her American friends hoped to lure Gertrude Jekyll to the United States, but after her last visit to the Chalet in 1902 she ceased to travel abroad. Although she was perennially short of funds ('always hard up', as Harold Falkner put it), she generally took a holiday, but these were undertaken with increasing reluctance as she grew older. These holidays were partly to give herself a change and a rest from work, but also to give the servants a holiday too, and also enable them to do some thorough cleaning. She loved the sea and often took her holiday somewhere on the coast, especially the Isle of Wight where she had been going since childhood. Her favourite month for travel seems to have been May. In 1904 she stayed at Tintagel in Cornwall; Cornwall was an old stamping-ground, and at one time she owned a holiday cottage near Zennor, The Old Poorhouse, which she had inherited from Barbara Bodichon in 1891. She sold it five years later, no doubt on the assumption that she would not be able to maintain both it and Munstead Wood; she may also have used the proceeds from the sale to help finance the building work then in train.[30]

Sometimes she was a house-guest, as in May 1906, when Edward Hudson invited her to Lindisfarne Castle, probably for the inaugural house party. She travelled to Northumberland by train, accompanied by Lutyens; the tide was in, and he never forgot the sight of Hudson's valet struggling to carry her from the boat. During the First World War she was enticed away to Folly Farm, which had been lent to Lutyens for a rare summer holiday. She spent part of the day gardening, 'out of force of habit', and playing the pianola in the evening. It was perhaps fitting that Lutyens and his long-standing friend should have the opportunity of enjoying one of their most significant commissions; this was the only time Lutyens ever lived in a house he had designed.

Gertrude Jekyll had stayed with the Lutyens family before, in 1907, when they took a house in Sussex. Lady Emily told Lutyens that she turned up with 'delicious funny odd luggage which she would unpack all by herself at once'.[31] The imminent arrival of 'Bumps' necessitated a few special preparations, and Lutyens warned Lady Emily that she would bring with her a great deal of paraphernalia (she was not one for travelling light), which was sure to include a drawing-board and masses of writing impedimenta. He also cautioned that she liked to spend time in her room during the day 'doing things', so would require a table of some sort – if none were available, he suggested they engage a 'carpenter to wait on her'.[32]

When she was at home, the hours beween tea and dinner, when visitors had left and the last post had gone, were devoted to work in the garden or workshop or to the company of her friends. Lady Chance saw her two or three times a week for twenty years, until the First World War 'dislocated all our lives'. If it was summer, and fine weather, they would spend the early evening in the garden, but during the winter they would repair to the workshop and pore over scrap-books, 'of

An illustration of 'delicious funny odd luggage' appeared in Old West Surrey *(CED–UC Berkeley)*

which [Miss Jekyll] had a great number'.[33] There seems to have been a natural sympathy between these two ladies, perhaps founded on the fact that both were artists. On one occasion Lady Chance called with her cousin to find Lutyens there and in one of his 'freakish moods'. The party ended up playing 'parlour games', the amusement was such that none wished to 'leave off', and they were all invited to stay to supper. Unfortunately it was soon discovered that there was not enough food in the house for four, a not uncommon occurrence in a household run for one person and in the days before refrigeration, so '"Ned" dashed off on his bicycle to . . . [Orchards] and returned with a tail of cold salmon'.[34]

Dinner, or supper as it was often called in modest establishments such as Gertrude Jekyll's, was served in the dining room at half-past seven. Given the surprise Lutyens had at luncheon, quite what the meal would have consisted of can only be guessed at. However, her sister-in-law Agnes, Lady Jekyll, a noted hostess of the period, published a cookery book compiled from articles she had written for *The Times*, and it gives some indication of the type of food that might have been served.[35] On one occasion Lutyens and Lady Emily thought they would go and have a surprise dinner with 'Bumps', who was then living in The Hut. They spent the afternoon 'buying mutton chops, eggs, sponge cake, macaroons, almonds, and bulls'-eyes [a peppermint sweet], and turned up about 6'. Miss Jekyll was delighted to see them and 'bore the shock splendidly' – and no doubt with considerable amusement, as Lady Emily dropped the eggs getting out of the carriage. They all set to work 'cooking the chops and peeling the almonds and [making] tipsy cake' and after dinner sat in 'the big ingle-nook and drank a variety of intoxicating liquors, brewed at home by Bumps, ending with hot tumblers of elderberry wine', which Lady Emily recalled was 'the most delicious stuff you ever drank'.[36]

When she was alone Gertrude Jekyll usually read after dinner or, after 1926, listened to the radio her brother had installed for her (not without objections to 'another of those modern contrivances'). Much to her surprise, she found it 'an unexpected source of delight', especially during the long winter evenings. Normally she would retire at about eleven o'clock. Winter or summer, the pattern of her life seldom changed.[37]

Munstead Wood exemplified, as Sir Herbert Baker remarked, 'the best simple English country life' of the day, which was 'frugal yet rich in beauty and comfort'. But it was not country life in the great country-house tradition of popular perception – the preserve of the aristocracy or the very rich, for whom Lutyens built a number of grand houses. Gertrude Jekyll's way of life was very much in the tradition of the English landed gentry, such as would have been familiar to, and was indeed chronicled by, writers like Jane Austen and George Eliot. It was one of great charm and simplicity, fast disappearing in the 1930s, to vanish all but completely with the Second World War.

CHAPTER 7

The Nursery and Kitchen Gardens

Not all visitors who came to Munstead Wood were aware that in addition to the pleasure gardens there was a large orchard, kitchen garden and nursery, all within less than two acres. Gertrude Jekyll seldom wrote about these areas and they were not included on the detailed plan of the main pleasure gardens drawn for *Gardens for Small Country Houses*, but her own photographs and those taken by Herbert Cowley for *The Garden* and *Gardening Illustrated* paint a fascinating picture of this little-documented part of the gardens. The general layout suggests a piecemeal development – hardly surprising, given that the area was originally devoted to servicing the main pleasure gardens (through the nursery), and supplying the house with produce.

Following the success of *Wood and Garden* and, later, *Colour in the Flower Garden*, Gertrude Jekyll was able to create a number of new decorative borders and eventually about half an acre was turned over to ornamental purposes; with a half-acre orchard, this left just one acre for the kitchen garden and nursery. Jekyll used these new decorative borders, largely created after the turn of the century and after the main pleasure gardens had become well established, to continue her experiments in the use of colour in planting design and her search for new ways in which to use shrubs and herbaceous plants in decorative gardening – subjects she found endlessly fascinating and absorbing. She wrote about these new borders in numerous magazine articles, but with the exception of the Grey Garden none were described in any of her books, although *Colour in the Flower Garden* went into many editions. However, the many photographs of the ornamental gardens reveal the numerous and inevitable changes which occurred during the fifty years she gardened at Munstead Wood, and help to unravel many of the ambiguities in her published descriptions.

Originally a double dry-stone wall, known as the 'old wall' (31), marked the divide between the pleasure gardens and the working gardens, separating the old Peony Garden and the Spring Garden from the first broad cross-path that linked the garden yard on the west side of the garden to the stable-yard on the east. The old wall, probably built by Gertrude Jekyll herself in 1892, was about four feet wide at the base and its central cavity was filled with an old hedge-bank removed from the Kitchen Garden. Although it was only four and a half feet high, the wall

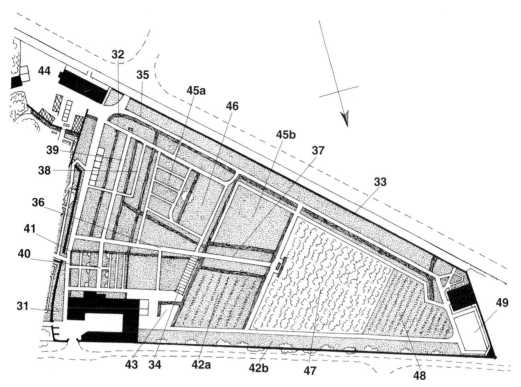

Plan for the nursery and kitchen gardens at Munstead Wood as they were in Gertrude Jekyll's day (Simon Dorrell)

31.	The Old Wall	39.	Summer Borders	45.	Nursery:
32.	Cypress Hedge	40.	Grey Garden		a) top nursery;
33.	Hascombe Border	41.	China Aster Garden		b) bottom nursery
34.	Larch Pole Pergola	42.	Kitchen Garden:	46.	Daffodils and Lily-of-
35.	Pansy Border		a) west bed;		the-valley
36.	Central Path		b) east bed	47.	Orchard
37.	September Borders	43.	Manure Heap	48.	Soft Fruit Bed
38.	Iris and Lupin Borders	44.	Main Garden Yard	49.	Hen Run

was richly planted with berberis, junipers, *Olearia × haastii* and Scotch brier roses that doubled its height and acted as a screen and windbreak.

In 1887 a hedge of *Chamaecyparis lawsoniana* was planted to give shelter from the north-westerly winds that swept across the garden (32). The hedge ran from the garden yard almost to the north-eastern tip of the garden, where the head gardener's cottage was later built, a distance of nearly five hundred feet. Although the plants were three feet high when purchased, they cost the modest sum of fifteen shillings (about £35 today) in a nursery stock sale; they were subsequently clipped to form a dense hedge about ten feet high and three deep that remained serviceable until the Second World War.[1] Two shorter hedges of yew and hornbeam provided further shelter and created a series of compartments that proved ideal for the nursery.

Head gardener, Albert Zumbach, trimming the cypress hedge near his cottage (from Gardening Illustrated, *14 July 1928)*

Between the Hascombe Road and the long cypress hedge lay a border four hundred and fifty feet long used as a stock bed for herbaceous plants (33). This did not have the elaborate colour scheme of the main flower border, but it was kept attractive for Sundays, when the Jekyll family from Munstead House used the path to walk to church. A second broad cross-path, partly covered by a larch pole pergola (34) used to grow gourds, ran between this border and the Kitchen Garden path, crossing the central path. At the end of the cypress hedge was a border devoted to pansies (35), which can be seen in a watercolour by Thomas Hunn. Gertrude Jekyll never commented on this pansy border in her writings, nor is she known to have photographed it, since it had disappeared by the mid 1920s, it may have been sacrificed when the summer borders and iris and lupin borders were created.[2] Possibly it was never intended as a purely decorative feature, but for use as a cutting border, to supply the house with flowers. Jekyll advised growing pansies in a 'northern facing border, where all flowers of purple and white colouring look their best', and mixing them with foxgloves, 'mulleins that do not open fully in sunlight, and tall evening primrose'.[3]

The central path (36) effectively split the working gardens into two segments and roughly separated the Kitchen Garden to the east from the nursery to the west. Why the central path, which terminated in the September borders, did not lead directly to the door in the south border is one of the mysteries of the garden's design. It may have been one of those 'awkward angles' to which Gertrude Jekyll referred, as most of the working gardens had been laid out before the high stone wall was built around 1892. Lining up the door with the central path would have destroyed the vista formed by the sweep of the bank of shrubs on the lawn that used the door as a focal point.

The September borders (37) were approached through an arch of laburnum, creating one of Gertrude Jekyll's most memorable 'garden pictures'. Although the borders, backed by hornbeam hedges, were primarily planted with early Michaelmas daisies, she deliberately set out to create a more pleasing tapestry by the addition of some yellow flowers. Clumps of pale primrose African marigolds and yellow and whitish-yellow snapdragons enlivened the array of misty blues, rich purples and dusty reds. Drifts of white moon daisies, often planted in association with purple asters, lightened the colour scheme and with the help of white hollyhocks and dahlias offset drifts of dark blue heliotrope and red *Sedum spectabile* at the borders' edge.[4] Copious amounts of grey foliage were also included, not only along the edges with drifts of white-flowered dianthus, *Stachys byzantina* and nepeta, but also in the body of the border with groups of artemisias, *Phlomis fruticosa* and even a silver willow.

Among the earliest borders developed in what had formerly been kitchen garden ground were those devoted to iris and lupins (38). These June borders, the subject of a memorable autochrome, seemed to sum up the essence of Gertrude Jekyll's style of planting.[5] They were partly backed by a yew hedge (to the north) and a hedge of flowering shrubs (to the south), which she later regretted had not been composed exclusively of guelder rose (*Viburnum opulus*) and flowering currant (*Ribes sanguineum*). Long before the advent of Russell lupins, Gertrude Jekyll had selected her own lupin strain with very large flowering spikes which she kept to a restricted colour range of pink, purple-red and blue, pale purple shading to white and, finest of all, 'Munstead white'. She was particularly fond of all those iris related to *Iris pallida*, of which she found the old pale-lilac variety Dalmatica (now known as *Iris pallida pallida*) the most useful in the general garden, because of its excellent leaves. On the whole these iris were too early in flower to be widely accommodated; the old variety 'Queen of the May', now lost to cultivation, was one of the few that were late enough, and because of its good 'rosy-lilac' colour it looked most effective with pink China roses (*Rosa* × *odorata* 'Pallida'). Planted among the lupins and iris were patches of blue *Anchusa azurea* 'Opal', with masses of white garden pinks and pansies along the edges. Gertrude Jekyll found the 'reddish satin-lustred' leaves of *Heuchera americana* invaluable as a ground-work for iris of the *squalens* type in red-purple and smoky yellow. To give the borders further substance white and yellow tree lupins were included, together with a hybrid called 'Somerset' which had been raised by Kelways of Langport.

The September borders framed by an arch of laburnum, with the head gardener's cottage in the distance, 1907 (CED–UC Berkeley)

An edge of stachys and grey-blue spikes of Lyme grass in the centre offset the pale lilac, purple and pale-pink asters in the September borders, 14 September 1907 (CED-UC Berkeley)

Running parallel with the iris and lupin borders, and probably created at the same time, were a set of borders devoted to summer flowers (39) with a 'hot' colour scheme of strong yellow, white and orange. Referring to the informal shrub hedge which formed the southern boundary of the iris and lupin borders, Gertrude Jekyll observed that 'some kind of hedge was wanted on both sides when a double flower-border was made'.[6] As the iris and lupin borders were bounded to the north by a yew hedge, which had been there for many years, she must have been referring to the new summer borders. Whatever the initial sequence of events may have been, these summer borders were originally composed of annuals such as China asters, snapdragons, godetias and zinnias. After a few years they were remade in a more mixed composition, probably because they were not very successful as annual borders, or perhaps as a labour-saving measure.[7] These double borders, flanking a path leading from the cypress hedge to the Grey Garden, appear to have been relatively narrow in relation to their length: Jekyll was engaged in another piece of *trompe-l'oeil*, using the restricted space and the rich colour scheme as a prelude to the cool and distant colours in the Grey Garden, cleverly concealed beyond the kink in the path. The colours gradually changed from red, orange and yellow to bold white patches of her own form of *Leucanthemum maximum*, followed by groups of purple

Graham Stuart Thomas's photograph of the summer flower borders, 6 September 1931. The yew arch at left is the entrance to the iris and lupin borders

erigerons, *Salvia × superba* and clary (*Salvia sclarea*), edged with drifts of sweet alyssum, ageratum and sea lavender.[8]

The summer borders led on to the cool and welcoming colours of the Grey Garden (40), laid out in front of The Loft. These borders, and the use of grey foliage in general, seem to have held a particular fascination for Gertrude Jekyll, as she wrote numerous articles about them. Her use of grey foliage as a foil for other plantings was copied by many designers, including Norah Lindsay who, according to Russell Page, carried the idea so far 'that some of her borders looked almost opalescent'.[9] She herself delighted in the rich yet cool tapestry of purple, blue and pink, lifted by touches of white, so welcoming to the eye after the violent colours of the summer borders.[10] The dark grey foliage of sea buckthorn (*Hippophaë rhamnoides*) was used to echo the grey-tinged weather-boarding of The Loft and to provide a backdrop to the four small beds, each about twenty-five feet long and nine feet wide. Tall pink hollyhocks and powder-blue ceanothus provided the background to drifts of artemisia, *Delphinium × belladonna*, and cascades of purple-flowered *Clematis* 'Jackmanii' were trained among globe thistles (*Echinops ritro*). Copious amounts of white flowers were used to contrast with the blue flowers and grey foliage, as can be seen in the autochrome of one of

The Grey Garden in front of The Loft, 1920s (courtesy Mary Bland)

the borders, where *Achillea ptarmica* 'The Pearl' and *Lilium longiflorum*, along with clouds of gypsophila, help to lighten the 'picture'.

Munstead Wood also had a garden devoted entirely to China asters (41), but Gertrude Jekyll's description in *Colour in the Flower Garden* is ambiguous, and she seems to have taken no photographs of it. It was enclosed by a hedge of lavender, with the four outer beds and the central bed edged in stachys. Before the Grey Garden was made a long lavender hedge (the lavender was used in pot-pourri) ran in front of The Loft, so it is entirely possible that the China Aster Garden was behind the Grey Garden. The asters were confined to 'those of the pure violet-purple and lavender colours, with whites', the planting arranged with the whites at the centre, fading into 'pale lavender lilac' succeeded by 'light purple' and ending with 'rich dark purple' at the garden's edge.[11]

The kitchen gardens were to the east of the September borders, and since the land had originally been a 'sandy field with a hard plough bed about eight inches down', considerable work had been required to rejuvenate the soil.[12] A broad path led from the stables to the Thunder-house, splitting the garden into two large beds. The western bed (42a) was much wider than the eastern (42b) but not as long, since the orchard occupied the lower end. At the top of the path, by the stables and the pig sties, was the manure heap (43), used in summer to grow vegetable marrows. The main garden yard (44), with the potting shed,

Mrs Cannon with hollyhock 'Pink Beauty' outside The Loft, late 1890s (CED–UC Berkeley)

greenhouses, cold frames and compost bins, was on the opposite side of the garden, near the Hascombe Road.

The potting shed served several functions, from the gardeners' 'mess' to a packing shed for plant orders. It also contained an engineer's shop, complete with a forge, where Gertrude Jekyll made to her own design, many of the small specialized tools used in the garden. Munstead Wood was run as efficiently and economically as possible, and much of the garden supplies were 'home made'. Three large bins in the garden yard were used for composting leaves collected from the lawns and the road, to be used in making seed and potting compost. Similarly, there was a large pit where ordinary garden rubbish was thrown and left to break down for use in compost-making and as a mulch for the ornamental beds. On wet days the gardeners made seed and pricking-out boxes out of wooden ones obtained from local shopkeepers. Garden labels were made from the butt ends of the pea- and bean-sticks which were gathered in the wood, shaved flat at

Delphinium × belladonna *in the Grey Garden, with arches of Rose 'La Guirlande' ('The Garland') framing the view west, 1907 (CED–UC Berkeley)*

one end and painted white. For larger labels, staves from old barrels were used, painted battleship grey with the lettering stencilled in white.[13]

The kitchen garden was not large (about a third of an acre of cultivated ground), and in 1927 additional vegetable beds were created in the orchard.[14] Towards the end of February onions, lettuce, tomatoes, cucumbers and annual flowers were sown in boxes in the greenhouses. Brick cold frames in the garden yard and wooden frames on the other side of the old wall were used to grow radishes and early carrots, sown in the first weeks of March.

Apart from a chapter in *Home and Garden* and several 'Kitchen Garden Notes' in *The Garden* during the First World War, Gertrude Jekyll wrote comparatively little about kitchen gardening, although she was 'by no means indifferent to the interest and charm of the kitchen garden'.[15] Most of the 'Kitchen Garden Notes' appeared in 1917, when the food situation in Britain was becoming increasingly desperate, thanks to the activities of German U-boats. Her notes included a

Vegetable marrows growing on the manure heap near the stables, around 1917. The head gardener's cottage is just visible in the distance (from The Garden, *12 June 1926)*

request that the Royal Horticultural Society should investigate the 'edible properties of Rhubarb leaves', following some deaths resulting from the leaves being used as a substitute for spinach at the suggestion of the National Training School of Cookery in their booklet *War-time Tips*. As she remarked to a friend, the First World War 'brought me an altered life': in 1917 she turned the main flower border over to potatoes and tomatoes, which she wrote about in *The Garden*.[16] Although the larger shrubs remained, the loss of the principal feature of the pleasure garden was no small sacrifice.

Not surprisingly, Gertrude Jekyll was more interested in unusual vegetables, and wrote enthusiastically about them in *Home and Garden* in an effort to bring them to wider notice. One such was sea kale, which cottagers used for greens in early spring. At Munstead it was grown in the pleasure gardens for its foliage as well as being forced for the table, and she also discovered that the 'crowded flower-bud, cut when at the most broccoli-like stage', made an excellent vegetable. She enjoyed a winter salad of dandelion greens, which she grew in trenches and blanched, like celery, to remove any bitterness.[17]

Bins for storing leaves in the garden yard, late 1890s (CED-UC Berkeley)

Because Gertrude Jekyll always seemed to be short of money, she grew some cash crops. The most profitable were daffodils for Easter and lily-of-the-valley. Between the 'top' (45a) and 'bottom' (45b) nurseries three large beds of daffodils and two of lily-of-the-valley (46) were grown for the cut-flower trade. In early spring the beds would be watered with a solution of pig manure, provided by the resident pig, which helped to produce sturdy flower stems. If Easter was late, the flowers would be cut and held back in the cool mushroom house; if early, the flowers would be put in a warm greenhouse to hasten their bloom. In 1928, sixty-three dozen bunches of daffodils and fifty dozen of lily-of-the-valley (a dozen stems to the bunch) were sent to local shopkeepers.[18]

There were also three long beds planted with Rose 'Zéphirine Drouhin' to provide flowers for pot-pourri making. To encourage more profuse blooming, young growths were tied down to a frame of small posts linked together by bamboo canes held in place by iron staples. The system was remarkably successful, and each year enough flowers were gathered to fill a fifteen-gallon cask with petals. To supplement the supply, climbing roses covering the fence behind the Hascombe border were also used. She had a ready market for her moist pot-pourri (different from the more common dry blend) and sold it for twenty shillings a gallon – sufficient to fill a large bowl.

The half-acre orchard (47) at Munstead was planted in a large block in staggered rows, to act as a wind-break. The fruit store in the stable-yard gave a continuous supply of cooking apples from the eight varieties grown, each with different qualities and uses, and different eating and keeping times. At least six varieties of dessert apple, which included 'Egremont Russet' and 'King of the Pippins', supplied fruit until Easter. Pears included the old French variety 'Catillac', which remains hard until April, and the finest of all, 'Doyenne du Comice'. The wall backing the spring vegetable bed was planted with gages, plums, pears, and the figs which Gertrude Jekyll loved best of all: her normally generous nature did not extend to figs.[19] She also had a bed of strawberries reserved for the table, and soft fruit (48) – an ordinary collection of raspberries and blackberries, blackcurrants, red and white currants, and gooseberries which were 'trained espalier fashion' to protect the gardener's hands from scratches. Besides the dessert gooseberry varieties there was an odd row of 'Ironmonger', used for jam-making, and one of 'Whinham's Industry' for pickling.[20]

Although the unusually large area of 'dressed ground' at Munstead Wood generated large quantities of surplus plants, Gertrude Jekyll probably never made a formal or even conscious decision to start a nursery. It doubtless began as a natural progression from exchanging spare plants with fellow-gardeners to supplying the needs of an increasingly busy garden design practice, but a desire to spread her selections to a wider public undoubtedly played some part in the establishment of a nursery which slowly evolved into a business.

From childhood she had had a keen eye for a good plant, and foreign travel had made her aware of a more diverse flora. In 1863 she collected iris from a Turkish cemetery on Rhodes, and twenty years later on Capri she found a small white periwinkle – now known as *Vinca minor* 'Gertrude Jekyll'. Closer to home, her interest in rural life had led her to cottage gardens where she found good herbaceous plants and old roses no longer considered fashionable. From these gardens came the briar roses grown everywhere at Munstead, and also a large rose of uncertain lineage used in The Hut garden.

There are still a number of plants in circulation which bear either the Munstead name or that of Gertrude Jekyll, although many more have been lost to cultivation. The most widely available plant she selected is the dwarf lavender 'Munstead', but the most famous is her strain of bunch primroses. The strain began in 1873 with her discovery of a white-flowered bunch primrose in a cottage garden; she crossed it with 'Golden Plover', a cultivated form, and for the next twenty-five years she crossed and re-crossed, restricting the strain to shades of white and yellow and discarding any unsatisfactory developments – a process which continued until the end of her life. On one occasion she tried to catalogue the various flower forms, but gave up after writing sixty different descriptions.[21] There was also another strain of Munstead primrose: in the 1890s she discarded a red strain she was working on, to concentrate on the whites and yellows, but after 1900 resumed her work with the reds. Progress was slow, and when in 1927 she finally had a flower pleasing to her in both colour and form she remarked to her gardener, 'I've waited twenty years for this day.'[22]

Gertrude Jekyll had her own strains or selections of many plants including a large white columbine, *Aquilegia vulgaris* 'Nivea' ('Munstead White'), still available today, and *Papaver somniferum* 'Munstead Cream Pink', a form of opium poppy which she sold to Vilmorin as seed.[23] Carter's also bought seeds from Munstead, so seed-collecting must have been a considerable activity which made its own contribution to garden finances.

What is most surprising about the nursery business at Munstead Wood was its scale. While it occupied only a half-acre of ground, its receipts (well over £300 a year) easily paid the wages of the four under-gardeners. The venture began in the early 1890s and Gertrude Jekyll produced a catalogue which ran into several editions, but only two copies are known to survive. An early one, probably dating from around 1905, lists more than three hundred plants, mostly shrubs and herbaceous plants but including twenty herbs and sixty alpines. The main business of the nursery, however, was to provide plants for garden design clients. When she drew up a planting plan for a garden, Gertrude Jekyll usually mentioned that she was able to supply plants 'a good deal to your advantage as to

A page from the Munstead Wood nursery catalogue, around 1905 (CED–UC Berkeley)

price and strength . . . of plant . . . compared to the usual nurseries' – an offer most clients found irresistible.[24] As the prices quoted in her catalogue were probably retail, she no doubt offered her design clients a discount that undercut trade prices, but she preferred this to remain a private matter.

Nursery stock lists from the 1920s given an idea of the scale of the business. In 1922, for example, the nursery could supply twenty-four *Choisya ternata*, twelve escallonias and twelve *Spirea prunifolia*, and in 1926 there were eleven types of roses, with no fewer than 100 plants of *Rosa gallica* available. The nursery was prepared to supply large quantities if required, such as 600 hollyhocks or 100 'Lady Lloyd' Michaelmas daisies.[25] Gertrude Jekyll had no problem supplying 330 plants of London Pride for fourteen shillings (roughly £35 today), which her client Amy Barnes-Brand thought 'marvellously cheap'.[26]

Nursery orders were recorded in small notebooks from which collecting sheets were prepared and handed to the head gardener at his morning briefing. After the orders had been made up and dispatched, the collecting sheet was returned to Gertrude Jekyll so that she could send a letter of explanation to her client, if necessary. As the orders were filled, the notebook listings would be struck off or amended, and the amount due for the plants transferred to the account books. Statements of account were then sent when the order or the project was complete. The plants were labelled and packed in wooden boxes obtained from local grocers and sent off by rail, then a cheap and efficient means of transport. Occasionally, as happens in even the best-run establishments, things went wrong, as when Amy Barnes-Brand received someone else's order. As Gertrude Jekyll said in her letter of apology, 'In all the thirty years I have been packing away plants, such a mistake has only happened once before'. She gave a flavour of the operations at Munstead when she added, 'If you were to see my packing shed on one of the busy days, with all the different lots of plants and the groups of labels and packing stuff, you would wonder that it did not happen oftener.'[27]

Francis Jekyll continued to run the nursery after his aunt died in 1932, but by 1941 labour had become so scarce and so restricted that he was unable to continue with the enterprise. When Munstead Wood was broken up and sold in 1948, a unique collection of very carefully selected herbaceous plants and shrubs was dispersed.

CHAPTER 8

Professional Garden Designer

It has been said that Gertrude Jekyll 'changed the face of England more than any, save the Creator himself and, perhaps, Capability Brown'.[1] Of course, in reality her influence on horticulture has spread, through the medium of the printed word, far beyond Britain, although she is often misunderstood and misinterpreted.

Gertrude Jekyll was an innovator and she instinctively turned, for inspiration, to the cottage gardens she had known since childhood. In looking to these 'little cottage gardens that help make our English waysides the prettiest in the temperate world', she was to some extent following fashionable artistic taste.[2] What might be termed reactionary nostalgia, of which the idealized watercolours of country cottages by artists such as Helen Allingham are merely one manifestation, was a significant driving force in Victorian Britain and lay at the heart of much of the Arts and Crafts Movement. Jekyll, with her training as an artist, wrote of what she knew well and of what she observed, measuring each fresh observation against her guiding principle of 'gardening for beautiful effect'. She was a broad-minded woman, something that is clear from her writings, and was prepared to use all manner of plants and devices if they fitted into, and contributed to, the effect she was seeking to create.

The Jekyll style was not a cheap form of gardening: it required not only money but a considerable amount of time and trouble to maintain the effects. Like the craftsmanship which lay at the heart of the Arts and Crafts Movement, it was an expensive luxury affordable only by the rich – and at this time many of the rich were the 'new rich', men who had made their fortunes in manufacturing or 'trade'. Consider the irony: the majority of Gertrude Jekyll's and the overwhelming majority of Sir Edwin Lutyens's clients were to be found, not among the 'old rich', aristocracy or gentry, many of whose fortunes had suffered from the fall in land values in the 1880s, but among the 'new rich' whose businesses were killing off the traditional craftsmanship they both valued so passionately.

Garden design was never a youthful ambition; Gertrude Jekyll entered the field only when the onset of myopia compelled her to lay aside her paint-brush and find a new outlet for her prodigious energies and talents. During the course of a career which spanned more than fifty years, she probably designed more than four hundred gardens – the exact number can never be known for certain. Although records for fewer than 250 gardens survive among her papers at the University of California at Berkeley, the list of her commissions prepared by her nephew Francis Jekyll in 1934 contains some 340 entries. Her nursery notebooks, now at the Godalming Museum, contain a wealth of incidental detail, from the extent of her nursery business, as discussed earlier, to the dates various plans were sent to clients, but fewer than 150 gardens are mentioned. There remain many, amounting to nearly one third of all those she is known to have designed, for which no records survive; in some cases all that is known is an address, or just a client's name.

Most of her gardens were created in the south-east of England, with relatively few in the north and fewer still in Scotland. A staggering seventy per cent of her commissions were within a radius of less than a hundred miles of London, well over thirty per cent in her own county of Surrey. Some clients found that her specific recommendations did not travel well. Her nephew noted 'that she had to be reminded that plants of border-line hardiness in Southern England must be replaced in the Eastern [United] States by others more able to withstand the rigours of a winter untempered by the Gulf Stream', as is also the case for most of Britain.[3] Climatic conditions defeated most attempts by American gardeners to replicate her ideas from reading her books, and even when they succeeded, the difference in the quality of the light, which in England is tinged with blue, largely destroyed the effect. Records survive for three gardens in the United States designed by her, but it is possible she did more work there than is generally acknowledged; her extensive contacts with The Garden Club of America and the frequency with which Americans visited Munstead Wood would seem to support this view.

Yet her first garden design commission was a distinctly modest affair. A mill boy from the Lancashire cotton town of Rochdale 'advertised in a mechanical paper' in 1870 that he would like a tiny garden in a window box. Her evident delight in planning this window box, which was only some three feet long and ten inches wide, is clear from her recollection of the story in *Wood and Garden*. The boy's letters were full of questions and his interest and enthusiasm were such that he needed to be restrained from killing his little garden with kindness. One can imagine, as she did with great pleasure, the joy it brought the recipient, whose life of relative poverty and hard work was in marked contrast to the genteel comforts of Munstead House. Her other early work was mostly done for friends such as the Blumenthals, Barbara Bodichon and Susan Mackenzie. These were probably not formal commissions, but small tokens of friendship and hospitality, something indicated by the lack of any significant documentation.

Garden design was something Gertrude Jekyll genuinely enjoyed doing and, unlike many of her contemporaries, she was not rich. Although William Robinson designed scarcely a dozen gardens, using Gravetye Manor as an example of his principles, just as Jekyll used Munstead Wood, he had made a fortune from property speculation and development, but preferred to concentrate his efforts on publishing. Ellen Willmott, of Warley Place in Essex, inherited a vast fortune, which she ultimately squandered on her passion for horticulture, and Reynolds Hole, Dean of Rochester, had a cathedral to run. Jekyll, lacking the financial security of her friends, found, almost by accident, that her interest in horticulture and gardening could be transformed into a profitable business to help supplement her slender financial resources.

The earliest garden for which any documentary evidence of her involvement survives is Crooksbury House, Lutyens's first major commission. The mutually beneficial relationship between the two begun at Crooksbury House in 1889 was to span forty years and range over more than fifty gardens. Although Gertrude Jekyll's reputation was already firmly established through her numerous magazine articles, it undoubtedly helped open the door to a career in garden design at an opportune moment. By the 1920s her renown was such that one client felt embarrassed asking for her help, likening it to asking 'Sir Joshua Reynolds to help me paint my stable doors'.[4]

Gertrude Jekyll's clients came from a number of sources, some through personal recommendation, others from the suggestion of an architect. Walter Brierley, unable to accept a garden design commission himself, generously recommended her as the 'best of garden designers'.[5] Brierley was a prolific architect in the North of England, continuing the practice established in 1750 by John Carr ('Carr of York'). He may have been introduced to her by Edward Hudson; when he built his own house in York, he turned to her for the garden design, and subsequently employed her on two other houses he built.

Lady Cowper of Hursley Park near Winchester showed some resourcefulness in obtaining Gertrude Jekyll's address from Hatchards, the Piccadilly booksellers. Other prospective clients wrote to the editors or publishers of magazines to which she was a contributor, hoping she might be persuaded to accept a commission. In a letter to the editor of *Gardening Illustrated* in which she sought help in designing a border for Ponds, her country house in Berkshire, Marjorie Goff described Gertrude Jekyll as 'a great authority on colour', citing her ability to describe the tone of colour 'accurately and perfectly'.[6]

On a number of occasions she answered queries from *Country Life* correspondents directly, as Hudson was aware that questions of garden design interested the majority of his readers. Allan Aynesworth, for instance, wanted suggestions for four small beds to give a sequence of flowering from spring to autumn, while Colonel Bailey of Bulcote Manor in Nottinghamshire wrote seeking planning advice for the whole garden of his Jacobean manor house. In this case Gertrude Jekyll quickly deduced that a major improvement would come from 'straightening . . . the edge of the shrubbery border on the west side of the lawn, which at present shows a line waving about with no apparent purpose'.[7]

What is most surprising about Gertrude Jekyll's work as a garden designer is that she seldom travelled to any of the sites involved, certainly after the First World War; even before the war, it is unlikely that she visited more than a couple of dozen of the commissions she worked on. In 1925, one of her most productive years, she wrote; 'I am old now [she was 81] and never . . . leave home, though I am still working at my desk and bench. I do designs and alterations of gardens now by plan and description only and have done this for the last few years with satisfaction to my clients.'[8] This, of course, is why she always requested a surveyor's plan; years of experience had taught her to be wary of clients' own rough plans, which usually turned out to be useless, resulting 'in my having to do the plan over and over again, so causing much more expense than if the plan forwarded had been right in the beginning'.[9]

When working for private clients, who accounted for more than sixty per cent of the gardens she created, she would send a sheet of specifications to ensure that she was given all the necessary information. The plan was to be drawn to a scale of one-sixteenth of an inch to one foot and should show the block plan of the house, together with any doors and important windows. Her instructions stressed the need to record 'roads, paths, flower borders and shrub clumps . . . [and] any important trees', which were to be named and the spread of the branches indicated. The levels of the site were also required, to be shown 'either by contours or figures on the plan at intervals, a datum being taken at the lowest level': if this should prove too exacting for the client, 'the surveyor would understand what would be required'.[10]

From the site plan supplied by the client, she usually prepared a general plan showing the basic layout of the garden, with the position of all proposed beds and borders clearly indicated with letters and numbers marked in red, to facilitate identification in correspondence and avoid any confusion. The scale she used in preparing layout plans varied, but one-thirty-second or one-sixteenth of an inch to a foot was most common. Such a small scale, while convenient to work on, tends to exaggerate dimensions, particularly those of paths and borders; it is also far too small for the preparation of planting plans, for which she nearly always used a scale of one-eighth of an inch to a foot, or occasionally one-quarter of an inch to a foot. The plans themselves were drawn on cartridge paper or on the thick white tracing paper Lutyens sent her, possibly for use on his work.[11] Naturally most clients wanted some idea of what Miss Jekyll's services would cost. As she told Mrs Temple-Richards of Wangford Hall, she found it impossible to 'quote the fee exactly till I see how much work is required, but it may be anything from 9 to 12 guineas' (probably £473 to £630 today); this seems to have been her usual fee for a garden design when no architect was involved.

Wangford Hall in Suffolk illustrates how she designed a garden without actually visiting the site. Her clients sent the requested plan, accompanied by sixteen photographs of the garden and house. Photographs often played a critical part in the design process, as they gave a good idea of what the house looked like and a flavour of the site, something which letters and plans could never convey. Recognizing that conditions on the ground might not always correspond exactly with the plans, she advised her clients not to take these 'as hard and fast, but as a guide to planting as nearly as the existing conditions allow'.[12]

Since the Temple-Richardses had taken Wangford on a short lease, there were limits to the amount of redesigning and gardening which could be undertaken. There was also another problem, as Mrs Temple-Richards explained: most of the windows overlooked the forecourt and they were obliged to retain the hedge of box and yew, even though it was in poor condition. Gertrude Jekyll considered

The south side of Wangford Hall, Suffolk, one of sixteen photographs Gertrude Jekyll received from Mrs Temple-Richards in 1929 (CED–UC Berkeley)

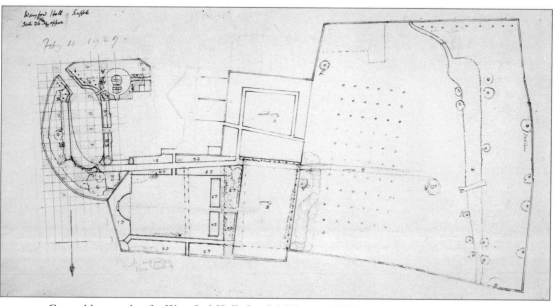

General layout plan for Wangford Hall, dated 4 February 1929, shows all the beds and borders clearly identified by a numbering system (CED–UC Berkeley)

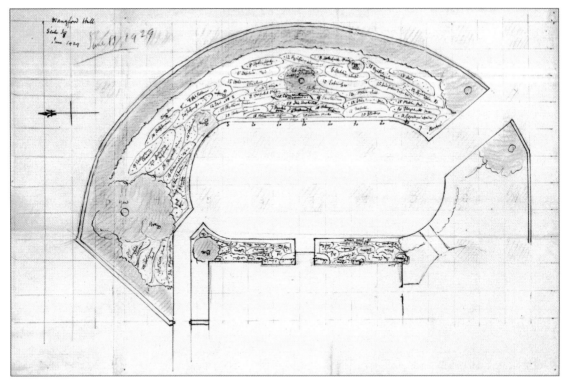

Detailed planting plan for the forecourt at Wangford Hall, 11 June 1929 (CED–UC Berkeley)

that 'the planting just within the entrance gate, and from there to the house, should be kept green and quiet, as a prelude to a bright display of flowers in the garden proper'.[13] For planting against the house wall she specified China roses and rosemary which, with drifts of London Pride and bergenia, would help to anchor the house more effectively to the site. Opposite the house, across the oval gravel forecourt, she recommended drifts of herbaceous plants to give a quick effect. A small area on the south side of the house was ingeniously transformed by creating a rotunda garden, screened from the drive and forecourt by Portugal laurels and *Viburnum tinus* – all very similar to the Walnut Lawn created at Folly Farm twenty years earlier. Her original idea was then altered, and the circularity of the lawn enhanced by giving it an edging of bergenia with odd patches of London Pride. Of course, designing by post can lead to confusion: Mrs Temple-Richards had to point out that there were no steps up into the summer-house – and did Miss Jekyll realize that the farmyards were on the other side of the wall in the rotunda garden?[14]

Gertrude Jekyll's finest gardens were invariably those she created when an architect provided the basic layout; and although she collaborated with many architects, her name is inextricably linked with that of Sir Edwin Lutyens.

Lutyens's genius in the creation and manipulation of space and his deep understanding of geometry resulted in a rigid framework when applied to garden design, in direct contrast but ideally suited to Gertrude Jekyll's essentially cottage-garden planting style of billowing borders which softened and set off neat lawns, crisp paving, and other architectural features. One of the few surviving gardens created by this formidable collaboration is Hestercombe House in Somerset (laid out in 1904 for The Hon. Edward Portman), which perfectly illustrates their combined talents. Lutyens designed an elaborate scheme centred around a large sunken garden, known as 'The Great Plat', flanked by two water gardens on a higher level. To enclose the garden he used a long pergola with alternating square and round piers which framed the view across Taunton Dene. Gertrude Jekyll softened the architecture of the pergola with Russian vine (*Fallopia baldschuanica*), jasmine and masses of climbing roses, while huge clumps of lavender, phlomis and santolina spilled out on to the path. As the pergola stood atop a retaining wall, with a border at its feet, she sketched the different plant silhouettes on her copy of the plan as she worked, to clarify her idea of the effect she was creating. On the client's copies of the plans the retaining walls and the borders at their feet were drawn on one sheet of paper which was then folded so that the wall became vertical, thus giving the client, who perhaps found ordinary plans confusing, a much better understanding of what was intended.

Lutyens's talents as a garden designer were employed to considerable effect at Folly Farm in Berkshire, where over the years he worked with two different owners on architectural additions. The garden was also developed in two stages, but most of the planting plans that survive are of the earlier commission, in 1906, for H. Cochrane. By March 1907 one of Gertrude Jekyll's working drawings shows garden areas adjacent to Lutyens's addition blocked in with her notes, and the rhododendron walk more fully detailed. Lutyens and Jekyll returned in 1912 at the request of the new owner, Zachary Merton, and much of the earlier garden was obliterated by a fresh scheme which included a canal garden, a parterre garden, a tank garden and, further to the west, an intricate sunken garden planted with roses and beds of rosemary.

In 1924 the partnership reached its apotheosis with Lutyens's grandest country house, and one of their last collaborations, Gledstone Hall in Yorkshire. Finding the original mansion impossible to alter, Sir Amos Nelson decided to engage Lutyens to build a new house on the estate. Costs rapidly spiralled out of control thanks to Lutyens's habitual failing of seriously underestimating his jobs, with the unfortunate consequence that the garden was never completed as originally envisaged. Its heart was a central sunken lily canal leading to a round reflecting pool on a slightly higher level. Jekyll immediately sensed that the massive sandstone retaining walls for the canal needed to be softened by planting, so as the wall was built, numerous pockets for plants were created. On either side of the canal (at ground level) she created broad double herbaceous borders leading to a pergola on a cross-axis, which flanked the reflecting pool and framed the view to the Pendle Hills in the distance. Unlike the canal garden at Folly Farm, the Gledstone example seems cold and forbidding; whether it would have worked any better had the scheme been completed as originally intended is open to debate.

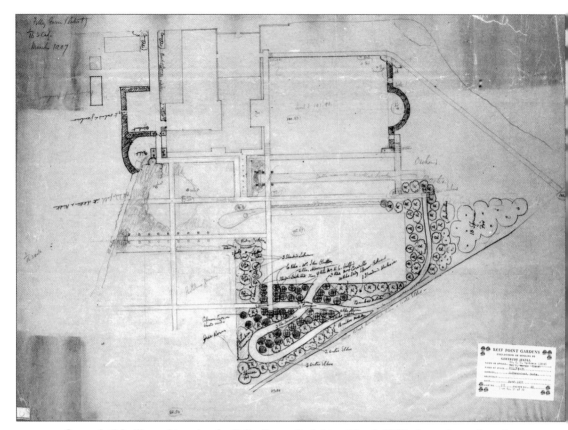

Gertrude Jekyll's working plan for Folly Farm, Berkshire, March 1907, shows the gardens that were replaced in 1912 by a canal, tank garden, and parterre garden (CED-UC Berkeley)

Since Gertrude Jekyll would clearly not travel to Yorkshire, all points needing clarification were dealt with by post; her enquiry as to the type of soil and colour of the stone resulted in the works manager dispatching samples for her to examine. Work began in 1925 and continued for about three years – a final Statement of Account was sent in August 1928. The planting plans cost Sir Amos 105 guineas (appoximately £5250 today), a fee considerably in excess of her usual charges, and negotiated by Lutyens on her behalf. The plants supplied from Munstead cost slightly less (£93 16s. 11d.); considering the quantities involved, this was remarkably cheap.[15]

Most gardens Edwin Lutyens and Gertrude Jekyll designed were large and grand, but occasionally they worked on a small scale, as at Millmead, in Bramley. No planting plans survive, but fragments reproduced in *Gardens for Small Country Houses* and Jekyll's own photographs illustrate the intention of the design. In 1905 she asked Lutyens to design for her the 'best small house in the

The north face of the tank garden at Gledstone Hall, North Yorkshire, 1934, designed by Lutyens for Sir Amos Nelson. The small pockets on the wall face were for plants (courtesy David Nelson)

A page from the planting notebook for Gledstone Hall, showing the number of plants required in the 'Parterre A' garden (Godalming Museum)

Garden front of Millmead, Bramley, seen from the middle terrace, 1908. The 'best small house' in the neighbourhood, it was designed by Lutyens in 1905 (CED–UC Berkeley)

whole neighbourhood', as a piece of speculative building. The ground fell away from the house, so several terraces were created, and the problem was to give 'each succeeding level . . . some individuality and distinctive interest, and yet . . . a comfortable sense of general cohesion', partly achieved by using a cottage-garden style of planting.[16] The project was a great success, and Harold Falkner recalled that he had 'never seen anything before, nor since, as perfectly developed, so exquisite in every detail, so much in so small a space'.[17]

Although so often associated with Lutyens, Gertrude Jekyll actually worked with nearly fifty other architects, among them such prominent names as Sir Herbert Baker, Charles Bateman, and Forbes and Tate. Harold Falkner remarked that she tended to overrate architects as a class, probably because she 'took Lutyens as her standard and thought that all his colleagues would be as interesting if not as entertaining' – which, of course, they were not.[18] She once described the difference between working with Lutyens and with Sir Robert Lorimer as that 'between quicksilver and suet'.[19] Lutyens was unusual: very few architects had his sureness of touch or his understanding of landscape, but some did take an active interest in garden design.

She also worked with many of the leaders of the Arts and Crafts Movement, including Sidney Barnsley, M.H. Baillie Scott and C.F.A. Voysey, as well as Lorimer and Brierley, and featured the work of several in *Gardens for Small Country Houses*. One of the first architects with whom she worked was Walter Sarel, about whom little is known.[20] Since Sarel was related to the More-Molyneuxes of Loseley House, she had probably known him since he was a child.

Gertrude Jekyll's work in 1925 for Sidney Barnsley at Combend Manor in Gloucestershire illustrates her way of dealing with an architect and reforming his preconceived ideas. The impetus to involve her at Combend probably came from Robert Weir Schultz, a friend of Barnsley's who supplied the introduction. From the first Barnsley certainly deferred to her regarding the concept of the garden, and actively sought 'any improvements in the general scheme and lay-out', adding that he hoped she would not hesitate to suggest any alterations to his proposals.[21]

To obtain further information as simply as possible, Gertrude Jekyll sent Barnsley a list of queries, with space left for his responses. In his original layout, Barnsley proposed building a seat on the upper terrace with a set of steps to the lower level, where a lily pool was intended as the prelude to an informal pond garden, probably formed from an existing horse-pond dominated by a group of poplars. Jekyll assumed from the spread indicated that they were 'black Italian not upright Lombardy' poplars, and invited confirmation – but Barnsley's reply that they were 'magnificent trees, about 3 feet diameter trunks' was evasively unhelpful. Always one for simplification, Gertrude Jekyll strongly deprecated the practice of planting in the joints of paving ('it makes a lot of work and trouble'), preferring to see 'the clean line of paving against turf'.[22] She could not however, persuade Barnsley to build a pergola along the south side to frame the view, a trick she and Lutyens had used to great effect at Hestercombe twenty years previously, and were currently proposing for Gledstone Hall. Barnsley was adamant that it would shut out the view across the valley.

The design was completed in little over a month, and in her letter accompanying the planting plans for the flower borders Jekyll explained that 'the red figures every ten feet are a useful guide in planting if a peg bearing the same number is put in each place'. If it should happen that 'any lengths do not exactly fit it is best to place the two end pegs and then it is easy to stretch or contract the spaces so as to distribute the error'.[23] Less than ten days later plans followed for the pond garden, which she thought would give the place 'the feeling of refined wild gardening, which seems to me right in character'. Along with her plan she considerately enclosed a description of each plant so that the client, Asa Lingard (a Bradford department-store owner), could better understand what was envisaged. The Lingards were 'charmed' by the proposals and Barnsley was equally enthusiastic, remarking that he could picture it as most beautiful in a few years' time; alas, he did not live to see it.

Gertrude Jekyll was sometimes introduced to an architect by his client; this was certainly the case with M.H. Baillie Scott, a prominent architect whose work was featured in *The Studio* magazine. Their relationship began in 1907 at Greenways in Berkshire, where they were brought together by the client, a Mr Spencer, and continued the next year at East Runton Hall in Norfolk; Baillie Scott regarded this as one of his best gardens and included illustrations of it in his own book, *Houses and Gardens*. As East Runton is near the sea and windswept, the garden was subdivided by walls of brick and flint, and to further reduce the effects of the wind, openings in the walls were fitted with ingenious doors made from the long Norfolk reed used in thatching. The client, Bertram Hawker, unfortunately had his own forthright ideas about the design of the gardens. His first objection was to a proposed rose garden outside the sitting room, which ended up as a spring garden with box edging. Attention moved on to the south lawn, overlooked by all the principal rooms of the house. Gertrude Jekyll wanted to turn this into four small grass parterres planted with lavender, rosemary and China roses, centred on a sundial surrounded by rose arches. Hawker would have none of it, and years later recalled how glad he was to have objected to these ideas.[24] She never saw the site, but Jekyll's instinct to break up the expanse of grass was in fact entirely sound.

A path led from the south lawn through an archway to the middle garden, and on to the tennis court at the northern end of the garden. Although it was overlooked by the study, the middle garden was intended to be part decorative and part working garden. The grass path was given a stone edge flanked by shrub borders, with soft fruit and flowers for cutting beyond: Hawker accepted the cutting borders and the fruit, but not the shrub borders. A fresh design was prepared, this time with a yew hedge laid out to form bays. Hawker accepted the outline design, but not the detailed planting – Gertrude Jekyll's working copy, marked 'thrown out', betrays a mild degree of irritation. Ironically, Hawker accepted a far more complex planting scheme a few days later.

Of all the gardens designed by Gertrude Jekyll an almost complete correspondence survives for only one, Woodhouse Copse at Holmbury St Mary in Surrey. The client, Amy Barnes-Brand, an actress, engaged the young architect Oliver Hill to design her a modest country cottage.[25] In Venice Oliver Hill had visited the famous garden on the island of Guidecca created by Gertrude Jekyll's

A photograph of the house at Woodhouse Copse, Surrey, sent by Amy Barnes-Brand to Gertrude Jekyll in 1926 (CED-UC Berkeley)

sister Caroline Eden, and when she returned to live in England Hill renewed the friendship. He was frequently asked to Agnes Jekyll's weekend parties at Munstead House and, of course, was taken to see Gertrude Jekyll, 'at whose feet [he] sat for the rest of her life', as he eloquently put it. His admiration for her was such that he 'suffered acute fear of boring her, but she was kindness itself'.[26]

Amy Barnes-Brand had read most of Gertrude Jekyll's books and was anxious to meet her, but Hill feared Miss Jekyll might find her boring and would only agree to take her to Munstead Wood if she had an intelligent question to ask. 'Do frogs make good mothers?' was not quite what he had in mind, but Gertrude Jekyll was charmed by her guest and later remarked to her that she had 'pleasantest remembrances' of her visit.[27] From this initial meeting in September 1926, the design for the garden began to evolve.[28]

Much of the garden's basic structure had already been laid out by Hill (who took no further part in the work) and remained intact apart from minor modifications to the shape of some of the beds and the amalgamation of three beds into one. The main flower borders were set between yew hedges on falling ground leading to a stream and a small woodland garden on the rising slope beyond. The arrangement of the colours was typically Jekyll, although she felt that the borders (sixty-three feet in length) were rather short for a 'really good

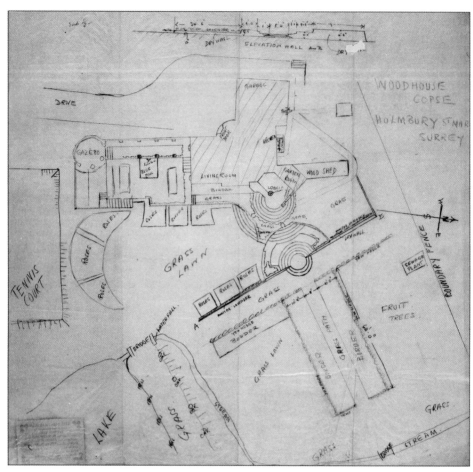

A rough site plan for Woodhouse Copse, probably sketched by Amy Barnes-Brand's husband for Gertrude Jekyll's use (CED-UC Berkeley)

effect'. The letter she sent with her plans is full of sound advice and detailed instructions for maintaining the borders as she intended, such as using *Clematis flammula* to cover delphiniums when out of flower. She felt her client's idea of including spring bulbs in the borders was a mistake: 'bulbs are so troublesome in a mixed border' that she always avoided them. Nor did she care for including flag iris, because of the way most go off and look untidy in the middle of summer.[29]

The previous season a hedge of lavender had been put in on the top of the dry-stone wall that held up the terrace, and the wall face had been planted with grey foliage plants to blend with the lavender. At the far end of the wall, near the house, gypsophila and *Centranthus ruber* (valerian) were proposed, to 'make a fine effect – well worth doing'.[30] All this proved to be just what Amy Barnes-Brand

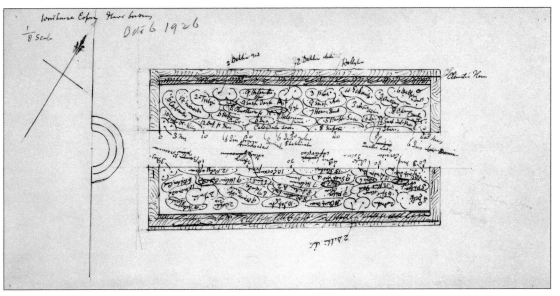

Gertrude Jekyll's plan for the double flower borders at Woodhouse Copse, 6 October 1926. She felt that the borders were 'rather too short to give a really good effect' (CED-UC Berkeley)

wanted, so arrangements were made for a haulage contractor to call at Munstead Wood with five wooden cases to take the plants to Woodhouse Copse.[31] The total cost of the plants for the borders and wall was £5 8s. 8d. (about £270 today), a remarkably good deal.[32] The plans cost a further four guineas (about £205): Gertrude Jekyll seems to have charged a fee of a guinea per sheet, although a single border plan, such as the peony and iris border, cost just half a guinea or 10s. 6d. This was considerably less than she had charged at Wangford Hall, but here she was merely drawing up planting plans rather than providing a full garden layout, which required much more work.

Towards the end of her life Gertrude Jekyll was forced to give up doing 'whole garden plans' in an effort to 'save her sight', as she wrote to Mrs Barnes-Brand, although she was still 'pleased to do flower borders'. Her sight had indeed deteriorated so much that she was nearly blind; as she explained, 'I do not actually see as I write, only a hazy line'.[33] This worsening of her sight probably explains the more limited part she played at Plumpton Place in Sussex, where Lutyens was carrying out renovation work for Edward Hudson. At Hudson's request Lutyens sent plans for Plumpton to Munstead in August 1928. Gertrude Jekyll's suggestions for planting were evidently warmly received; Hudson wrote to say he had 'gone through them with great interest' and found them 'most helpful'.[34] Her ideas harmonized with his own, his feeling being that the effect should be 'simple throughout the place' and not 'the swagger sort of gardening'.

Of the four hundred or more gardens that Gertrude Jekyll designed few remain today in any recognizable form. Times have obviously changed in the sixty and more years since her death in 1932, but Russell Page's observation in 1962 that he could think of few English gardens made since her death that 'did not bear the mark of her teaching' is even more valid today. In our modern world it may not be possible to exactly reproduce Gertrude Jekyll's planting designs, nor perhaps is it appropriate to do so, but it is entirely possible to distil the essential spirit from her work as a garden designer and from her writings; and it is in the way we arrange our gardens and use colour in them, the way we consider the form of plants and use them to soften the hard lines of garden architecture, that her work lives and endures.

CHAPTER 9

An Eloquent Pen

A critic for *The Studio* magazine expressed it well when he claimed that Gertrude Jekyll had 'the trained eye of the artist as well as the eloquent pen of the ready writer'.[1] Of all her many accomplishments, it was her books and articles that spread her name to a wider world and served to preserve the legacy of her home and garden at Munstead Wood. A happy combination of critical observation and a direct prose style elevated her writings from the commonplace to the realm of garden literature. She was the recipient of several honours in her lifetime, but one award was exclusively for her books: in 1929 she received the George Robert White Medal of Honor from the Massachusetts Horticultural Society in recognition of her achievement in writing books which changed the 'whole tone of horticultural literature'.[2] As a holder of this prestigious award, she was in the company of two other distinguished writers and colleagues, William Robinson and Mrs Francis King.

In the introduction to her first book, *Wood and Garden*, Gertrude Jekyll modestly explained that she had put forth the volume even though 'there are already many and excellent books about gardening'. Disclaiming any literary ability or botanical knowledge, she declared that her simple goal was to share with others 'the enduring happiness that the love of a garden gives. . . . For the love of gardening is a seed that once sown never dies.' *Wood and Garden* was the product of years of practical experience that had slowly evolved into 'gardening for beautiful effect', where both garden and woodland were treated in a pictorial way.

Prior to the publication of her first book, she had contributed articles to weekly gardening magazines such as *The Garden* and *Gardening Illustrated*.[3] In 1881, the year her signed contributions first appear in print, she embarked on a series of nearly seventy short pieces devoted initially to house plants and winter gardens; by the time it concluded the following year, her subjects had expanded to include hardy border plants, no doubt in response to the accolades bestowed upon her Munstead House border. Her pieces appeared so frequently in *The Garden* that it is likely she was considered a regular correspondent. By June 1885 she had started to enhance her contributions with her own photographs, but after this prodigious start her output of articles diminished significantly over the next twelve years or so, no doubt because her attention and energies were absorbed by Munstead Wood. It was only after the publication of nearly a dozen books that the steady output of articles was resumed; by 1912 she was contributing to a wide range of publications.

In April 1896, after fifteen years of writing about gardening, she began a remarkable series for the *Guardian* newspaper: the fruits of her experience in laying out her garden at Munstead Wood during the early 1890s were set forth in thirteen articles, modestly signed 'G.J.'[4] The title, 'Notes from Garden and Woodland', may have derived from John Ruskin's book *Hortus Inclusus, Messages from the Wood to the Garden* (1887). Gertrude Jekyll admirably heeded Ruskin's message of unity of the arts and honesty in workmanship, not only in her artistic approach to garden design and related home-making arts, but in her eloquent writing style. 'There is always in February some one day', she began her first instalment, when 'one smells the yet distant, but surely coming, summer.' From February to the last days of winter, these articles guided the reader on an evocative seasonal tour of Munstead Wood, without actually mentioning its name or location. When the series concluded the following March, she had no doubt awakened the sympathies of untold numbers of admirers – and she also had the makings of a worthwhile book. Using the articles as the backbone, she reorganized the text to better advantage, in a more obvious monthly format. She created a chapter for February by splicing together the first and last articles and, without rewriting already-published sentences, she augmented some topics and introduced specific references to the Munstead Wood garden, also adding new chapters, including one for January. There were no illustrations accompanying the original articles, but she brought her book to life with sixty-six of her own photographs.

With the publication of *Wood and Garden: Notes and Thoughts, Practical and Critical, of a Working Amateur* by Longmans, Green and Company in 1899, she 'took the world by storm', as one critic expressed it.[5] *Country Life* hailed it as 'one of the most delightful books upon the garden published for a long time', although the reviewer for *The Garden* sniffed that the book was essentially one for the amateur, opining that 'a professional would . . . .learn little [and] find nothing new'.[6] Readers delighted in a forthright prose which pinpointed the attributes and evils alike in gardening. The gentle tone in which she offered encouragement while firmly reinforcing the dictum that mastery of gardening comes from diligence and determination, not from the wave of a wand, contrasts with her admonishment of those who were less thoughtful than herself: 'It may be safely said that no colour can be called artistic in itself; for in the first place, it is bad English, and in the second, it is nonsense.'[7] Her 'love of precision in the use of the English language' (as a friend stated it) earned her the respect of her readers, but was a source of consternation to her editors.[8] One admitted that he 'would rather have clipped the wings of an archangel' than cut her prose when it was slightly too long to fit his layout conveniently.[9]

So eager was the reception of this volume that it was reprinted five times by the year's end.[10] It also opened the floodgates on a stream of admirers wanting to visit Munstead to see for themselves the woodland idyll. 'When I wrote something about my garden in my books,' Gertrude Jekyll confided to an American friend, 'it was in the hope of encouraging others to try and make their own surroundings pleasant, but by no means to advertise this as a place to be seen. Anything the garden can show or teach can be better seen in the books than on the ground itself.'[11]

To the delight of her many disciples a new book, *Home and Garden*, followed in January 1900. It received even more praise than the first, possibly because it went far beyond the confines of her gardening to present a more personal side of the author, lauding the alliance of house, garden, and copse. The reviewer for *The Garden* paid her a somewhat back-handed compliment when he remarked that though the space devoted to gardening matters was limited, the advice was always sound.[12] A greater testimonial came from *Country Life*, which devoted nearly three pages to its review. The core of the book – 'Miss Jekyll's appreciation of the poetry of craftsmanship and the dignity of common tools' – and her wise counsel of patience, evaluation, and suitability, whether of plants or of building, formed the nucleus of the author's thesis. The reviewer was undoubtedly E.T. Cook, editor of *The Garden*, who cherished the memory of a 'never-to-be-forgotten afternoon' in July 1899 when he had the rare privilege of seeing the 'thoughtful idyll' which was 'the physical embodiment of Miss Jekyll's spirit, as this book is the literary expression of it'.[13]

The proprietor of *Country Life* magazine, Edward Hudson, had accompanied Cook that afternoon to Munstead Wood, and was subsequently to play an important role in Gertrude Jekyll's life. Hudson, with a strong personal interest in gardens and in country matters generally, had founded the magazine in 1897.

Edward Hudson, proprietor of Country Life *magazine (from* Country Life, *26 September 1936)*

He combined a finely-tuned artistic sense with a penchant for perfectionism and an extraordinary instinct in the selection of his associates. When he inherited the family printing business, he quickly saw the possibility of using full-plate photography to illustrate his favourite themes of country houses and country pursuits.[14] Hudson also sensed the scope of Gertrude Jekyll's extraordinary accomplishments, and his respect for her came to be rivalled only by that which he felt for Edwin Lutyens, to whom Miss Jekyll introduced him in 1900. Hudson not only commissioned several houses and gardens from Lutyens, but championed his work in the pages of *Country Life*, as he did Gertrude Jekyll's books. A direct result of his visit with Cook was an unusually long (ten pages) feature on Munstead Wood, illustrated with the full-plate photographs for which *Country Life* was noted, together with four of her own more candid snapshots.[15]

Shortly after this visit, Gertrude Jekyll began to work with Cook as co-editor of *The Garden*, which Robinson had recently sold to Country Life. It is unclear how the co-editors apportioned their responsibilities, and she relinquished hers after two years (January 1900 to December 1901). She possessed incisive editorial skills, but soon discovered that the work aggravated her worsening eyesight, and cut into time that might have been better spent on her own writing than on commissioning and editing the work of others. During her tenure many interesting features were published, such as a series running from August 1900 to March 1902 devoted to her brother Walter Jekyll's garden in Jamaica.

While editing *The Garden* with Ernest Cook, Gertrude Jekyll also began to contribute articles and garden notes to *Country Life*. During her long association with Country Life, which lasted until shortly before her death in 1932, she wrote more than a hundred signed articles and published nine books. Whether she penned the regular 'In the Garden' feature is subject to speculation, but the inclusion of her own photographs in the column from December 1900, together with her distinctive prose style, seem strong indications that she did.[16] Her first contribution to the magazine was not a gardening article, but a letter accompanied by a snapshot of an unfortunate weasel caught in a mole-trap.[17] The first signed article, which appeared in 1901, was devoted to a playhouse for children, illustrated with a sketch and plan.[18] Amusements for children resurfaced in 1908 in her book *Children and Gardens*, which Lutyens suggested to her. It was based in part on memories of her own childhood amusements, such as cowslip-ball-making, and her uncondescending prose carefully introduced children to the mysteries of plans, sections and elevations, using sketches of Munstead cats as examples. A more important feature appeared in August 1901 with an article on the house and garden at Orchards, just up the road from Munstead Wood, a pivotal commission she and Lutyens had completed a few years earlier.

About the time that Gertrude Jekyll began contributing to *Country Life*, Hudson founded Country Life Library, a book-publishing venture that capitalized on the high-quality photographic reproductions used in the magazine. *Gardens Old and New* (1901–7), *The Gardens of Italy* (1905), *In English Homes* (1904) and other sumptuous folios perfectly captured the Edwardian era, but the publication of *The Century Book of Gardening* in 1900 marked Hudson's acknowledgement of the public's appetite for practical gardening books. Cook

In Children and Gardens, *Gertrude Jekyll's niece, Barbara Jekyll, demonstrates the art of making a primrose ball, 1901 (CED–UC Berkeley)*

wrote or edited a number of books under the imprint of Country Life Library, but Hudson obviously saw the value of enhancing his list with titles by such a popular author as Gertrude Jekyll, and beginning in June 1901 with *Wall and Water Gardens*, with few exceptions her subsequent books were published by Country Life Library. *Wall and Water Gardens* was not limited to the philosophies but very much concerned with the practicalities of gardening. It was uniform in size (9 in by 5¾ in) and design with the two earlier volumes published by Longmans, but set apart by a welcome improvement in the quality of the photographic reproductions. Sadly, while the illustrations were of superior quality, only a dozen photographs are actually Gertrude Jekyll's.[19] It is interesting to speculate on the reasons for Gertrude Jekyll's move from Longmans. Certainly Hudson was a friend, and shared her regard for quality; perhaps the financial arrangements were an improvement. Another significant factor may have been the prospect of wider sales afforded through Country Life's arrangement with Charles Scribner's for American distribution of the titles.

Lilies for English Gardens, published in November 1901, and *Roses for English Gardens*, which followed six months later, are examples of books commissioned by Country Life that Gertrude Jekyll might not have written otherwise. They were

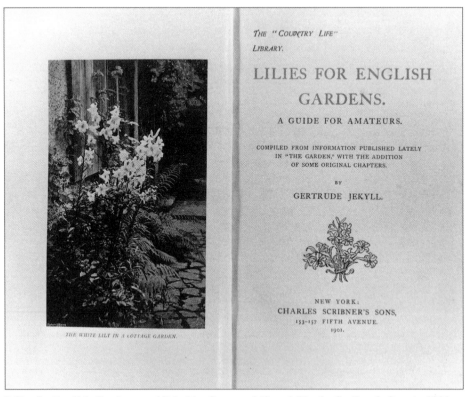

THE WHITE LILY IN A COTTAGE GARDEN.

THE "COUNTRY LIFE" LIBRARY.

LILIES FOR ENGLISH GARDENS.

A GUIDE FOR AMATEURS.

COMPILED FROM INFORMATION PUBLISHED LATELY IN "THE GARDEN," WITH THE ADDITION OF SOME ORIGINAL CHAPTERS.

BY

GERTRUDE JEKYLL.

NEW YORK:
CHARLES SCRIBNER'S SONS,
153-157 FIFTH AVENUE.
1901.

Lilies for English Gardens, *published by Country Life and Charles Scribner's Sons in 1901*

Annuals and Biennials *(1916) and* Colour Schemes for the Flower Garden *(1925)*

practical books, not compendiums of botanical information of little value to 'working amateurs'. *Lilies* was based on information she gathered from circulars sent by lily growers; in addition to her own photographs, she selected illustrations from Ellen Willmott and others, and plates by Henry G. Moon.[20] *Roses* was co-written with Edward Mawley and illustrated primarily with photographs solicited from *Country Life* readers: although Jekyll had many rose studies in her albums, they did not necessarily represent all the species and hybrids needed for the book. Precise to the point of humour, she requested good photographs of roses, either as cut flowers arranged 'in plain glasses, or vases without pattern, and a plain background' or growing in the garden, when they should be photographed without 'ironmonger's stock, garden seats, bicycles, or family pets'.[21] The last book that Gertrude Jekyll prepared to commission for Country Life was *Annuals and Biennials*, which appeared in 1916. Although it was never as popular as the others – partly because it came out during the war, also perhaps because it was without her own illustrations – like many of her other books it was still in print at the time of her death in 1932.

One of the themes that Gertrude Jekyll returned to repeatedly in her articles for *Country Life, The Garden*, and other magazines was the use of colour in the flower garden. She set forth her theories on the harmonious relationship of colours in 1882, when she detailed for *The Garden* her success in creating a flower border at Munstead House that was 'painted with living flowers'. One correspondent took exception to her claim that she had accomplished it using only hardy plants, and likened her efforts to those of the 'bedding man'. In response she published planting plans showing suggested groupings from spring through to autumn, and extended an invitation to the doubter to see for himself her eminently practical work.[22] The following year William Robinson included her article, which she had expanded slightly with additional comments, in the first edition of *The English Flower Garden*, and for the next fifty years the chapter appeared unaltered in all editions of the book, until the last, in 1933. It may be that Robinson did not have the courage to remove it from later editions; but perhaps it is more likely that her theories on the subject, which never wavered, stood the test of time.

Twenty-five years after the publication of her first article on colour theory, she decided to devote a book to the subject, which was to prove her most popular and influential. When *Colour in the Flower Garden* appeared in 1908, it was greeted with rapture. The horticulturist and garden writer E.A. Bowles recommended it as required reading for 'every gardener as well as gardening amateur'.[23] It proved so enduring that (having gone through seven editions) it was still in print in 1932. A new title was adopted for the third (1914) edition, *Colour Schemes for the Flower Garden*, and for the sixth edition (1925) a dust jacket was added, featuring an autochrome of the Dutch Garden at Orchards rather than one of Munstead Wood. The text refined and developed topics introduced in earlier books, but despite its title had less to do with colour than with the seasonal arrangements of gardens.

Colour in the Flower Garden exerted a profound influence on writers and gardeners on both sides of the Atlantic. For many American readers this book, widely available in libraries and bookshops through Scribner's, was their introduction to Gertrude Jekyll. Mrs Francis King, who did more than any other American writer to champion Gertrude Jekyll and her literary accomplishments, claimed that it 'represented the highest achievement in gardening art'.[24] Mrs King was herself the author of many excellent gardening books, and in her work for the vast Garden Club of America network she continually stressed Gertrude Jekyll's importance. While gardeners wrestled with the problems of duplicating her advice, writers were quick to sense the importance of her contribution to garden literature. Among the many inspired by her example was Marion Cran, author of numerous light-hearted volumes on gardening, whose tribute to Gertrude Jekyll was expressed in her statement that 'she wrote everything with restraint, with abundant knowledge, and ever a twinkle of fun'.[25] Louise Beebe Wilder, one of America's most important garden writers, painted a glowing portrait of her mentor: 'Miss Jekyll made us believe ourselves artists in embryo with a color box to our hands and a canvas ready stretched before us. She opened up to us a new delight in gardening and new possibilities in ourselves and set us a most radiant and enticing example.'[26]

The plans and suggestions for single-colour gardens included at the back of the book, almost as an afterthought, inspired untold numbers of gardeners to attempt the creation of all-blue or all-red borders. But the arrangement of plants as exemplified in the main hardy flower border at Munstead Wood, and the expertise necessary to maintain the picture, proved more challenging. Julia Cummins, who laid out her garden with 'Miss Jekyll hung upon [her gardener's] flank like a gadfly', soon discovered that the likeness of her border to Gertrude Jekyll's began and ended 'with a slight similarity in length and cross-path'.[27] American gardeners found the practical application of her advice difficult of achievement in their more widely variable climates; Mrs Wilder's book *Colour in My Garden* (1918) delightfully recounted her own trials, tribulations, and occasional minor successes with many of Gertrude Jekyll's recommendations.[28]

One American who acted on the message of the book was the renowned horticulturist Henry Francis du Pont, creator of the garden at Winterthur, in Delaware. 'Follow Miss Jekyll's shape of beds and arrangements of colours,' he scribbled next to the plan of the aster garden in his copy of *Colour in the Flower Garden*. Inspired by her books and her articles in *Gardening Illustrated*, which he clipped and annotated, he visited Munstead Wood, as did many other keen followers. The notebook jottings for one of his visits included suggestions for using clematis to create a 'pulled-over Jekyll effect behind the Delphinium', such as he had seen in the Grey Garden.[29]

In addition to dealing with the practical aspects of gardening, Gertrude Jekyll wrote three books that show her profound knowledge of garden design. In each she collaborated with a co-author, and once with an artist. *Some English Gardens*, which Longmans published in October 1904, offers an insight into her critical evaluation of Old English gardens, their design, planting, and ornamentation.[30] It is illustrated with George Elgood's paintings of houses and gardens she had visited in her youth, such as Great Tangley Manor. The candour of the comments seems to suggest that she may have revisited several while working on the book, perhaps even the Irish and Scottish examples added to a new edition in 1905 – yet in fact all was done from notes supplied to her by Elgood.[31]

Gertrude Jekyll's comment about her own Michaelmas daisy borders, illustrated by Elgood in the book, gets to the root of her gardening objectives: 'Like all the best flower gardening it is the painting of a picture with living plants, but unlike painting, it is done when the palette is empty of its colours.'[32] Although the subject-matter of the book is ostensibly gardens, her frequent comments on the merits of the buildings they belong to demonstrate her considerable appreciation of architecture. 'Wonderful are these great stone houses of the early English Renaissance – wonderful in their bold grasp and sudden assertion of the new possibilities of domestic architecture!' was her comment on Montacute in Somerset. The obelisk-shaped finials, she wryly noted, show that the designer had borrowed 'straight from the Italians everything except their marvellous discernment'.[33]

While *Colour in the Flower Garden* inspired amateur gardeners on planting aspects, *Gardens for Small Country Houses* opened their eyes to garden architecture and practical considerations of garden design. Written with Lawrence Weaver as part of Country Life's series on the design and repair of small country houses old and new, the attractive quarto-sized book, which 'filled a place, hitherto empty, on the bookshelves of the garden-loving public', soon became a standard reference work on the Arts and Crafts philosophy of design. It capped years of fulmination among critics regarding the 'formal' versus the 'naturalistic' approach to gardens. The controversy fizzled out in the face of this practical volume. Illustrations of recent work by Inigo Triggs, C.E. Mallows and Edwin Lutyens balanced examples of Old English gardens such as Owlpen Manor and Packwood House, and Gertrude Jekyll's drawings of site plans and border plantings rounded out the volume. After its publication in October 1912 a revised edition followed three months later, with an expanded introduction and additional measured drawings which 'could not be completed in time for the first edition'.[34] The appearance of a sixth edition in 1927 attested to the continuing value of the book.

During the First World War Gertrude Jekyll produced *Garden Ornament* (1918), an illustrated folio devoted to sundials, gates, pergolas, dipping wells, sculpture, orangeries, garden seats and the like, drawn from the picture resources of Country Life Library – 'quite the most useful reference book on the subject'.[35] The idea was a development of two articles written for *Country Life*, but this was primarily a picture-book, with more discerning captions.[36] The inclusion of chapters on parterres, flower borders, wall gardening and Japanese gardens, however, struck an odd note in an otherwise cohesive work, and a revised edition in 1927 ironed out some of these shortcomings, substituting a chapter on Hispano-Moorish gardens for the Japanese one. While the picture selection remained substantially unaltered, the captions were more descriptive and discerning. The change in focus of the new edition can be attributed to Gertrude Jekyll's co-author, Christopher Hussey, the renowned Country Life writer who elevated architectural criticism to an art-form. Recent work by Harold Peto and Edwin Lutyens fared well ('a brilliant effect of light and shade'), while such mild criticisms as 'the steps at too steep an angle to be entirely satisfactory' and 'the stairs might have been given greater width' were typically applied to the historical examples. In a few instances, her remarks smack of horticultural-show judging: 'Oil jar is well placed but its effect is spoilt by overgrowth.' Her greatest severity was reserved for examples of rampant ivy at its worst: 'A building of uncommon interest blotted out by overgrowth'.

Yet another side of Gertrude Jekyll's wide-ranging interests was portrayed in *Old West Surrey*, published by Longmans in July 1904. This lengthy chronicle of rural life developed themes she had merely touched on in earlier books. Claiming that her native Surrey was then 'overrun', 'thickly populated', and 'robbed of its older charms of peace and retirement' (and thus quite unlike her memories of idyllic childhood days), she set out to provide a record of 'the common things of daily use' that were no longer in favour. She assembled more than three hundred illustrations for the book, and exhaustive enterprise that involved taking approximately two hundred new photographs and culling through old ones dating back to the 1880s. 'The hasty critic might, perhaps, think it almost absurd to give photographs of such homely and familiar objects as a sewage-pump, a five-barred gate, or a pocket-lantern', said one reviewer, but went on to express the opinion

Gertrude Jekyll's sketch for the spine of Old West Surrey *(RHS Lindley Library)*

that these curios would soon be of inestimable value – which has proved to be the case.[37]

Old West Surrey is the only one of Gertrude Jekyll's books for which the original manuscript and printer's page proofs are known to survive. With few exceptions the manuscript, handwritten in her neat script on ordinary letter-writing paper, mirrors the published text. Her ability to express herself directly without the need for extensive rewriting is rare. She made very few corrections to the printer's proofs, but her patience with the designer who laid out the typeset text with the illustrations must surely have worn thin. While checking the page proofs she noticed a photograph was positioned lopsidedly on the page – 'possibly this block would be better with the horizontal lines kept parallel with the lines of the text?' In another case, she politely pointed out that the illustration was upside down.[38]

In addition to writing and illustrating her books, Gertrude Jekyll played a decisive part in their appearance. Her designs for the characteristic gold stamping on the cloth spines and covers of her books, and the line drawings on the title page, originated with *Wood and Garden* and were carried through on most of her other books, regardless of the publisher.[39] These attractive decorations evolved from the patterns she had used in her silver repoussé work, wood inlay, and, to a

A page from the original manuscript for Old West Surrey, *published by Longmans, Green in 1904 (Surrey Local Studies Library)*

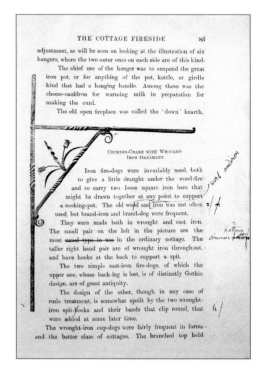

A page proof for Old West Surrey, *with Gertrude Jekyll's notations, 1904 (Surrey Local Studies Library)*

Original sketch for spine and cover of Home and Garden *(1900) (RHS Lindley Library)*

lesser extent, embroidery. Her appealing design for the cover of *Home and Garden*, showing cats crouched beneath a spreading tree, also appeared in a bedroom fireplace at Munstead Wood.

Little is known about the fees Gertrude Jekyll commanded for her writing, but for a two-thousand word article in *The Times* in 1910 she received a fee of five guineas (roughly £262 today), and this was probably quite typical.[40] Through her American friends she was commissioned to write six articles about wild gardening, winter gardens, borders, and other familiar topics for the *Bulletin of the Garden Club of America* in 1919, for which she received the then considerable sum of $100 each.[41] Although the subjects were ones she covered time and time again in other magazines, these articles were prepared afresh. The original handwritten manuscripts are as 'clean' as the one for *Old West Surrey*: the only change made was the addition of her name on the by-line. Kate Brewster, the *Bulletin*'s editor, was later rewarded with a memorable day at Munstead Wood when she met Gertrude Jekyll and saw her famous garden.[42]

Because her books were in print for decades, rather than months or years, Gertrude Jekyll was able to revise them frequently. Generally such revisions were slight – changing a photograph or adding a paragraph of text – and she rarely turned an old book into an entirely new one, as many authors might have done. To *Wall and Water Gardens*, however, she added five new chapters in 1920; and

A manuscript page for 'The Conservatory or Winter Garden', an article published in the Bulletin of the Garden Club of America *(1920)*

for the final edition, which she worked on just prior to her death, more chapters were added, necessitating a new name – *Wall, Water and Woodland Gardens*. A second edition of *Children and Gardens* was brought out posthumously, and in a regrettable attempt to freshen up an older title, Country Life replaced more than half of Gertrude Jekyll's photographs with new ones, mainly of children in more up-to-date clothing. When in 1925 Batsford issued a new edition of *Old West Surrey* (then long out of print), it was renamed *Old English Household Life*, and this was one of the rare occasions on which Gertrude Jekyll rewrote, as opposed to revised, her text. When Lutyens was asked to review the book, he penned a charming tribute to his friend: 'There is an extreme satisfaction in opening a book with the conviction that no disappointment is possible.'[43]

After 1918, by which time she had had a dozen books published, Gertrude Jekyll redirected her literary energies to hundreds of articles, which are now almost inaccessible; fortunately Francis Jekyll and G.C. Taylor published a selection in *A Gardener's Testament* (1937). Although she wrote articles steadily from the 1880s, the bulk of her output, sometimes as many as forty articles or 'notes' a year, were published during the late 1910s and throughout the 1920s, when pieces on the use of grey foliage and other familiar subjects appeared simultaneously in *The Garden* and *Country Life*. By the mid-1920s she was writing almost exclusively for *Gardening Illustrated*. Her last article, entitled 'The South Border Door', appeared on 26 November 1932, just twelve days before she died.

CHAPTER 10

The Legacy of Munstead Wood

In 1919 Gertrude Jekyll wrote to her friend Mrs Francis King that ' "The War" has brought me an altered life. . . . The cost of labour is ruinous – and everything else. I am seventy-five, as good as half blind and with very little strength all around. I am only thankful that it is myself alone, no family. What happens to an old woman does not really matter, and if it must be, I shall face it quite cheerfully, as my way of paying for the war and its good ending'.[1] This sad lament reflected not only her poor health but also the state of her finances, which had been in decline for some years. Lutyens, when he visited her in August 1917, had been 'rather shocked at her appearance, so aged I thought but she was fussed at a party – so I let everything go – & promised to go to her on Monday. . . . She is worried about her affairs – & says she must give up Munstead.'[2]

The advent of the First World War in August 1914 brought inflation in its wake. It may be hard to believe today, but in 1914 the pound sterling had exactly the same purchasing power it had had in 1815, the year Napoleon was defeated at Waterloo. For a century the careful management of the Bank of England had held off inflation, but with the outbreak of war the currency rapidly lost more than a third of its value, which for people such as Gertrude Jekyll, who by the standards of the day could not be considered rich, had devastating consequences.[3] In 1919 the American heiress Louise du Pont Crowninshield noted that Miss Jekyll's finances were in such a perilous state, she was 'in danger of not being able to afford to keep her garden'. Probably at the instigation of Mrs Crowninshield, The Garden Club of America came to the rescue by awarding Gertrude Jekyll the staggering sum of $10,000 (about £75,000 today), 'in token of appreciation of her work and friendship'.[4]

Gertrude Jekyll had only a modest private income, even though at her death in 1932 her estate was valued at just over £20,000 – equivalent to about a million pounds today.[5] Even before 1914 she may have been living beyond her means in maintaining her large staff – nine full-time and one part-time – and cannot have relied solely on her private income, which can scarcely have been more than £1,000 a year.[6] Most of her income went on her servants' wages: at the end of her life the annual wage bill amounted to more than £830, a not inconsiderable sum.

*Herbert Cowley's snapshot of Gertrude Jekyll in her Spring Garden, 1918 (*Gardening Illustrated, *17 December 1932)*

In 1926 her head gardener was paid £4 per week and the under-gardeners and groom twenty-five shillings per week (or £65 per year), thus the combined outdoor wage bill was more than £533 a year, not including overtime paid to the gardeners during such busy periods as hedge-cutting. Although her gardeners were not liable to income tax before the Second World War, Gertrude Jekyll was. Ironically, it was her niece's husband, the Chancellor of the Exchequer Reginald McKenna, who in 1912 introduced a surtax to pay for Dreadnought battleships (a tax which was inevitably christened 'McKenna dues'). Jekyll paid both income tax and surtax, and on at least one occasion an Inspector of Taxes from the Inland Revenue called on her – the gardeners prudently hid any new tools for the duration of his visit.[7]

As Gertrude Jekyll grew older she became increasingly reclusive. As her nephew recalled, 'those who court isolation may find it recoil upon them with a vengeance' in the evening of their life. Occasionally she made new friends, such as Sir Henry and Lady Wood (of Promenade Concerts fame), who were introduced to her by Gerald and Betty Balfour (Lady Emily Lutyens's sister); nevertheless, her circle of friends inevitably narrowed. In the circumstances, she must have found the rekindling of her friendship with Logan Pearsall Smith particularly welcome.

Smith, an American by birth, had often visited Munstead Wood in the early years of the century in the company of James Britten, an official in the Botanical

Department of the British Museum and an old friend of Gertrude Jekyll. Years later Smith was to recall that their friendship was a 'kind of cat-and-dog relationship', with Britten, who was an 'irascible, fault-finding little man', playing the role of the cat, and Miss Jekyll that of 'the big, good-natured dog'. On many occasions Smith would listen with some alarm to Britten's fault-finding; as they paused to argue about some plant or flower, the 'cat would begin to spit, the dog would growl', and then they would walk on just as before. Smith was a writer and a specialist in the English language, a subject which greatly interested Gertrude Jekyll and of which she had considerable knowledge. In *Old West Surrey* she had included a chapter on the country dialects and patterns of speech found in the area, and she also recorded some details of the lives of the simple country people.

As is often the case with friendships, Gertrude Jekyll and Logan Pearsall Smith's lives diverged; Britten died, and they saw nothing of one another for many years. Returning to live in the area about 1930, Smith was asked to lunch at Munstead House, and although Miss Jekyll was 'quite unable to receive most visitors', she left word that she would none the less be glad to see him.[8] Smith vividly recalled being taken across the Bramley Road and 'shown the key, allowed to open the gate . . . and so found admittance into the great wood. . . . Walking along shadowy paths, I came at last on a glade of lawn, and saw Miss Jekyll's house before me. All was hushed in silence; there was not a soul about.' He soon found himself 'in the presence of the Gertrude Jekyll I had known of old. She seemed more feeble in body, of course, but her mind was still alert; her eyes still twinkled behind her heavy glasses, the sound of her deep chuckle was quite as rich as ever'. She was delighted to see her old friend, but he found that 'it was not of her profession that she wanted to talk', and when he introduced the subject, 'she gazed at me through her spectacles with an almost stony look; a veil of fatigue, or boredom with all the garden-chatter of the world, seemed to dim her face.'[9]

In anticipation of his visit she had prepared a list of words to be debated. Despite her age she 'was ready as ever for a scrap, and it was impossible, or almost impossible, when she held to a view strongly, to make her give way an inch'. In all these debates Smith, who now played the role of the cat, got the better of her only once, on the difference between 'drive' and 'ride' in a modern context, of which Gertrude Jekyll was not very enamoured. On his next visit she took her revenge by appealing to him, as 'an authority', to explain to her the derivation of the word 'epergne'. Smith fell straight into the trap, remarking that it was 'a French word' (which of course it is not, but merely a corruption). As he took his leave, on what was to prove his last visit, she walked him to the open door, where they stood for a moment. 'Miss Jekyll looked at me with her plain, but splendid face', which reminded Smith (somewhat incongruously) of an 'ancient, incredibly aristocratic rhinoceros gazing gravely out from amid a tangle of river reed'. Advising him to go and look at 'a big patch of blue meconopsis behind the tool-shed', she regretted not being able to show him personally. She 'laughed her jolly laugh' and asked him to 'come see me again soon'.[10]

In the last year of her life there was a marked decline in Gertrude Jekyll's health; a wheelchair (a gift from Lutyens) enabled her to continue to see the

The south front of Munstead Wood from the Green Wood Walk, 1899. Groups of cistus among the rhododendrons provide summer interest (CED–UC Berkeley)

The "Blowdiphino Splendax"!

Caricature of Gertrude Jekyll by
her neighbour, S. Pleydell-Bouverie
(Dumbarton Oaks Studies in
Landscape Architecture Photo
Archive)

garden, but she resented having to use it. As she told Ellen Willmott, she found it frustrating not being able to do 'all the little things about the garden that want doing directly you notice them . . . [that it] would seem silly to call a man to do'. She complained, 'I fret at being hauled about in wheeled chairs instead of the leisurely prowls of close intimacy with growing things.'[11] By spring 1932 her health had declined considerably: a letter from Amy Barnes-Brand at the end of March, with an order for plants, brought a swift reply, but in an unsteady hand. Although she wrote that she was 'glad to hear from you again', she explained she was 'a very poor creature just now . . . the Doctor is coming every day'. She had been in bed for a fortnight and could expect to be there for another week or so, but hoped to be 'able to get about a little when the days are warmer'.[12]

When Lutyens came to Godalming for Herbert Jekyll's funeral in September 1932, just two months before Gertrude's death, he found her 'self-possessed and herself' but 'very feeble [and her] hands had shrunk a great deal and had a slight shake'.[13] They were never to meet again; Gertrude Jekyll died in the evening of Thursday, 8 December. At her funeral four days later, the congregation included the ninety-four-year-old William Robinson, and Ellen Willmott. The coffin was draped with a gold and white linen pall, designed by her brother and worked by their mother when she was herself more than seventy. Most appropriately, the lesson was taken from the Revelation of St John the Divine, chapter 21, verses one to seven: 'And I saw a new heaven and a new earth. . . .' She was buried in the churchyard at St John's, Busbridge, beside her brother; the gardeners, who acted as pallbearers, had lined the grave with moss raked from the lawns at Munstead Wood.

Lutyens, who designed her gravestone, simply inscribed with the words

'ARTIST
GARDENER
CRAFTSWOMAN'

penned a very moving foreword for Francis Jekyll's biography of his aunt, published in 1934. In describing his old and valued friend he paid tribute to her 'clear logical brain', her 'unfailing modesty and self-possession', and her 'wit and intelligent sympathy to all who worked with, for, and under her'. He remarked upon 'her faith in that godliness from which she knew the best alone could spring . . .' and concluded by observing that she could be 'described fitly as a grande dame' – which would no doubt have amused her greatly.[14]

In 1938 Nellie B. Allen, an American landscape architect who had first visited Munstead Wood in 1921, returned to call on Francis Jekyll, whose home it had become. After enquiring about the time of her return to London, Francis offered Mrs Allen the opportunity to prolong her stay, as he had to go out: 'Wouldn't you like to be all alone here in the evening's glow, and do just as you like – go anywhere, do anything?' How could she resist such a tempting offer? It proved to be 'the climax of the greatest dream I could have possibly imagined', to be able to wander through the house and garden at will. 'The air was laden with fragrance of roses clambering everywhere (even to the very tree tops) . . . and all the time I felt G.J. was there with me.' As a memento of her visit and a token of her many years of friendship with Gertrude Jekyll, Francis gave Mrs Allen a pair of his aunt's gardening boots, as immortalized in Nicholson's famous portrait. She kept them safe in her Manhattan apartment for many years, half-forgotten, and toward the end of her life generously donated them to the Guildford Museum.[15]

The advent of the Second World War in September 1939 marked the beginning of the end for Munstead Wood. Labour restrictions during the war forced Francis Jekyll to give up the nursery in 1941, and heavy taxation after the war proved the final impossible burden for the Jekyll family. There were no generous American benefactors this time, and in 1948, on the first two days of September, the contents of the house were sold at auction by Alfred Savill and Sons. The property was broken up: the house and pleasure gardens were left intact, but the working gardens were split into three units. Until his death in 1965 Francis retained The Hut for his own occupation; thereafter the Jekyll family's ownership of Munstead Wood came to an end.

The Second World War changed the world forever, in a way Gertrude Jekyll could neither have envisaged nor understood, even though to be a designer of gardens is a salutary lesson in the transient nature of human endeavour – for a garden is the most ephemeral of all art forms and, it often seems, carries the seeds

Nellie B. Allen's snapshot of the
overgrown garden at Munstead Wood,
1938 (courtesy Blair McMorrow)

of its own destruction in its very creation. Gertrude Jekyll's legacy is the gardens she designed, but these gardens have suffered the same fate that befell her own at Munstead Wood. Today we must be content to study her work as a garden designer through the many plans left among her papers, although their very survival seems to have been largely an accident of chance. In 1948 the landscape architect Beatrix Farrand purchased Gertrude Jekyll's papers for her Reef Point Gardens Library from a list of duplicate books offered by the Massachusetts Horticultural Society in Boston. Mrs Farrand, a niece of the novelist Edith Wharton, had visited Munstead Wood in 1895 and the acquisition fifty years later of these papers – 'the entire output of Gertrude Jekyll's long and distinguished career' – crowned a lifetime of admiration for her and for her considerable accomplishments as a garden designer.[16]

The journey of these papers to the United States is still shrouded in mystery. After Francis Jekyll had used his aunt's papers and correspondence to write her biography, he gave them to the Royal Horticultural Society's Red Cross Sale of botanical books in September 1940, along with a collection of her gardening books – an act of considerable generosity. Because of bomb damage at Vincent Square during the London blitz the sale was held by post, circulars being sent to members worldwide, including many in the United States. Regrettably, no

Beatrix Farrand in her library, mid-1920s (CED-UC Berkeley)

purchaser was noted for the Jekyll papers; it may be that Francis Jekyll withdrew them from the sale and offered them privately, although rumours still circulate about their having been rescued from a bonfire.[17]

Having acquired the papers, Beatrix Farrand repaired the fragile ones, then sorted and labelled them, storing the collection in large flat steel files. She used the papers in her school of landscape studies at Reef Point Gardens, Bar Harbor, Maine, her intention being that students should learn to understand the nature of the design process by studying original documents, especially those of an eminent gardener. Mrs Farrand's purpose was sadly short-lived, and in 1955, because of problems with the town of Bar Harbor, she dramatically disbanded the Reef Point Gardens Corporation, dismantled her garden, distributed her plants to friends, and had her house torn down. She then actively sought an institution for her library, of which the Jekyll papers were only a part. She seems to have offered them to her client Mildred Bliss, of Dumbarton Oaks in Washington, DC, who gladly accepted the offer, but for some unknown reason nothing came of it. Beatrix Farrand, then 83 and somewhat disillusioned, eventually donated all her books and papers to the school of landscape architecture at the University of California at Berkeley.[18] Her own papers remained in storage until 1974, when a graduate student 'discovered the existence of the material' and wrote a thesis upon it.[19] Gertrude Jekyll's papers lay unused in the archives for many years, although they were catalogued by the late Betty Massingham in 1978.

Betty Massingham, through her biography of Gertrude Jekyll published in 1966 by Country Life, helped to reintroduce her to a new generation of gardeners. Although her stock never fell quite as low as Sir Edwin Lutyens's, she became a rather unfashionable figure in the years after the Second World War, regarded as irrelevant to changed times. Even so, some writers and designers of considerable repute such as Margery Fish, Russell Page and the American Lanning Roper, held her in high esteem long before her current resurgence of popularity began.

But it is her books that have really preserved her reputation, and captured her genius. For many years they remained eagerly sought after in the antiquarian book trade and commanded high prices, even though they had gone into many editions and countless impressions. In 1964 Elizabeth Lawrence, a North Carolina garden writer, made the first anthology of Gertrude Jekyll's writings, published under the title *Gertrude Jekyll on Gardening*. This helped to pave the way for the Massingham biography two years later, but it was not until the books began to emerge from copyright in 1982 that they were almost all reprinted and thus made available to a much wider audience than those who could afford the second-hand prices.

Christopher Hussey thought Gertrude Jekyll 'the greatest artist in horticulture and garden-planting that England has produced – whose influence on garden design has been as widespread as Capability Brown's in the eighteenth century'.[20] But her influence spread further than the garden: the impression she made on the young Lutyens was so great that she effectively shaped much of his early work, although she would have been the first to deny any such suggestion. From their early rambles around the Surrey countryside they both concluded that 'Georgian architecture is part of country tradition', something which, while it would have horrified Pugin, paved the way for Lutyens to turn to the classical style as he grew older, thus influencing much of the country-house movement in the inter-war years and helping to fuel the Georgian revival.[21]

At the very heart of Gertrude Jekyll's many works and endeavours lay the example of her own home, Munstead Wood. As they walked down some shady glade towards the house she had had built, surrounded by the garden she had created, Logan Pearsall Smith once asked Gertrude Jekyll if she really enjoyed it all. It is difficult for any artist, be they painter, writer, or even gardener, 'to possess [their] own possessions', since the creator of the work sees, only too clearly, the imperfections. 'When I come out here . . . ,' she replied, 'I see what's wrong; I get cross about it – it's my own fault sometimes, sometimes the gardeners'. But . . . now and then when I am thinking of something else I come round the corner suddenly on the house and garden, I catch it unawares. It seems to me all right; and then I enjoy it – I enjoy it very much, I can tell you.'[22]

Gertrude Jekyll's Munstead Wood lasted just fifty years, and one of the most frequently asked questions is why she made no effort to preserve her garden after her death. Lanning Roper, writing in *Country Life* in 1967, answered the question in a manner she would have wholeheartedly endorsed: 'In some cases gardens are so personal and so poetic in their conception that their spirit dies with the owner. . . . A garden is a picture painted with flowers and foliage. Each year and each season there is a slightly different picture, but when the painter is gone the picture may easily alter increasingly with the years until it becomes a bad reproduction.'23 Gertrude Jekyll realized that a garden is a living thing, and she appreciated that her garden, which she had created and which was so much a part of her, could never outlive her. To seek to preserve it, or pickle it in aspic, was a futile nonsense.

Yet, in a way, she did preserve it. Her career as a photographer, which came to an end with the First World War, captured the garden as it was being developed, and her writings have sent the message of her teaching echoing down the years. In the pages of her many books, the relevance of her work to the modern gardener shines through. Although she believed that gardening was a form of art, as has been demonstrated, she was also well versed in the practical application of her

September borders at Munstead Wood, 1907 (CED–UC Berkeley)

ideas, what might be called the 'craft of gardening', and there is scarcely an aspect of it that she does not cover in some way.

Above all, Gertrude Jekyll never lost sight of what a garden is for or, as she termed it, the 'idea of a garden'. To her, 'no artificial planting [could] ever equal that of Nature', but from nature one might learn the 'importance of moderation and reserve, of simplicity of intention, and directness of purpose', a message firmly rooted in the principles of the Arts and Crafts Movement, of which, though by no means an obvious part, Jekyll was such a striking example. It is a message which can be applied as well to her house as to her garden. As she wrote in 1896, the year she began to build Munstead Wood: 'After all, what is a garden for? It is for "delight", for "sweet solace", for "the purest of all human pleasures; the greatest refreshment of the spirits of men"; it is to promote "jucundite of minde"; it is to "call home over-wearied spirits". So say the old writers, and we cannot amend their words, which will stand as long as there are gardens on earth and people to love them.'[24]

APPENDIX I

List of Commissions

This list has been compiled from three sources : the commissions list in Francis Jekyll, *Gertrude Jekyll: A Memoir* (London, Jonathan Cape, 1934); from the Reef Point Gardens Collection, College of Environmental Design Documents Collection, University of California at Berkeley, California, USA; and notebooks in the Godalming Museum collection. Entries are arranged in alphabetical order by the name of the property; or, if this is unknown, by the surname of the client.

Abbreviations used

Brown   Jane Brown, *Gardens of a Golden Afternoon* (London, Allen Lane, 1982)
CL   *Country Life*
F numbers indicate the folder numbers for plans now held in the Reef Point Gardens Collection
G   *Garden* magazine
GC   *Gardeners' Chronicle*
GD   *Garden Design*
GFSCH   Gertrude Jekyll and Lawrence Weaver, *Gardens for Small Country Houses* (London, Country Life, 1912)
GI   *Gardening Illustrated*
GM   *Gardener's Magazine*
N numbers indicate a notebook now in the Godalming Museum collection
RHS   *Journal of the Royal Horticultural Society*
RIBAD   Margaret Richardson, *Catalogue of the Drawings Collection of the Royal Institute of British Architects: Edwin Lutyens* (Farnborough, Gregg International, 1973)
Weaver   Lawrence Weaver, *Houses and Gardens by E. L. Lutyens* (London, Country Life, 1913)

Amersfoort
Berkhamstead, Herts
Client Walter Cohen
1911. N24
(may have been known as Fairhill)

Amesbury Abbey
Amesbury, Wiltshire
Client Colonel Sir Edmund Antrobus
Date unknown. N2
Ref. CL7 (1902):272; Jekyll, *Garden Ornament*: 219, 257, 360.

Amport House
Andover, Hants
Architect E. Lutyens
Client Mrs Sofer Whitburn
1923. F173; RIBAD

Angerton Hall
Morpeth, Northumberland
Architect E. Lutyens
Client J.H. Straker
1905, 1910. F225/7

Apple Tree Farm
Address unknown
Client unknown
1924. N4

Arundel Castle
Arundel, West Sussex
Client Duke of Norfolk
1902. F25
Ref. CL 36 (1914): 746, 782

Ashby St Ledger's
Nr Rugby, Northants

Architect E. Lutyens
Client Hon. Ivor Guest
1905. F47; RIBAD
Ref. CL 110 (1951): 496; Weaver: 158

Ashwell Bury House
Ashwell, Herts
Architect E. Lutyens
Client Mrs Wolverley Fordham
1908. F70; N35; RIBAD
Ref. CL 101 (1951): 810

Aston Rowant House
Aston Rowant, Oxon
Client Sir W. Chichele-Plowden
1892
Ref. GC ii 1907: 196–197; GM 1907: 929–32

Banacle Copse
Culmer, Witley, Surrey
Architect W. Sarel
Client Mrs Sheppard
1895. F6

Banacle Edge
Witley, Surrey
Client Dr Theodore Williams
1895

Barrington Court
Ilminster, Somerset
Architect Forbes and Tate
Client Colonel A.A. Lyle
1917. F129; N3
Ref. CL 16 (1904): 414; 63 (1928):
370; 64 (1928): 332; 123 (1957):
495; 128 (1959): 184

Barton Hartshorn Manor
Buckingham, Bucks
Architect R. Lorimer
Client Colonel Trotter
1908
Ref. CL 34(1913): (27 Sept 1913
Supplt) xxii; Peter Savage, *Lorimer
and the Edinburgh Craft Designers*
(1979): 25

Barton St Mary
Forest Row, East Grinstead, West Sussex
Architect E. Lutyens
Client Sir G. Munro Miller
1906. F51; N37
Ref. Weaver: 170

Basildon Park
Pangbourne, Berks
Architect E. Lutyens
Client Major J.A. Morrison
1919. F156; RIBAD

Beacon House
Droxford, Hants
Client Mrs Douglas Hamilton
1926. N2

Bear Place
Twyford, Berks
Client Henry Nicholl
1896. F7A

Belgrade, Yugoslavia. *See* Postfach

Berlin
17 Rauchstrasse, Berlin, Germany
Client unknown
1923. N31

Berrydown
Ashe, Hants

Architect E. Lutyens
Client Archibald Grove
1897. RIBAD

Bestbeech St Mary
Wadhurst, East Sussex
Client Julian Leacock
1926. F197

Birchgrove. *See* Tangley Way

Birkenhead
172 Preston Road, Birkenhead,
Merseyside
Client N.F. Dean
1923

Bishopbarns
St George's Place, York,
North Yorks
Architect W. Brierley
Client Walter Brierley
1905. F42

Bishopthorpe Paddock
Bishopthorpe Road, York,
North Yorks
Architect W. Brierley
Client Mr Green
1907. F67
Ref. CL 65 (1929): 50; 91 (1941):
510; 130 (1960): 566

Blagdon Hall
Seaton Burn, Northumberland
Architect E. Lutyens
Client Viscount Ridley
1928. F221; RIBAD
Ref. CL 112 (1951): 188, 396

Bointon Hall
Bointon, Rugby, Warwks
Client Mrs Shaw
Date unknown. N36

(Le) Bois des Moutiers
Varengeville-sur-Mer, Seine
Inférieure, France
Architect E. Lutyens
Client M. Guillaume Mallet
1904. F36
Ref. CL 169 (1980): 1418, 1494;
174 (1982): 90; Weaver: 21

Bonaly Tower
Colinton, Lothian, Scotland
Client Mrs Ogilvie
1926. F207

Borlases
Twyford, Berks

Client N.L. Davidson
1918. F134

Boveridge Park
Cranborne, Dorset
Client C.W. Gordon
1920. F136; N13

Bowerbank
Wimbledon, London
Architect W. Hewitt
Client Arthur Carr
1914. F117; N19

Braboeuf Estate
Guildown House, Guildford,
Surrey
Architect E. Lutyens
Client Mrs Bowes Watson
1907. F61

Brackenbrough
Calthwaite, Cumbria
Architect R. Lorimer
Client Mrs Harris
1904. F37; N9

Bradstone Brook
Guildford, Surrey
Architect J.H. Norris
Client Mrs C.M. Wigan
1921. F163

Brambletye
East Grinstead, West Sussex
Architect Forbes and Tate
Client Mrs Guy Nevill
1919. F155
Ref. CL 111 (1951): 726

Bramley House
Bramley, Guildford, Surrey
Client Colonel Ricardo
1905. F40

Bramleys (formerly Orchards)
Little Kings Hill,
Great Missenden, Bucks
Architect E. Willmott
Client Ernest Willmott
1913. F112; N23

Bridge Farm
Byfleet, Surrey
Client unknown
1916. N2

Broad Oak
Seale, Farnham, Surrey
Client Lady Mayo Robson
1920

Buckhurst Park
Withyham, East Sussex
Architect E. Lutyens
Client Robert Benson
1903

Bulcote Manor
Bulcote, Notts
Client Colonel B.E. Bailey
1922. N6
Ref. CL 52 (1922): 385

Burgate
Dunsfold, Surrey
Client Mrs Bateson
1919. F133; N14

Burgh House
Well Walk, Hampstead, London
Architect Seth, Smith and Monro
Client Dr Williamson
1912. F101; N24

Burningfold Farm
Dunsfold, Surrey
Architect H. Chalton Bradshaw
Client R.R. Faber
1922. F166; N11

Burnt Axon
Burley, Hants
Architect Read and MacDonald
Client Colonel H.B. Strang
1925. F184

Burrows Cross. See Hazelhatch

Burwood House
Cobham, Surrey
Client Mrs Nuggatt
1928. F225

Busbridge Park
Goldalming, Surrey
Architect E. George
Client P. N. Graham
1904. F38

Busbridge Rectory
St John's Church, Busbridge,
Godalming, Surrey
Client Revd E. Larner
1914. F48; N9

Busbridge War Memorial
St John's Church, Busbridge,
Godalming, Surrey
Architect E. Lutyens
1922

Butts Gate
Wisborough Green, West Sussex

Client the Misses Davidson
1920

Caen Wood Towers
Highgate, London
Architect L.R. Guthrie
Client Lady Waley Cohen
1920. F137; N12
Ref. GC ii (1928): 307, 309–11

Caesar's Camp
Wimbledon Common, London
Client Sir George Gibb
1906. F50; N36

Calkins, Mr
Address unknown
1926. N2
Ref. G 90(1926): 535–6, 551–2

Cambridge
80 Chesterton Road, Cambridge,
Cambs
Client Revd C.M. Rice
1916

Camilla Lacey
Dorking, Surrey
Client E. Leverton Harris
1901. F18

Camley House
Maidenhead, Berks
Architect Miss Eggar
Client Mr Rothbart
1921. N12

Castle Drogo
Drewsteignton, Devon
Architect E. Lutyens
Client Julius C. Drewe
1915. F128
Ref. GC 192 no 10 (1982):
21–25; CL 95 (1943): 69; 98
(1944): 200, 244; 106 (1948): 30;
157 (1974): 779; RHS 1975:
426–29

Chalet de Sonzier (Chalet
Blumenthal)
Les Avants, Switzerland
Client M. Jacques Blumenthal
1880

Chalfont Park
Gerrards Cross, Bucks
Architect E. Lutyens
Client Mrs Edgar
1912. RIBAD

Chamberlaynes
Bere Regis, Wareham, Dorset

Client Mrs J. Edmonds
1919. N15

Chart Cottage
Seal, Sevenoaks, Kent
Architect M. Taylor
Client Bernard Blunt
1911. F93; N26

Charterhouse School
Godalming, Surrey
Client Revd Gerald Rendall
1898. F8
See also The Red House

Chatham Cemetery (grave for
Captain F.G. Bird, RN)
Maidstone Road, Chatham, Kent
1923. F209

Chesterton Old Hall
Bridgnorth, Shrops
Client Mrs Thompson
1919. N25

Cheswick
Hedgerley Dean, Bucks
Client E.T. Cook
1902. F29

Chinthurst Hill
Wonersh, Surrey
Architect E. Lutyens
Clients Aemilia Guthrie, 1893;
Hon. Mrs Wilbraham Cooper,
1903. F4; RIBAD

Chisbury
Address unknown
Client C.D. Heatley
Date unknown. F225/5

Chislehurst
57 Elmstead Lane, Chislehurst,
Greater London
Client E. Borthwick
1924. N31

Chownes Mead
Cuckfield, West Sussex
Architect Norman and Burt
Client K.M. Carlisle
1920. F141; N12

Close Walks
Midhurst, West Sussex
Client Revd F. Tatchell
1907. F64; N9

Combend Manor
Elkstone, Gloucs
Architect S. Barnsley

Client Asa Lingard
1925. F185

Compton War Memorial
Compton, Surrey
1920

Copford Hall
Colchester, Essex
Client Mrs Brancker
1920

(The) Copse
Brook, Godalming, Surrey
Client R.W. Williamson
1913. F111

Copybold Cottage
Haslemere, Surrey
Client Mrs Richardson
Date unknown. N36, 39

Corner House
Beckenham, Kent
Client Francis Hooper
1910. N29

Cotmaton
Lindfield, West Sussex
Client Kate Leslie
1902

Cotswold Cottage. *See* Resor
House

Cottage Wood
Walton-On-Thames, Surrey
Client D.E. Round
1932. F213

(The) Court
St Fagan's, Cardiff, Wales
Client Lady Llewellyn
1925. F192; N10

Court Lodge
Knockholt, Kent
Client Mrs Langley Smithers
1922. N4

Coworth Park
Sunningdale, Berks
Clients Lady Alice Stanley, 1909;
Countess of Derby, 1913
F57; N23, 33, 36

Crooksbury House
Farnham, Surrey
Architect E. Lutyens
Client Arthur W. Chapman
1891. F5; RIBAD
Ref. CL 8 (1900): 336; 96 (1943):

596, 640; 141 (1966): 54; Weaver:
xvi, 1

Crossways Cottage
Busbridge, Godalming, Surrey
Client Mr Pullman
Date unknown. F225/6A, 6B

Culmer
Witley, Surrey
Client Miss H. Eastwood
1914. F116; N23

Culmer Corner
Witley, Surrey
Client J. H. Eastwood
1910. F89

Daneshill
Basings, Hants
Architect E. Lutyens
Client Walter Hoare
1903
Ref. Brown: 167; Weaver: 119–22

Deanery Garden
Sonning, Berks
Architect E. Lutyens
Client Edward Hudson
1901. F19; RIBAD
Ref. CL 141 (1917): 54; GFSCH:
17; Weaver: 53

Didswell Place
Welwyn, Herts
Client Mrs Buckley
1920

(The) Dormy House
Walton Heath, Surrey
Architect E. Lutyens
Client G.A. Riddell
1906
Ref. GFSCH: xxxvii

Drayton Wood
Drayton, Norfolk
Architect W.A. Dunham
Client Lieut-Colonel O'Meara
1921. F162

Drumbanagher
Newry, Co. Down, Ulster
Client Lady Muriel Close
1911

Duffell
Brockham Green, Betchworth,
Surrey
Client Mrs Davidson
Date unknown. N2
See also Friars Hill

Dungarth
Honley, Huddersfield, West Yorks
Architect G.H. Crowther
Client Mrs James Sykes
1920. F135

Durbins
Guildford, Surrey
Client Roger Fry
1910. N29

Durford Edge
Petersfield, Hants
Architects Unsworth and Triggs
Client J.P. Gabbatt
1923. F179; N11

Durmast
Burley, Hants
Client Miss Baring
1907. F65; N29, 37

Dyke Nook Lodge
Whatley Road, Accrington,
Lancs
Architect W. Brierley
Client H.V. Blake
1907. F68

Eartham House
Chichester, West Sussex
Architect E. Lutyens
Client Sir William Bird
1906. RIBAD

East Haddon Hall
East Haddon, Northants
Architect E. Lutyens
Client C. Guthrie
1893. RIBAD
Ref. GM 1915: 186–87

East Runton Hall
East Runton, Cromer, Norfolk
Architect M.H. Baillie Scott
Client Bertram Hawker
1908. F69; N35

Elmhurst. *See* Groesbeck
House

Enbridge Lodge
Kingsclere, Hants
Client Mr Grant
1892

Enton Hall
Witley, Surrey
Architect J.H. Norris
Client Major S. Chichester
1922. F165; N6

Enton Lodge
Witley, Surrey
Client J.H. Eastwood
1901. F12

Esholt
Sheffield, South Yorks
Architect E. Lutyens
Client A.J. Hobson
1905. N38

Fairhill
Berkhamstead, Herts
Architect E. Willmott
Client W.S. Cohen
1911. F94

Faslane
Gareloch, Strath, Scotland
Client Mrs MacFarlan
1928. N10

Fawkewood
Sevenoaks, Kent
Client Mrs Best
1919. F150; N41

Felbridge Place
East Grinstead, West Sussex
Architect E. Lutyens
Client H. Rudd
1916. F127
See also New Chapel House

Field House
Clent, Stourbridge, West Mids
Architect Forbes and Tate
Client A. Colin Kenrick
1914. F115; N17

Field Place
Dunsfold, Surrey
Client Mrs Bateson
1904. F34; N9

Firgrove
Godalming, Surrey
Client Alfred W. Mellersh
1907. F59; N35

Fishers
Wisborough Green, West Sussex
Client Captain J.W. Greenhill
1922. F167; N6

Fisher's Gate
Withyham, East Sussex
Client Countess De La Warr
1924. N31

Fishers Hill
Hook Heath, Woking, Surrey

Architect E. Lutyens
Client Rt. Hon. Gerald Balfour
1901. F15
Ref. Weaver: 60

Folly Farm
Sulhamstead, Berks
Architect E. Lutyens
Clients H. Cochrane, 1906;
Zachary Merton, 1912
F52; N38
Ref. CL 51 (1922): 112, 146;
58 (1925): 812; 63 (1928): 643;
125 (1958): 1004; 130 (1960):
6; 157 (1974): 1230; Weaver:
275

Fountain Hall
Pencaitland, Lothian, Scotland
Client Sir Thomas Dick-Lauder
1903. N2

Fox Hill
Elstead, Surrey
Client Mrs Hamilton
1923. F176

Fox Steep
Crazies Hill, Wargrave, Berks
Architect O. Hill
Client Mrs Van Der Bergh
1923. F175; N8
Ref. CL 63 (1928): 31

Foyle Riding Farm
Oxted, Surrey
Client A.C. Houghton
1920. N14

Frant Court
Tunbridge Wells, Kent
Architect G. Streatfeild
Client Miss Thornton
1914. F119; N18

Frensham Place
Frensham, Surrey
Client Sir Arthur Pearson
1909. F82

Friar's Hill
Elstead, Surrey
Client Mrs Davidson
1902. F21

Fulbrook House
Elstead, Surrey
Architect E. Lutyens
Client Gerard Streatfeild
1897
Ref. CL 13 (1902):52; Weaver: 21

Fulmer Court
Beaconsfield, Bucks
Client Mrs Oswald Watt
1913. F113; N16

(The) Garden
A series of articles under the
general title 'The joy of making a
new garden'.
1926, 1927. N3
Ref. G 90 (1926): 569, 581, 599,
630; G 91(1927): 2, 35, 99, 189
See also Calkins; Gorselands;
Kinder

Garden Court
Guildford, Surrey
Architect M.H. Baillie Scott
Client H.G. Steele
1915. F124

Gazely
Marlow, Bucks
Client Revd M. Graves
1895

Girton College
Cambridge, Cambs
Client Lady Stephen
1920. F139

Gishurst Cottage
The Heath, Weybridge, Surrey
Client G.F. Wilson
1881

Glasgow
150 Balshagray Avenue, Jordanhill,
Glasgow, Strath, Scotland
Client Mary Stuart
1924

Glebe House
Cornwood, Devon
Client Allan Aynesworth-
Anderson
1922, 1925 & 1927. F225/14; N6
See also Old Parsonage, Otford, Kent

Glebe House, Connecticut, USA
See Old Glebe House

Gledstone Hall
West Marton, North Yorks
Architect E. Lutyens
Client Sir Amos Nelson
1925. F195; N10; RIBAD
Ref. CL 77 (1934): 374, 400; 170
(1980): 2292

Glenapp Castle
Ballantrae, Strath, Scotland

Client Mrs Stock
1902. F23

Glottenham
Robertsbridge, East Sussex
Client B. Leigh Smith
1890

Godalming Police Station
Godalming, Surrey
1914

Goddards
Abinger Common, Surrey
Architect E. Lutyens
Client Sir Frederick Mirrielees
1899
Ref. CL 15 (1904): 162; Weaver: 35

Golands House
New Chapel, Lingfield, Surrey
Architect unknown (plan
unsigned)
Client H. Rudd
1920. F151; N14

Golders Green Cemetery
London
Client R. H. Philipson
1915

Gorse Bank
Enton Green, Witley, Surrey
Client P. Whateley
1914. N19

Gorselands
Highcliffe, Dorset
Client unknown
1926. N2
Ref. G 90 (1926): 661

(The) Grange
Hindhead, Haslemere, Surrey
Client Mrs Crossley
1905. F39; N23

Grayswood Hill
Haslemere, Surrey
Architect J.H. Howard
Client W. J.H. Whittall
1920. F144; N6, 8, 31
Ref. CL 80 (1935): 326; 88 (1939):
175; 126 (1958): 6

Great Blow. *See* Middlefield

Great Enton
Witley, Surrey
Client J.H. Eastwood
1883

Great House
Hambledon, Surrey
Client Mrs Readhead
1922. F171; N14

Great Meadow. *See* Holmwood

Great Roke
Witley, Surrey
Client Mrs Dixon
1910. N29

Greenways
Devenish Road, Sunningdale,
Berks
Architect M.H. Baillie Scott
Client A. Spencer
1907. F63

Greenwich, Connecticut, USA
See Resor House

Groesbeck House
Perintown, Ohio, USA
Client Glendinning B. Groesbeck
1914. F120; N20

Groote Schuur
Rondebosch, Cape Town, South
Africa
Architect H. Baker
Client Rt Hon. Cecil Rhodes
1898
Ref. CL 32 (1912): 420; 56 (1924):
32; Baker, *Architecture and
Personalities* (London 1944), 96

Hale House
Ockley, Surrey
Client Mrs Powell
1902. F24

Hall Cottage
Frensham, Surrey
Architect H. Falkner
Client Harold Falkner
1924. N31

Hall Place
Shackleford, Godalming, Surrey
Client E. Horne
1903. F30

Hangerfield
Witley, Surrey
Client Captain Crawford
1885

Hanley Court
Bewdley, Worcs
Client Mrs Wakeman-Newport
1901. F14

Harbledown Lodge
Canterbury, Kent
Client Canon Holland
1890

Hascombe Court
Hascombe, Surrey
Architect J.D. Coleridge;
Landscape architect Clare
Nauheim
Client Sir John Jarvis
1922. F170; N11
Ref. GD 1930 No 3: 103–13; CL
92 (1941): 554

Hascombe Grange
Godalming, Surrey
Client Mrs Henderson
1913. F110

Hatchlands
Guildford, Surrey
Client Lord Rendel
1900, 1914. F17; N21
Ref. CL 39 (1916): 176; 114
(1952): 870; 183 (1987): 182

Hawkley Hurst
Petersfield, Hants
Architect G. Streatfeild
Client Mrs Clive Davies
1914. F114

Hazelhatch
Shere, Surrey
Architect E. Lutyens
Client Hon. Emily Lawless
1897

Heathcote
Ilkley, West Yorks
Architect E. Lutyens
Client Ernest Hemingway
1907. F66; RIBAD
Ref. CL 28 (1910): 54; 39 (1916):
308; 58 (1925): 570; 145 (1968):
711; Weaver: 183

Heath Cottage
Puttenham, Guildford, Surrey
Client Bruce Gosling
1913. F108
(also known as Kilnfield)

Heath House
Headley, Epsom, Surrey
Architect E. Lutyens
Client Edward Hudson
1920. F140

Heatherside House
Camberley, Surrey

Client Mrs Walter Leaf
1909. F86; N33

Henley Park
Henley-on-Thames, Oxon
Architect C.R. Daw
Client Mrs Reade Revell
1909. F83; N32, 35

(The) Hermitage
Effingham, Surrey
Client Susan Muir-Mackenzie
1891. F3

Hestercombe
Cheddon Fitzpaine, Somerset
Architect E. Lutyens (gardens only)
Client Hon. E.W.B. Portman
1904. F77; N9, 36; RIBAD
Ref. CL 24 (1908): 486, 522; 61
(1927): 598, 638; 111 (1951): 1239;
160 (1975): 822; *Journal of the
Institute of Landscape Architects* 61
(1963): 8–11; *Landscape Design* 133
(1981): 26–27; Weaver: 40

Heywood House
Abbeyleix, Eire
Architect E. Lutyens
Client Sir E. Hucheson Poe
1910. RIBAD
Ref. CL 45 (1919): 16, 42

High Barn
Hascombe, Surrey
Architect R. Lorimer
Client Hon. Stuart Pleydell-
Bouverie
1901. F16; N35

Highcroft
Burley, Hants
Client Miss Sarrin
1906. F55

Highdown Sanatorium.
See King George V Sanatorium

Highlands
Haslemere, Surrey
Client Hon. Mrs E. Gibson
1915. F125

Highmount
Fort Road, Guildford, Surrey
Architect D.G. Round
Client Walter Neall
1909. F84; N4, 27
Ref. GFSCH: 46–54

Hill Hall
Theydon Mount, Epping, Essex

Client Lady Hudson
1928. F225/13
Ref. CL 20 (1906): 18; 41 (1917):
448, 472, 496

Hillside
Goldalming, Surrey
Client Gedley Robinson
1897

Hillside
Penarth, Glamorgan, Wales
Client J. Croisdale Kirk
1924. N31

Hill Top
Fort Road, Guildford, Surrey
Client Mrs Walter Neall
1921. F161; N6

Hollington House
Newbury, Berks
Client E. Fergus Kelly
1908. F72; N34

Holmwood
Hambledon, Surrey
Architect A.G.J. Harbour
Client Mrs Wentworth Martin
1923. F174; N31

Holywell Court
Cliff Road, Eastbourne, East Sussex
Architect Murray and Hay
Client Mrs Hornby Lewis
1918. F131

(The) House Farm
Sandling, Hythe, Kent
Client Mrs Murray
1914. N19

Hughes Memorial Church
(Wesleyan Chapel)
Goldalming, Surrey
1903. F33

Hursley Park
Winchester, Hants
Client Sir George Cowper
1925. F186
Ref. CL 12 (1902): 776; 26 (1909):
562, 598; 34 (1913): 679

Hydon Heath
Hambledon, Surrey
Client National Trust
1915

Hydon Ridge
Hambledon, Surrey
Architect S. Towse

Client C.E. Denny
1911. F95; N24

Ickwell House
Biggleswade, Beds
Client Colonel Hayward Wells
1926. F200; N18

Ide Hill
Sevenoaks, Kent
Client National Trust
1921

Kedleston Hall
Kedleston, Derbys
Client Earl of Curzon
1923. F177
Ref. CL 10 (1901): 240; 181(1986)
30: 96; 47(1990): 56

Keston
High View Road, Sidcup, Kent
Architect P. Leeds
Client F. Eastwood
1916

Kew
61 The Avenue, Kew, Greater London
Client Edward Jekyll
1920

Keyham Hall
Keyham, Leics
Client Mrs Baxter
1916

Kildonan
Barrhill, Ayrshire, Scotland
Client Mrs Euan Wallace
(Barbara Lutyens)
1924. F183; N31

Kilmeena
West Byfleet, Surrey
Client F. Littleboy
1918. F132; N41

Kilnfield. *See* Heath Cottage

Kinder, Mr
Burgess Hill, West Sussex
1926. N2
Ref. G 90 (1926): 692

King Edward VII Sanatorium
Midhurst, West Sussex
Architect Adams and Holden
Client by public subscription
under the patronage of HM King
Edward VII
1908. F74; N5, 28, 36
Ref. CL 26 (1909): 701

King George V Sanatorium
Milford, Surrey
Architect unknown
Client Metropolitan Sanatorium
Board
1922. N2

King's Arms Hotel
Godalming, Surrey
Client Miss Botham
1915

Kingston upon Thames
28 Albany Park Road, Kingston
upon Thames, Surrey
Client R. Antill
1921

Kingswood
Shere, Surrey
Client J.W.B. Sexton
1920. F143; N14

Knebworth House
Stevenage, Herts
Client Earl of Lytton
1907. F61; N38; RIBAD
Ref. CL 1 (1897): 694; 19 (1906):
486, 522; 149 (1970): 68; 152
(1971): 386

Knole
Cranleigh, Surrey
Client Sir George Bonham
1888

Kylemore
Bradley, Humberside
Client W.H. Thickett
1918. F130

Lainston House
Winchester, Hants
Architect Forbes and Tate
Client Mr Harvey
1922. F172; N11
Ref. CL 45 (1919): 252

Lambay Castle
Lambay Island, Co. Dublin, Eire
Architect E. Lutyens
Client Hon. Cecil Baring (Lord
Revelstoke)
1907. F56; RIBAD
Ref. CL 66 (1929): 86, 120;
Weaver: 204

Lascombe
Puttenham, Surrey
Architect E. Lutyens
Client Colonel Spencer
1895

Lees Court
Faversham, Kent
Landscape architect G.H. Mawson
Client Mrs Reginald Halsey
1909. F80; N30
Ref. CL 52 (1922): 178

Legh Manor
Cuckfield, West Sussex
Client Sir William and Lady
Chance
1918. N15
Ref. CL 70 (1931): 672

Legh Manor
Address unknown (possibly
Cuckfield, West Sussex)
Client M.H. Kent
1931. F210

Lenton Hurst
Nottingham, Notts
Client Mrs Player
1911

Letchworth Garden City, Herts
Architect C.M. Crickmer
Client Mrs Firth
1907. F59A

Lewtrenchard Manor
Lewdown, Tavistock, Devon
Architect W. Sarel
Client Revd Sabine Baring-Gould
1928. F216; N10

Leybourne
Witley, Surrey
Client Sir Owen Roberts
1902. F22

Leys Castle
Inverness, Highlands, Scotland
Client Mrs Ogilvie
1920. F138; N13

Lillingstone Dayrell
Bucks
Client Hon. Mrs Douglas-Pennant
1910. N29

Limerick
Clogrenmon Terrace, Ennis Road,
Limerick, Eire
Client Mrs Handyside
1914. N19

Lindisfarne Castle
Holy Island, Northumberland
Architect E. Lutyens
Client Edward Hudson
1911. F91; N11, 29; RIBAD

Ref. CL 33 (1913): 830;
Weaver: 127

Lindsey House. *See* London

Little Aston Hall
Little Aston, Staffs
Architect Bateman and Bateman
Client J.H. Birch
1914. F121

Little Beverley
Canterbury, Kent
Client Miss Taylor
1925. N31

Little Cumbrae Island
Firth of Clyde, Strath, Scotland
Architect C.E. Bateman
Client Evelyn S. Parker
1916. F126

Little Haling
Denham, Bucks
Architect W. Sarel
Client Mrs Acland Hood
1927. F204; N31

Little Hay
Burley, Ringwood, Hants
Client Lady Isobel Ryder
1907. F60

Little Hoe
Rake Hanger, Petersfield, Hants
Client Mr Gabbatt
1929. F214

Little Munton
Sunningdale, Berks
Architect W. Sarel
Client Mrs Acland Hood
1924. N31

Little Tangley
Guildford, Surrey
Architect E. Lutyens
Clients Cowley Lambert, 1899;
Mrs Hooper, 1908; Miss Simon,
1921. F11; N6, 9, 35

Little Wisset
Hook Heath Road, Woking, Surrey
Architect W. Sarel
Client Miss Bayley
1931. F211

Littlecote
Lindfield, West Sussex
Client Kate Leslie
1907. F58
(also known as Oak Lee)

Llanfawr
Holyhead, Gwynedd, Wales
Client Mrs Jane Adeane
1890

(The) Lodge
Thames Ditton, Surrey
Client Sir Guy Campbell
1895

London
35 Hamilton Terrace,
St John's Wood
Client W. M. Foster
1923. N8

London
38 Hamilton Terrace,
St John's Wood
Client Sir Lawrence Weaver
1920

London
50 Kensington Park Road,
Kensington
Client A. Leaver
Date unknown. F225/9; N32

London
Lindsey House, 100 Cheyne Walk,
Chelsea
Architect E. Lutyens
Client Sir Hugh Lane
1910
Ref. GFSCH: 64

London
Mostyn Road, Merton Park,
Architect J.S. Brocklesby
Client G.H. Hadfield
1913. N19

London
23 Vale Avenue, Chelsea
Client Lady Helena Acland Hood
1917. N15

London
Wilbraham House, Wilbraham
Place, Sloane Street,
Architect O. Hill
Client Ludley Scott
1923. F178; N11

Longwood House
Winchester, Hants
Client Countess of Northesk
1882

Loseley House
Guildford, Surrey
Client William More-Molyneux

1905. F46
Ref. CL 77 (1934): 544; 146
(1968): 802, 894

Lower Eashing
Godalming, Surrey
Client Mr Turnbull
1884

Lower House
Bowlhead Green, Witley, Surrey
Client Lady Guillemard
1915. F122

Lukyns
Ewhurst, Surrey
Client Mrs Dugald Clerk
1914. F118

Manchester
Sutton, Ashley Road, Bowdon,
Gt Man
Client R. Okell
1884

(The) Manor House
Mells, Somerset
Architect E. Lutyens
Client Sir John and Lady
Horner
1902
Ref. Brown: 166; CL 112 (1951):
444

(The) Manor House
Upton Grey, Hants
Architect Ernest Newton
Client Mr Best
1908. F73; N33, 35

(The) Marches
Willow Brook, Eton, Berks
Architect E. Lutyens
Client E.L. Vaughan
1926. F199

Marks Danes
Bruton, Somerset
Architect A.J. Pictor
Client Mrs Torrance
1919. F147; N14

Marsh Court
Stockbridge, Hants
Architect E. Lutyens
Client Herbert Johnston
1905. F44; N9; RIBAD
Ref. CL 20 (1906): 306; 33 (1913):
562; 71 (1932): 316, 354; 141
(1966): 71; 145 (1968): 711;
Weaver: 75

Marylands
Hurtwood, Surrey
Architect O. Hill
Client Mr and Mrs Warner
1929. F212
Ref. CL 70 (1931): 452

Mayhurst
Maybury Hill, Surrey
Client Miss Graham
1895

Mells Park House
Mells, Somerset
Client Rt Hon. Reginald
McKenna
1926. F201; RIBAD
Ref. CL 92 (1941): 444

Merdon Manor
Hursley, Winchester, Hants
Client Captain Cowper
1925. F188

Merrow Croft
Guildford, Surrey
Architect W. Sarel
Client Mrs Pike Pease
1912. F98; N23

Middlefield
Great Shelford, Cambs
Architect E. Lutyens
Client Henry Boyd
1908
Ref. Brown: 170

Milford House
Milford, Surrey
Client Robert Webb
1896

Mill House
Wylye, Wilts
Client unknown
1920s. N2 (no entry found)

Millmead
Snowdenham Lane, Bramley,
Surrey
Architect E. Lutyens
Client Gertrude Jekyll
1904
Ref . CL 21(1907): 674; G (1919):
130–131; GFSCH: 1–9; Weaver:
164

Milton Court
Dorking, Surrey
Client unknown
Date unknown. F225/12
Ref. CL 10 (1901): 528

Minnickfold
Dorking, Surrey
Client Mrs McLaren
1898

Monkswood
Godalming, Surrey
Architect Forsyth and Maule
Client J.A. Moir
1912. F100; N26

Monkton House
Singleton, West Sussex
Architect E. Lutyens
Client William James
1903. RIBAD
Ref. CL 178 (1984): 700; 179
(1985): 751; Weaver: 123

Monkton Farleigh
Bradford-on-Avon
Client L. Thornton
1907. N9

(The) Moorings
Hindhead, Haslemere,
Surrey
Client Mrs Russell
1906. F53

Mostyn Road. *See* London

Moulsford Manor
Moulsford, Oxon
Client Mrs Mayo Robson
1909. F81; N33

Mount Stewart
Newtonards, Co Down, Ulster
Client Edith, Marchioness of
Londonderry
1920. F146; N13
Ref. CL 78 (1934): 356, 380; 145
(1968): 1261, 1302; 161 (1976): 934;
167 (1979): 646, 754, 1406; (1990) 6:
72, 20: 180; GD 1938: 33, 8–13; GC
ii 1960: 240–41, 245; ii 1962: 80–81;
RHS 1935: 521–31; 1950: 241–43

Muir-Mackenzie, Lord
May have been for his town house,
27 Cumberland Terrace, Regents
Park, London
1903. N2

Munstead
Busbridge, Godalming, Surrey
Client H. Shearburn
1890. N23

Munstead Corner
Busbridge, Godalming, Surrey

Client C. D. Heatley
Architect E. Lutyens
1895

Munstead Grange
Busbridge, Godalming, Surrey
Architect E.W. Mountford
Clients E.W. Mountford, 1902;
F.S. Staples, 1912, 1915
F26, 99; N4, 21, 26

Munstead House
Busbridge, Godalming, Surrey
Architect J.J. Stevenson
Client Julia Jekyll
1877
Ref. G22 (1882): 191–93; 23
(1883): 295–99

Munstead Oaks
Busbridge, Godalming, Surrey
Client Lady Victoria Fisher-Rowe
1913. F107; N7

Munstead Rough
Busbridge, Godalming, Surrey
Client W.R. Pullman
1899. F13

Munstead Wood
Busbridge, Godalming, Surrey
Architect E. Lutyens
Client Gertrude Jekyll
1883. F1; RIBAD
Ref. GFSCH: 36–45; CL 8 (1900):
730

Nashdom
Taplow, Bucks
Architect E. Lutyens
Client Princess Alexis Dolgorouki
1909. RIBAD
Ref. CL 32 (1912): 292; Weaver: 238

Nettleston
Exact address unknown
Client unknown
1903. N39

(The) Neuk
Aboyne, Grampian, Scotland
Client Mrs Smithson
1924. N2

New Chapel House
Lingfield, Surrey
Client H. Rudd
1916. F123; N41
Ref. CL 60 (1926): 631

New Place
Haslemere, Surrey

Architect C.F.A. Voysey
Client Sir Algernon Methuen
1902. F27
Ref. G 1921: 388–89; Mabel
Parsons, *English House Grounds*
(London, 1924), 49–53; RHS 108
(1983): 229–33

New Place
Botley, Shedfield, Hants
Architect E. Lutyens
Client Mrs A.S. Franklyn
1906. F49; N38; RIBAD
Ref. CL 27 (1910): 522; Weaver: 175

Newnham College.
See Sidgwick Memorial

Newlandburn
Lothian, Scotland
Client Lord Ruthven
1905. F45

Normanswood
Farnham, Surrey
Clients Mrs Russell, 1898;
Miss Russell, 1919

North Munstead
Busbridge, Godalming, Surrey
Client Captain Sampson
1924. F181; N11
Ref. CL 55 (1924): 400; 56 (1924): 913

Nurseries
Solihull, Warwicks
Client Hewitt and Co
1924

Nurses House. *See* Culmer

Oak Lee
Lindfield, West Sussex
Client Kate Leslie
1907. F58
See also Littlecote

Oaklands
Cranleigh, Surrey
Client Mrs Thompson Hankey
1882

Oaklands
Wilmslow Park, Wilmslow,
Cheshire
Client H.O. Wood
1921. F224/6

Old Croft
Godalming, Surrey
Client Revd D. Hyland
1910. N29

Old Glebe House
Woodbury, Connecticut, USA
Client Annie Burr Jennings
1926. F196

(The) Old Lighthouse
St Margaret's at Cliffe, Kent
Architect unknown (plans
unsigned)
Client Sir W. Beardsell
1925. F193

(The) Old Parsonage
Gresford, Clwyd, Wales
Architect Forbes and Tate
Client G.C. Bushby
1919. F149

Old Parsonage
Otford, Kent
Client Allan Aynesworth-
Anderson
1922. N41
Ref. CL 52 (1922): 290
See also (The) Glebe House
(Devon)

Orchards
Godalming, Surrey
Architect E. Lutyens
Clients Sir William and Lady
Chance, 1899; Lady Elizabeth
Taylor, 1918
N15; RIBAD
Ref. CL 10 (1901): 272; 23 (1908):
522; Weaver: 23

Orchards, Great Missenden,
Bucks. See Bramleys

Oroszvar
Moson Megye, Hungary
Architect E. Lutyens
Clients Princess Stephanie of
Belgium and Countess De Longay
1913. F105

Osbrooks
Capel, Surrey
Client Mrs Schluter
1904. F32; N36

Palace Cottage
Beaulieu, Hants
Client Mrs Stuart Wortley
1921. N15

Papillon Hall
Market Harborough, Leics
Architect E. Lutyens
Client Frank Belville
1903. RIBAD

Ref. CL 31: (Supp. 4 May 1912)
xiv; Weaver: 112–18

Parc des Sports
Versailles, France
Client J.H. Hyde
1924. F182

Pasture Wood
Address unknown
Client R. Potter
Date unknown. F225/4

Pasturewood House
Holmbury St Mary, Surrey
Architect E. Lutyens
Client Sir Frederick Mirrielees
1899
Ref. Brown: 164

Pednor House
Chesham, Bucks
Architect Forbes and Tate
Client H.S. Harrington
1919. F148; N15

Penheale Manor
Egloskerry, Cornwall
Architect E. Lutyens
Client Captain P. Colville
1920. F142; RIBAD
Ref. CL 57 (1925): 484, 524; 68
(1930): 569; 69 (1931): 35

Peperharow Park
Godalming, Surrey
Client Earl of Middleton
1908. F71
Ref. CL 58 (1925): 1002; (1990)
33: 52

Peter Jones Ltd
Club House, Teddington,
Middlesex
Client Peter Jones Ltd
1920. N2

Phillimore's Spring
Crazies Hill, Berkshire
Client unknown
1870

Phillips Memorial
Godalming, Surrey
Architect T. Turner
Client Borough of Godalming
1912. F97; N21

Pinecroft
Graffham, Petworth, West Sussex
Client Mrs Powell
1908. F75; N36

Place of Tilliefour.
See Tilliefour

Plumpton Place
Plumpton, East Sussex
Architect E. Lutyens
Client Edward Hudson
1928. F222; RIBAD
Ref. CL 73 (1933): 522

Pollard's Park
Chalfont St Giles, Bucks
Client A. Grove
1906. F41

Pollard's Wood
Fernhurst, Surrey
Architect J.E. Forbes
Client J.E. Forbes
1908. F76; N9

Ponds
Seer Green, Beaconsfield, Herts
Client Mrs James Goff
1928. F217; N10

Postfach
Belgrade, Serbia, Yugoslavia
Client M.S. Ilitch
1928. F215

Presaddfed
Holyhead, Gwynedd, Wales
Client Mrs W. Fox-Pitt
1909. F78

Prior's Field
Puttenham, Guildford, Surrey
Architect C.F.A. Voysey
Clients F.H. Chambers; Leonard
Huxley
1900
(formerly known as Prior's Garth)

(The) Priory
Hitchin, Herts
Architect W. Sarel
Client Lady Hudson
1928. F218

(The) Priory
Seaview, Isle of Wight
Architect E. Lutyens
Client unknown
1927. F220; RIBAD; Sketch-book
Godalming Museum, 1903

Purley
Church Road, Purley,
Greater London
Client Mrs Watson
1905. F43

Puttenham Priory
Puttenham, Surrey
Client C.F. Wood
1919. F154; N21

Putteridge Park
Luton, Beds
Architect E. Lutyens
Client Sir Frank Cassel
1911. F92

Quedley
Shottermill, Haslemere, Surrey
Architect Miss Eggar
Client Mrs Ericsson
1921. N12

Queen's Dolls' House
Architect E. Lutyens
Client Gift from nation to HM
The Queen
1920. F226; RIBAD
Ref. CL 55 (1924): 202, 242; 58
(1925): 129; 65 (1929): 812; 128
(1959): 1292
(now at Windsor Castle, Berks)

Reading
75 Tilhurst Road, Reading, Berks
Client A.C. Bartholomew
1887

(The) Red House
Effingham, Surrey
Architect E. Lutyens
Client Susan Muir-Mackenzie
1891. RIBAD

(The) Red House
Charterhouse School, Godalming,
Surrey
Architect E. Lutyens
Client Revd H.J. Evans
1896
See also Charterhouse School

Redcliff
Whittingehame, Prestonkirk,
Lothian, Scotland
Client R.A.L. Balfour
1925

Reflections
Echo Pit Road, Guildford, Surrey
Client Mrs Tucker
1929

Renishaw Hall
Renishaw, Derbys
Architect E. Lutyens
Client Sir George Sitwell
1910. F88; N24; RIBAD

Ref. CL 8 (1900): 560; 83 (1937):
476, 506; 101 (1946): 46; 162
(1976): 522

Resor House
Greenwich, Connecticut, USA
Client Stanley Resor
1925. F191
(also known as Cotswold Cottage)

Richards, Miss C.D.
Address unknown
Date unknown. N15

Richmond
Address unknown
Architect H.P. Adams
Client unknown
Date unknown. F225/8

Rideway
Tittlerow, Maidenhead, Berks
Client L. Gilau
1922

Rignalls Wood
Great Missenden, Bucks
Architect Adams and Holden
Client Sir Felix Semon
1909. F79; N29, 33

Rochdale, Lancs
Client unknown mill boy
1877
Ref. Jekyll, *Wood and Garden*: 185

Roysted
Highdown Heath, Godalming,
Surrey
Clients Mrs Sessions and H.J.
Shindler
1926. F198; N10

Ruckmans
Oakwood Park, Surrey
Architect E. Lutyens
Client Miss Lyell
1894. N36
Ref. Weaver: 5

Runton Old Hall. *See* East Runton
Hall

St Edmund's Catholic Church
Godalming, Surrey
1910. N29

Salisbury
North Canonry, Salisbury, Wilts
Client Canon Swayne
1884

(The) Salutation
Sandwich, Kent
Architect E. Lutyens
Clients Gaspard and Henry Farrer
1911
Ref. Brown:171; CL 132 (1962):
564, 650; 170 (1981): 849; 174
(1983): 506, 616; Weaver: 256–60

Sandbourne
Bewdley, Worcs
Client Mrs Wakeman-Newport
1912. F102; N8

Scalands
Robertsbridge, East Sussex
Client Barbara Bodichon
1877. F2 (interior plans)

Seymour Court
Marlow, Bucks
Client T. Wethered
1895

Shepherd's Well
Forest Row, East Sussex
Client Mrs Frost
1910

Shorncliffe Camp
Moore Barracks, Folkestone, Kent
Client War Office, under the
direction of Lieutenant-Colonel
Freyberg
1929

Sidgwick Memorial
Newnham College, Cambridge,
Cambs
Client Miss Clough
1911. F90; N24
Ref. CL 150 (1970): 1704

South African War Memorial
Delville Wood, France
Architect H. Baker
Client Government of the Union
of South Africa
1925. F194

South Corner, Wimbledon,
London. *See* Caesar's Camp

South Luffenham Hall
Stafford, Staffs
Client Mrs Nugent Allfrey
1926. F202

Southernway
St Martha's, Guildford, Surrey
Client Sir John Snell
1923. F168; N8

Spain
Dendromecon
Address unknown
Client unknown
1925. N40

Springwood
Godalming, Surrey
Client Dr S. Wilkinson
1931

Stanstead House
Glemsford, Suffolk
Architect E. Lutyens
Client Mrs Bird
1923

Stilemans
Godalming, Surrey
Architect C. Nicholson
Client Dr E.P. Arnold
1909. F87; N4, 15, 32
Ref. CL 81 (1936): 63

Stonepitts
Seal, Sevenoaks, Kent
Architect G.L. Kennedy
Clients Lady Rhondda and Mrs
Archdale
1925. F189

Stowell Hill
Templecombe, Somerset
Client Mrs McCreery
1925. F190
Ref. CL 61 (1927): 147

Stratton Audley
Bicester, Bucks
Client Colonel G. Gosling
1895

Stratton Park
Micheldever, Hants
Client Earl of Northbrook
1895
Ref. CL 141 (1966): 80; 35 (1914): 839

Strood Park
Horsham, West Sussex
Client Mrs Buckley
1928. F219

Struy Lodge
Beauly, Highland, Scotland
Client Countess of Derby
1911. F106; N24, 29

Stubbings
Maidenhead, Berks
Client E.R. Squales
1910. N29

Sullingstead
(now High Hascombe)
Hascombe, Surrey
Architect E. Lutyens
Client Sir Charles Cook
1924. N31
Ref. CL 31 (4 May 1912 supp):
xxvii; Weaver: 11–12

Sunningdale. *See* Greenways

Sutton Place
Guildford, Surrey
Client Lady Northcliffe
1902. F28
Ref. CL 4 (1898): 824; 8 (1900): 854;
35 (1914): 198, 234; 71 (1932): 202

Tangley Way
Blackheath, Guildford, Surrey
Architect M. Horder
Client J.W. Kennedy
1921, 1923, 1928. F164; N11, 18
(also known as Birchgrove and
Thatched House)

Tarn Moor
Witley, Surrey
Client Mr Dunn
1905

Temple Dinsley
Hitchin, Herts
Architect E. Lutyens
Client H.G. Fenwick
1909. RIBAD
Ref. CL 29 (1911): 562; Weaver:
221–31

Thatched House. *See* Tangley Way

The Old Poorhouse
Zennor, Cornwall
Client Barbara Bodichon,
Gertrude Jekyll
1870s

Thorncombe Park
Bramley, Surrey
Client Edward Rowe Fisher-Rowe
1896. F7; N36

Thorpe Hall
Louth, Lincs
Client Mrs Brackenbury
1906

Three Fords
Send, Surrey
Architect F. Hodgson
Client Mrs Claud Serocold
1926. F205; N18

Tigbourne Court
Witley, Surrey
Architect E. Lutyens
Client Sir Edgar Horne
1899. RIBAD
Ref. CL 18 (1905): 414; Int. Studio
17 (1902): 21–24; Weaver: 41–47

Tilecotes
Marlow, Bucks
Client Mr Graves
1895

(Place of) Tilliefour
Gordon, Grampian, Scotland
Architects H. Wardrop and
R. Lorimer
Client Mrs Moncrief Paterson
1924. N31

Townhill Park
Bitterne, Southampton, Hants
Architect L.R. Guthrie
Client Lord Swaythling
1912. F103; N4, 22
Ref. CL 53 (1923): 536; 74 (1933):
394; Lady Rockley, *Historic
Gardens of England* (London,
1938): 256–57

Trenance
Summerhouse Road,
Godalming, Surrey
Client T. P. Whately
1914. N19
See also Gorse Bank

Tresserve
Aix-les-Bains, Sevoire, France
Client John Bellingham
1902. F20

Trouville Hospitals.
See War Cemeteries

Tunworth Down
Basingstoke, Hants
Client Mrs Claud Chichester
1919. F152; N25

Tylney Hall
Rotherwick, Nr. Hook, Hants
Architect R.W. Schultz
Client Mrs Lionel Phillips
1906. F54; N9
Ref. Arch. Review 16: 81–85; GC I
1905: 257–59

Uplands
Brook, Witley, Surrey
Client Arnold Williams
1907. F62; N37

Upper Ifold House
Dunsfold, Surrey
Client Lady Cynthia Mosley
1921. F160; N6

Vale Wood Farm
Haslemere, Surrey
Architect O. Hill
Client Oliver Hill
1927
Ref. CL 77 (1934): 298

Vann
Hambledon, Surrey
Architect W.D. Caroe
Client W.D. Caroe
1911. N24
Ref. CL 159 (1975): 1394; 179
(1985): 1816

(The) Vicarage
Milford-on-Sea, Hants
Client unknown
1927. F203; N31

(The) Vicarage
Witley, Surrey
Client Revd J.E. Eddis
1895

Viceroy's House
New Delhi, India
Architect E. Lutyens
Client Imperial Government of
India
1912. N2
Gertrude Jekyll made trees for
the model of this commission
and may have given general
advice on the gardens, although
no documentary evidence
survives.

Walsham House
Elstead, Surrey
Client A.C. Kenrick
1920. F145; N12

Wangford Hall
Brandon, Suffolk
Client Mrs Temple Richards
1929. F223; N10

War Cemeteries
Architect E. Lutyens
Client Imperial War Graves
Commission
1918. F157, 158; N14
Sites listed are: Auchonvillers,
Gezaincourt, Corbie La Neuville,
Hersin, Frenvillers, Trouville,
Warlincourt Halte

Wargrave Hill
Wargrave, Berks
Client Captain E.J. Jekyll
1868

Warren Hurst
Ashtead, Surrey
Architect P. Leeds
Client Mrs Henry Sams
1913. F104; N19

Warren Lodge
(now Warren Mere)
Thursley, Surrey
Architect E. Lutyens
Client Robert Webb
1903. F31
Ref. CL 164 (1977): 638

Waterlow, Mrs
Address unknown
Date unknown. N36

Waterside Copse
Liphook, Hants
Client A.H. Scott
1913. F109; N21

Watlington Park
Watlington, Oxon
Client Viscount Esher
1922. F169; N11
Ref. CL 125 (1958): 18, 60

Westaway
Godalming, Surrey
Client Mrs Fleming
1898

West Barsham
Norfolk
Architect Page and Holton
Client J.A. Keith
1926. F206

Westbrook
Godalming, Surrey
Client Thackeray Turner
Date unknown. N4

Westcliffe-on-Sea
5 Hall Park Avenue, Westcliffe-on-
Sea, Essex
Client W. Bruce Peart
1928

West Dean Park
West Dean, West Sussex
Client Mrs William James
1898. F9
Ref. CL 6 (1899): 112; 170 (1980):
1378, 1462; G 34 (1888): 317–18;

GC ii 1901: 1; ii 1905: 273–74; 186
no 10 (1979): 16–17

West Surrey Golf Club
Milford, Surrey
Client J.H. Eastwood
1910. N24, 29

Whinfold
Hascombe, Surrey
Architect R. Lorimer
Client Lionel Benson
1897. F10

White House
Wrotham, Kent
Client Miss M. Rowe and Miss
Edith Taylor
1919. F153; N25

Whiteways
Brockham Green, Surrey
Client Mrs Williamson
Date unknown. N9

Widford
Wydown Road, Haslemere,
Surrey
Client H.A. Barrett
1925. F187; N31

Wilbraham House. See London

Wilderness
Sevenoaks, Kent
Client L.M. Faulkner
1925

Winchester War Memorial
Winchester, Hants
Architect H. Baker
Client Winchester School
1923. F180; N11
(now Winchester College)

Wingstone
Manaton, Devon
Client Mrs Galsworthy
1908. F225/10; N36

Winkworth Farm
Hascombe, Surrey
Architect E. Lutyens
Client Mrs Lushington
1893

Wisley (now The Royal
Horticultural Society Garden)
Wisley, Surrey
Client G.F. Wilson
1881
Ref. CL 2 (1897): 319; 8

(1900): 304; 10 (1901): 101; 14
(1903): 254; 30 (1911): 683; 37
(1915): 119; 45 (1919): 799; 48
(1920): 143

Woodcote
Whitchurch, Hants
Architect Crickmay and Sons
Client R.F. Nicholson
1911. F96

Wood End
(now Orchards)
Witley, Surrey
Architect E. Lutyens
Client Lady Stewart
1892

Wood End
Ascot, Berks

Client J.B. Stevenson
1919. F159

Woodhouse Copse
Holmbury St Mary, Surrey
Architect O. Hill
Client Amy Barnes-Brand
1926. F208; N10, 18 RHS Lindley
Library (letters) Ref. CL 60
(1926): 593

Woodlands
Saltburn-by-Sea, North Yorks
Client C.W. Littleboy
1926. N31

Woodlea
Virginia Water, Berks
Client Mrs Bartlett
Date unknown. F225/11; N9

Woodruffe
Worplesdon Hill, Brookwood,
Surrey
Client Mrs Johnstone
1909. F85; N32

Woodside
Chenies, Bucks
Architect E. Lutyens
Client Adeline, Dowager Duchess
of Bedford
1893. RIBAD
Ref. CL 39 (1916): 767; Weaver: 7

Wrystone. *See* Wingstone

Yew Tree Hall
Forest Row, East Sussex
Client Miss Rumbold
1921. N6

APPENDIX II

Commissions Listed by Architect

Adams and Holden
King Edward VII Sanatorium
Rignalls Wood

Adams, Percy H.
Richmond, a garden

Baker, Sir Herbert
Groote Schuur
South African War Memorial
Winchester War Memorial

Barnsley, Sidney H.
Combend Manor

Bateman and Bateman
Little Aston Hall

Bateman, Charles E.
Little Cumbrae

Bradshaw, H. Chalton
Burningfold Farm

Brierley, Walter H.
Bishopbarns
Bishopthorpe Paddock
Dyke Nook Lodge

Brocklesby, J.S.
Mostyn Road, Merton Park

Caroe, W.D.
Vann

Crickmay and Sons
Woodcote

Crickmer, Courtenay M.
Letchworth Garden City

Coleridge, J.D.
Hascombe Court

Crowther, G.H.
Dungarth

Daw, Clifton R.
Henley Park

Dunham, W.A.
Drayton Wood

Eggar, Miss
Camley House
Quedley

Falkner, Harold
Hall Cottage

Forbes, J.E.
Pollards Wood

Forbes and Tate
Barrington Court
Brambletye
Field House
Lainston House
Old Parsonage (The)
Pednor House

Forsyth and Maule
Monkswood

George, Sir Ernest
Busbridge Park

Guthrie, L. Rome
Caen Wood Towers
Townhill Park

Harbour, A.G.J.
Holmwood

Hewitt, Walter
Bowerbank

Hill, Oliver
Fox Steep
Marylands
Vale Wood Farm
Wilbraham House, Sloane
    Street (London)
Woodhouse Copse

Hodgson, Fred
Three Fords

Horder, Morley
Tangley Way

Howard, J.H.
Grayswood Hill

Kennedy, G.L.
Stonepitts

Leeds, Percy
Keston
Warren Hurst

Lorimer, Sir Robert
Barton Hartshorn Manor
Brackenbrough

High Barn
(Place of) Tilliefour
Whinfold

Lutyens, Sir Edwin
Amport House
Angerton Hall
Ashby St Ledger's
Ashwell Bury House
Barton St Mary
Basildon Park
Berrydown
Blagdon Hall
(Le) Bois des Moutiers
Braboeuf Estate
Buckhurst Park
Busbridge War Memorial
Castle Drogo
Chalfont Park
Chinthurst Hill
Crooksbury House
Daneshill
Deanery Garden
Dormy House (The)
Eartham House
East Haddon Hall
Esholt
Felbridge Place
Fishers Hill
Folly Farm
Fulbrook House
Gledstone Hall
Goddards
Hazelhatch
Heathcote
Heath House
Hestercombe
Heywood House
Lambay Castle
Lascombe
Lindisfarne Castle
Lindsey House, 100 Cheyne
    Walk, Chelsea (London)
Little Tangley
Manor House, Mells
Marches (The)
Marsh Court
Middlefield
Millmead
Monkton House
Munstead Corner
Munstead Wood
Nashdom
New Place, Hants
Orchards, Godalming

Oroszvar
Papillon Hall
Pasturewood House
Penheale Manor
Plumpton Place
Priory (The), Isle of Wight
Putteridge Park
Queen's Dolls' House
Red House (The),
    Charterhouse, Godalming
Red House (The), Effingham
Renishaw Hall
Ruckmans
Salutation (The)
Stanstead House
Sullingstead (now High Hascombe)
Temple Dinsley
Tigbourne Court
Viceroy's House
War Cemeteries
Warren Lodge
Winkworth Farm
Wood End
Woodside

Mawson, G.H.
Lees Court

Mountford, E.W.
Munstead Grange

Murray and Hay
Holywell Court

Newton, Ernest
Manor House (The), Upton
    Grey

Nicholson, Sir Charles
Stilemans

Norman and Burt
Chownes Mead

Norris, J.H.
Bradstone Brook
Enton Hall

Page and Holton
West Barsham

Pictor, A.J.
Marks Danes

Read and Macdonald
Burnt Axon

Round, D.G.
Highmount

Sarel, Walter
Banacle Copse
Lewtrenchard Manor
Little Haling
Little Munton
Little Wisset
Merrow Croft
Priory (The), Herts

Schultz, Robert Weir
Tylney Hall

**Scott, Mackay Hugh
    Baillie**
East Runton Hall
(Runton Old Hall)
Garden Court
Greenways, Sunningdale

Seth, Smith and Monro
Burgh House

Stevenson, John James
Munstead House

Streatfeild, Grenville
Frant Court
Hawkley Hurst

Taylor, M.
Chart Cottage

Towse, Stanley
Hydon Ridge

Turner, Thackeray
Phillips Memorial

Unsworth and Triggs
Durford Edge

**Voysey, Charles Francis
    Annesley**
New Place (Surrey)
Prior's Field

Wardrop, Hew
(Place of) Tilliefour

Willmott, Ernest
Bramleys (Orchards)
Fairhill

Notes

1. A Walk in the Garden

1. Jekyll and Hussey, *Garden Ornament*, p. 1; Jekyll and Weaver, *Gardens for Small Country Houses*, p. xlvii.
2. Jekyll and Weaver, *Gardens for Small Country Houses*, p. 36.
3. This arrangement of avenues and cross paths may have been inspired by Melbourne Hall in Derbyshire, which drew praise from Jekyll in *Some English Gardens* for its 'extremely ingenious . . . plan [which] so cleverly concealed the limits' of the small ten acre site (p. 18).
4. Jekyll, *Wood and Garden*, p. 51.
5. Jekyll and Weaver, *Gardens for Small Country Houses*, p. 43.
6. Jekyll, *Wood and Garden*, p. 151.
7. Jekyll, *Colour in the Flower Garden*, p. 14.
8. Jekyll, *Wood and Garden*, p. 70.
9. Jekyll, 'Hardy Azaleas', *The Garden*, 82 (28 December 1918), p. 478.
10. Jekyll, *Wood and Garden*, p. 48.
11. Jekyll, 'Native Ferns in the Garden IV', *Gardening Illustrated*, 53 (24 January 1931), p. 81.
12. Jekyll, *Wood and Garden*, p. 142.
13. David Pleydell-Bouverie, 'Miss Jekyll and I', *House and Garden*, June 1988, p. 111.
14. Jekyll, 'A Young Heath Garden', *Country Life*, 38 (2 October 1914), p. 464.
15. Jekyll, *Wood and Garden*, p. 146–47.
16. Jekyll, *Colour in the Flower Garden*, p. 21.
17. Charles Liddell, a British Museum librarian, supplied the name, but he probably meant Sigismonda, daughter of Tancred, King of Salerno. Tancred ordered the death of his squire after his daughter married him, but when Sigismonda learned of her father's deed, she poisoned herself; her dying wish was that she and her husband be buried in a common sepulchre. Lutyens adopted the idea of a cenotaph, or empty tomb, to honour 'The Glorious Dead'.
18. Jekyll, 'Michaelmas Daisies', *Gardening Illustrated*, 52 (29 November 1930), p. 775.
19. Jekyll, 'The Nut Walk in Spring', *Gardening Illustrated*, 49 (26 May 1928), p. 324.
20. Jekyll, *Roses for English Gardens*, p. 23.
21. Jekyll, 'Magnolias stellata and conspicua', *Gardening Illustrated*, 52 (7 June 1930), p. 381.
22. Jekyll, 'The Yew Cat', *Gardening Illustrated*, 49 (15 October 1927), p. 641.
23. Jekyll, 'Borders of Spring Flowers', *The Garden*, 68 (21 October 1905), p. 257, shows the earliest photograph of the Spring Garden.
24. Massingham, *Miss Jekyll*, p. 68.
25. Jekyll, *Wood and Garden*, p. 268.
26. Jekyll, *Colour in the Flower Garden*, 3rd edn (1914), p. 88.
27. Brenda Colvin, *Land and Landscape* (London, John Murray, 1947), p. 122.
28. T.H.D. Turner, preface to Gertrude Jekyll, *Colour Schemes for the Flower Garden* (Woodbridge, Antique Collectors' Club, 1982).
29. Jekyll, *Colour in the Flower Garden*, p. 55.
30. Aldred Scott Warthin, letter, *Bulletin of The Garden Club of America*, October 1913. Mrs Warthin was president of the Garden Club of Ann Arbor, Michigan.
31. Jekyll, *Wood and Garden*, p. 210; 'Colour in the flower border', *The Garden*, 83 (20 September 1919), p. 450.
32. Jekyll, *Colour in the Flower Garden*, p. 24.
33. Ibid., p. 54.
34. Jekyll, *Wood and Garden*, p. 210.

2. The Seed Is Sown

1. Lord Riddell, 'Miss Gertrude Jekyll', *Country Life*, 60 (17 November 1926), pp. 805–6.
2. Caroline Jekyll (1837–1928), Edward Joseph Jekyll (1839–1921), Herbert Jekyll (1846–1932), Walter Jekyll (1849–1929).
3. Jekyll, 'Some Early Reminiscences', in F. Jekyll and G.C. Taylor, *A Gardener's Testament*, p. 3.
4. Jekyll, 'My Own Young Days', *Children and Gardens*, pp. 1–2.
5. Captain Edward Jekyll (1804–1876), Julia Hammersley Jekyll (1812–1895).
6. Barbara Leigh Hunt, later Madame Bodichon (1827–1891).
7. Jacques Blumenthal (1829–1908), or 'Monsieur' as he was called, was a composer of songs and an instructor, as well as a Court pianist.
8. Fiona Halpin and Al Weil, *Hercules Brabazon Brabazon 1821–1906*, exh. cat. (London, Chris Beetles, 1989). See also C. Lewis Hind, *Hercules Brabazon Brabazon, 1821–1906, His Art and Life* (London, George Allen, 1912).
9. Jekyll, letter to Mrs Combe, 17 May 1906, and letter to Brabazon, 13 December 1889, cited in Massingham, *Miss Jekyll*, pp. 52–53, 106.
10. George Leslie, *Our River*, as cited in F. Jekyll, *Gertrude Jekyll*, p. 83.
11. Ibid., pp. 83–84.
12. On 7 May 1877 a conveyance was signed for '18 acres, 2 rods, 16 perches and one eighteenth of another perch', then in the ownership of Edward Rowe Fisher-Rowe of Thorncombe Park (Somerset House, H. M. Probate Registry, will of Mrs Julia Jekyll, 1896). Gertrude Jekyll later carried out commissions for the Fisher-Rowe family.
13. Ian Nairn and Nikolaus Pevsner, *The Buildings of England: Surrey* (London, Penguin Books, 1962), p. 322.
14. John James Stevenson (1831–1908) is credited with introducing the Queen Anne style to London (Alastair Service, *Edwardian Architecture and Its Origins*, London, Architectural Press, 1975, p. 101). The Jekyll family owned a copy of Stevenson's book *House Architecture*. Some of the commissions they might have seen include the Red House, 141 Bayswater Road (1871), 8 Palace Gate, Kensington (1873), 42–58 Pont Street, Chelsea (1877), 1–2 Lowther Gardens, Knightsbridge (1878).
15. F. Jekyll, *Gertrude Jekyll*, p. 105.
16. Jekyll, *Wood and Garden*, p. 194.
17. F. Jekyll and G.C. Taylor, *A Gardener's Testament*, p. 4.
18. John Thomas Bennett-Poe (1846–1926). Jekyll, 'John T. Bennett-Poe', *Gardening Illustrated*, 48 (19 May 1926), p. 312. See also *The Garden*, 61 (28 June 1902), p. 1.
19. William Robinson (1838–1935); Dean Samuel Reynolds Hole (1819–1904).
20. Jekyll, 'Some Plants from Algeria', *The Garden*, 19 (19 February 1881), p. 202.
21. William Goldring (1854–1919), 'Munstead, Godalming', *The Garden*, 22 (26 August 1882), p. 191.
22. 'Plan of a Garden', *The Garden*, 23 (31 March 1883), pp. 298–99.
23. Goldring, p. 192.
24. Jekyll, 'Munstead Bunch Primroses', *The Garden*, 82 (22 June 1918), p. 242.
25. Ibid., p. 191.
26. F. Jekyll, *Gertrude Jekyll*, p. 110.
27. 'Plan of a Garden', p. 299.
28. Jekyll, 'Colour in the Flower Garden', *The Garden*, 82 (25 November 1882), pp. 470–71.
29. Goldring, p. 191.

3. Picture Perfect

1. Her elder sister Caroline Eden's photographs of her garden in Venice were published in *The Garden* (19 September 1919, p. 259) and their youngest brother Walter photographed his garden in Jamaica for the same magazine. See also Frederick Eden, *A Garden in Venice* (London, Country Life; New York, Charles Scribner's Sons, 1903).
2. Cadmium bromide (Bromo) was used in the preparation of gelatin-silver bromide emulsion, and Pyrogallic acid (Pyro) was used as a developing agent.
3. 'Notes', *The Photographic Gazette. The Journal of the West Surrey Photographic Society*, ed. George H. James, vol. 1, no. 2 (March 1893), pp. 1–2.
4. Alice Pleasance Liddell (1852–1934) studied art with Ruskin when he came to Oxford in 1869. After Mary and Charles Newton had travelled to the Near East

with Jekyll in 1863, they spent the following summer with Alice's parents, Dean Henry and Mrs Liddell of Christ Church, Oxford (Anne Clark, *The Real Alice*, New York, Stein and Day, 1981, pp. 96, 120).

5. Julia Margaret Cameron (1815–1879) took up photography late in life, but soon made a name for herself with her evocative portraits of women and children.

6. F. Jekyll, *Gertrude Jekyll*, p. 115.

7. Brian Coe, *The Birth of Photography. The Story of the Formative Years 1800–1900* (London, Ash and Grant, 1976), p. 43.

8. Paul Martin, *Victorian Snapshots* (London, Country Life, 1939), pp. 12–14. Martin was a wood engraver who turned to photography in 1884.

9. Lot 499, Munstead Wood sale catalogue, Alfred Savill and Sons, 1–2 September 1948. Courtesy of Primrose Arnander.

10. The Collins camera was invented by S.D. McKellen, the father of the modern camera. 'An Improvement in Cameras for Photographic Purposes', Patent 6688, 23 April 1884, British Patent Office, Leeds, Yorkshire. Advertisements for the camera disappear after 1895, and in recent years only three Collins cameras have come up for auction (1/2 plate Collins camera, Lot 66, Christie's, 3 May 1984; 1/1 plate Collins camera, Lot 150, Christie's, 4 October 1984; and another in January 1991). Colin Harding, Kodak Curator, National Museum of Photography, Film and Television, Bradford, Yorkshire, interview with Judith B. Tankard, 1992; Michael Pritchard, Christie's South Kensington, telephone interview with Judith B. Tankard, February 1995.

11. Jekyll, *Children and Gardens*, pp. 98–99.

12. James M. Reilly, *Care and Identification of 19th-Century Photographic Prints* (Rochester, NY, Eastman Kodak Company, 1986), pp. 4–10 for description of processes.

13. Dan Johnson, Library Photographic Service, University of California, Berkeley, July 1992, letter and interview with Judith B. Tankard, 3 August 1992.

14. The six albums were donated in 1956 by American landscape architect Beatrix Farrand. She acquired them for £18 from a local bookseller shortly after the Munstead Wood sale in 1948. They were among eleven that were offered at the sale.

She used them in her Reef Point Gardens Library, in Bar Harbor, Maine, until the time of her donation. See Judith B. Tankard, *Annotated Catalog of Gertrude Jekyll's Six Photo-Albums at the College of Environmental Design Documents Collection*, 1990.

15. Mrs C.W. Earle, *More Pot-Pourri from a Surrey Garden* (London, Smith, Elder, 1901), p. 208. Mrs Earle's *Pot-Pourri* books, which had no illustrations, were less popular than Jekyll's.

16. Peter Henry Emerson (1856–1936) worked about the same time as Jekyll was learning about photography, but Henry Peach Robinson (1830–1901) was of an earlier generation.

17. 'Extreme and always progressive myopia', cited in F. Jekyll and G.C. Taylor, *A Gardener's Testament*, p. 6.

18. Jekyll, *Home and Garden*, p. 278.

19. Jekyll, 'Spring in Winter', *The Garden*, 27 (21 February 1885), p. 141.

20. 'Group of Heart-Leaved Saxifrages', *The Garden*, 27 (13 June 1885), p. 541.

21. 'Romneya Coulteri', *The Garden*, 29 (6 March 1886), p. 207.

22. See Judith B. Tankard, 'A Perennial Favourite: "The English Flower Garden",' *Hortus* 17 (Spring 1991), pp. 74–85 for detailed information on Jekyll's photographic assignment for Robinson's book.

23. Jekyll, *Wood and Garden*, p. 194.

24. *The Garden*, 28 (17 October 1885), p. 395.

25. 'Holly Stems in an Old Hedge-Row', *Wood and Garden*, p. 153.

26. 'Horse Chestnuts at Busbridge, Surrey', *The Garden*, 31 (23 April 1887), p. 367.

27. 'Scotch Firs Thrown on to Frozen Water by Snowstorm', *Wood and Garden*, p. 27. This is a rare example of a dated photograph.

28. 'The Old Path up the Hill', *Country Life*, 35 (14 February 1914), pp. 228–30.

29. E.V. Lucas, 'Miss Gertrude Jekyll', *Country Life*, 71 (14 May 1932), p. 535.

30. Lumière autochromes were exhibited for the first time at the annual exhibition of the Royal Photographic Society in 1907 (*Country Life*, 28, 3 December 1910 Supplt, p. 14).

31. Jekyll, 'A Border of Irises and Lupines', *The Garden*, 76 (21 December 1912), p. 639.

32. When a box of autochromes was discovered

at the Country Life offices some years ago, it was assumed that they were Gertrude Jekyll's; however, her habit was to keep her photographic plates in her studio at Munstead Wood, so it is unlikely that she would have left any at Country Life. The frontispiece of *Gardens for Small Country Houses* (1912) was the first of those autochromes to be published, and several more followed in books and articles, but not all. These autochromes are of great interest as they are the only known colour photographs of Jekyll's garden taken during her lifetime, and more than likely were taken by Herbert Cowley.

33. Herbert Cowley (1885–1967) trained at Swanley Horticultural College and Kew; he served as assistant editor (1910–1915), then editor (1915–1926) of *The Garden*, and editor of *Gardening Illustrated* (1923–1936). He contributed to *Country Life* and may have served as gardening editor between 1911 and 1919. See Judith B. Tankard, 'Gardening with "Country Life"', *Hortus* 30 (Summer 1994), pp. 72–86.

4. A Passion for Domestic Architecture

1. Herbert Baker, *Architecture and Personalities* (London, Country Life, 1944), p. 16.
2. Jekyll and Elgood, *Some English Gardens*, p. 8.
3. Designs and Carvings Scrapbook, Lindley Library, London; 'Little State Bedroom at Berkeley Castle, December 1868', from album of watercolours and drawings 1856–1872, William Drummond, London.
4. Priory Farm (Isle of Wight) notebook (1903), Godalming Museum.
5. The school was later built in Bramley. Annabel Freyberg, *World of Interiors*, November 1991, pp. 45–46; J.R. Palmer, Headmaster, St Catherine's School, letter to Martin A. Wood, 9 January 1992.
6. Jekyll, letter to Alice Morse Earle, 27 June 1904, cited in 'BBG's Gertrude Jekyll Letters', *The Year's Highlights: Handbook of the Brooklyn [New York] Botanic Garden*, 40 (Winter 1984), pp. 4–9.
7. John Ruskin, letter to Jekyll, cited in F. Jekyll, *Gertrude Jekyll*, pp. 112–13.
8. W. Galsworthy Davie and W. Curtis

Green, *Old Cottages and Farmhouses in Surrey* (London, B.T. Batsford, 1908) is an excellent example of this type of study.
9. Jekyll's notation on reverse of photograph, Surrey Local Studies Library, Guildford.
10. Jekyll, *Home and Garden*, p. 45.
11. Jekyll, *Old West Surrey*, p. 201.
12. Jekyll, *Home and Garden*, p. 51. The bridges were in Eashing, Elstead, Somerset, Stopham, Tilford, and Unstead.
13. Jekyll's notation on reverse of photograph, Surrey Local Studies Library, Guildford.
14. Illustration, *Old West Surrey*, p. 274.
15. Jekyll, letter to W. Robinson, 23 December 1883, Mea Allan papers, Gravetye Manor.
16. 'Loseley, Bowling Green and Summer Tea-House', *The Garden*, 30 (20 November 1886), p. 473; 'Garden-front, Loseley, Surrey', *The English Flower Garden*, 3rd edn (London, John Murray, 1889).
17. Jekyll, *Home and Garden*, pp. 15–16.
18. Edwin Lutyens (1869–1944), foreword to F. Jekyll, *Gertrude Jekyll*, p. 7.
19. Ibid.
20. *Old Cottage and Domestic Architecture in South-West Surrey* (Guildford, Billings and Sons, 1889). See Roderick Gradidge, 'Influential Origins', *Country Life*, 184 (30 August 1990), p. 93.
21. E.L. Lutyens, 'The Work of the Late Philip Webb', *Country Life*, 37 (8 May 1915), p. 618. Between 1890 and 1892 Lutyens executed renovations at nearby Little Tangley, designing a coachhouse and stable.
22. Baker, *Architecture and Personalities*, p. 16.
23. Margaret Richardson, 'List of Works by Sir Edwin Lutyens', in *Lutyens*, Arts Council exh. cat., p. 192, dates the Winkworth barn renovation as 1895.
24. Lutyens, letter to his wife, 3 February 1900, in Percy and Ridley, *Letters of Edwin Lutyens*, pp. 84–85.

5. A Sagacious Client

1. Lutyens, foreword to F. Jekyll, *Gertrude Jekyll*, pp. 8–9.
2. Peter Savage, *Lorimer and the Edinburgh Craft Designers* (Edinburgh, Paul Harris, 1980), p. 25.
3. Folder 1, CED.
4. Jekyll, *Home and Garden*, p. 18.
5. Jekyll's photograph of the newly built pergola (published in 'Formation of

Pergola with brick pillars', *The Garden*, 41, 30 January 1892, p. 107 and in Robinson, *The English Flower Garden*, 1893 edn, p. 152) confirms that it was built before the high wall or the enclosure wall around the garden yard.

6. Munstead Wood Sketch-book, 1892–93, leaf 17, RIBAD.

7. Jekyll, *Old West Surrey*, p. 43.

8. Jekyll, *Home and Garden*, p. 295.

9. See illustration in Jekyll and Weaver, *Gardens for Small Country Houses*, pp. 44–45.

10. Jekyll, *Children and Gardens*, p. 88.

11. Savage, *Lorimer*, pp. 25, 115. Lorimer may have been intrigued by the old barn, because in 1901 he had received a commission from S. Pleydell-Bouverie to build a new house (High Barn) in Hascombe that used as its centre-piece two old barns.

12. At Great Dixter, for instance, he supervised the moving of a timber-framed town hall from a nearby village to the modest farm, where he magically eased it into the setting.

13. Lutyens, letter to Jekyll, 4 March 1909, folder 1, CED.

14. William Robinson, *Mushroom Culture* (London, George Routledge, 1870).

15. Jekyll, *Children and Gardens*, p. 88; Jekyll, 'Corydalis and Welsh Poppy', *Country Life*, 44 (31 August 1918), p. 179.

16. Jekyll, *Wood and Garden*, p. 169.

17. Savage, *Lorimer*, p. 25.

18. Frederick Müntzer, the building contractor, also worked for Lutyens and was a frequent visitor to Munstead Wood. Wendy Hitchmough, *C.F.A. Voysey* (London, Phaidon, 1995), pp. 85, 88.

19. Jekyll, *Home and Garden*, pp. 13, 16, 17.

20. Lutyens, letter to his wife, 15 April 1897, cited in Percy and Ridley, *Letters of Edwin Lutyens*, pp. 42–44.

21. Jekyll, *Home and Garden*, p. 9. If the drawings did survive until Lutyens's death in 1944, they were subsequently discarded by A.S.G. Butler, who prepared the three-volume *The Lutyens Memorial: The Architecture of Sir Edwin Lutyens* (London, Country Life, 1950). Between 1950 and 1952 Butler had the awesome task of trawling through nearly 80,000 drawings which Robert Lutyens had donated to the RIBA. Inevitably, perhaps, Butler's choices

leaned heavily towards Lutyens's classical work, rather than his earlier vernacular, mock-Tudor style, which was unfashionable in the 1950s.

22. Jekyll, *Home and Garden*, pp. 18–19.

23. Lutyens, letters to his wife, 11 February 1897 and 15 April 1897, cited in Percy and Ridley, *Letters of Edwin Lutyens*, pp. 26, 42.

24. Jekyll, letter to W. Robinson, 23 December 1883, Mea Allan Papers, Gravetye Manor.

25. Martha Houghton, 'Impressions of English Gardens in 1928', *Bulletin of The Garden Club of America* (November 1928), pp. 34–38.

26. Jekyll, letter to W. Robinson, 23 December 1883, Mea Allan Papers, Gravetye Manor.

27. Jekyll, *Home and Garden*, p. 7.

28. Falkner, as cited in Massingham, *Miss Jekyll*, pp. 69–70.

29. Elisabeth Lutyens, *A Goldfish Bowl* (London, Cassell, 1972), p. 70.

30. Savage, *Lorimer*, p. 109.

31. Jekyll, letter to W. Robinson, 23 December 1883, Mea Allan Papers, Gravetye Manor.

32. At some point prior to the late 1960s, all the first floor leaded windows were altered, so that every other oak mullion was replaced by a steel mullion which created a 'rippling' effect that was never intended by Lutyens. Roderick Gradidge, letter to editor, *Country Life*, 170 (3 December 1981), p. 1971.

33. Even though Munstead Wood had many 'modern' amenities, as late as 1967 it only had two bathrooms (one upstairs and one down), and one near the larder. Michael Hanson, 'Houses by a Master Architect', *Country Life*, 142 (21 December 1967).

34. Jekyll, *Home and Garden*, p. 13.

35. Pevsner and Nairn, *Surrey*, p. 322.

36. Jekyll, *Home and Garden*, p. 10.

6. At Home

1. F. Jekyll, *Gertrude Jekyll*, p. 102.

2. Alice Morse Earle, *Old Time Gardens* (New York, Macmillan, 1901). Mrs Earle was the author of numerous books on American Colonial life; Jekyll, letters to Earle, 15 May and 27 June 1904, cited in 'BBG's Gertrude Jekyll Letters', *The Year's Highlights: Handbook of the Brooklyn* [New York] *Botanic Garden*, 40 (Winter 1984), pp. 4–9.

3. Jekyll, letter to unidentified friend,

presumably Mrs Francis King, 10 July 1908, as cited in F. Jekyll, *Gertrude Jekyll*, p. 136.

4. Jekyll, letter to unknown correspondent, 3 October (no year), collection of Judith B. Tankard; F. Jekyll, *Gertrude Jekyll*, p. 186.

5. Jakob and Margrit Zumbach were old and trusted retainers of Jacques Blumenthal. In his will Blumenthal left them a generous annuity in recognition of their 'many years of faithful and devoted service'. Her Majesty's Probate Registry, Somerset House, Will of Jacques Blumenthal, 1908.

6. In retirement Zumbach and his family ran a boarding-house on the south coast which Gertrude Jekyll may have helped him to buy. The venture was short-lived, however, and the family moved to Deal, in Kent, where Zumbach died on 8 May 1931, age 57.

7. Lutyens, letter to his wife, 8 August 1933, cited in Percy and Ridley, *Letters of Edwin Lutyens*, p. 430.

8. Frank Young (27 June 1907–15 June 1988) had also worked for Herbert Jekyll, and left Munstead Wood in 1933. William John Hawkes died 13 February 1929 (aged 76); Fred Boxall died 16 September 1930 (aged 78).

9. F. Jekyll, *Gertrude Jekyll*, p. 162.

10. Jekyll, *Children and Gardens*, p. 94.

11. Jekyll, *Home and Garden*, p. 292.

12. F. Jekyll, *Gertrude Jekyll*, p. 174; Jekyll, letter to Mrs Huttenbach, Witley, 21 June 1930, collection of Rosamund Wallinger.

13. Lutyens, letter to his wife, 9 August 1909, cited in Percy and Ridley, *Letters of Edwin Lutyens*, p. 174.

14. Jekyll, letter to James Britten, Keeper of the Department of Botany at the British Museum, as cited in Massingham, *Miss Jekyll*, p. 131.

15. F. Jekyll, *Gertrude Jekyll*, pp. 207–8; Mary Lutyens, *Edwin Lutyens by His Daughter* (London, John Murray, 1980), p. 27; 'A Revived Accomplishment', *Bulletin of The Garden Club of America* (March 1928), p. 106.

16. Marion Cran, *I Know a Garden* (London, Herbert Jenkins), p. 74.

17. Massingham, *Miss Jekyll*, p. 97.

18. Jekyll, letter to Nellie B. Allen, 22 June 1921, Guildford Museum.

19. Kate Brewster, 'Gertrude Jekyll: The Patron Saint of All Gardens', *Home Acres*, 16 (February 1929), p.117.

20. Louisa Y. King, *Bulletin of The Garden Club of America*, January 1928, p. 1.

21. Anna Gilman Hill, *Forty Years of Gardening* (New York, Frederick A. Stokes, 1938), p. 274; Professor Harshberger had visited Munstead Wood in 1923.

22. Harold Falkner, cited in Massingham, *Miss Jekyll*, p. 70.

23. F. Jekyll, *Gertrude Jekyll*, pp. 158–60.

24. Edith Wharton, *A Backward Glance* (New York, Charles Scribner's Sons, 1933), p. 250.

25. Victoria Glendinning, *Vita, the Life of V. Sackville-West* (London, George Weidenfeld and Nicolson; New York, Alfred A. Knopf, 1983), p. 85.

26. Lutyens, letter to his wife, 28 August 1917, cited in Percy and Ridley, *Letters of Edwin Lutyens*, p. 354.

27. Even after Gertrude Jekyll's death, her sister-in-law Agnes Jekyll continued to welcome Garden Club of America visitors to Munstead Wood.

28. Aldred Scott Warthin, letter cited in *Bulletin of The Garden Club of America*, October 1913.

29. Mrs Francis King, *From a New Garden* (New York, Alfred A. Knopf, 1928), pp. 96–97. Most letters are now lost, but examples are cited in F. Jekyll, *Gertrude Jekyll*, in which Mrs King is referred to as 'an American friend'.

30. Katharine Heron, letter to Martin A. Wood, 13 November 1994.

31. Lutyens, letter to his wife, 27 August 1907, cited in Percy and Ridley, *Letters of Edwin Lutyens*, p. 141.

32. Lutyens, letter to his wife, cited in Sally Festing, *Gertrude Jekyll*, p. 181.

33. F. Jekyll, *Gertrude Jekyll*, p.161.

34. Ibid., p.162.

35. Lady Jekyll, *Kitchen Essays* (London, Thomas Nelson and Sons, undated but circa 1922).

36. Lady Emily Lytton, letter to the Revd Whitwell Elwin, 22 September 1896, cited in Percy and Ridley, *Letters of Edwin Lutyens*, p.12.

37. F. Jekyll, *Gertrude Jekyll*, pp. 191, 195.

7. The Nursery and Kitchen Gardens

1. Jekyll, 'A Cypress Hedge', *Gardening Illustrated*, 46 (21 June 1924), p. 375.

2. Thomas Hunn's undated watercolour,

'Pansy Garden, Munstead Wood, Surrey', was exhibited in May 1990 at Christopher Wood Gallery, London.

3. Jekyll, as cited in F. Jekyll and G.C. Taylor, *A Gardener's Testament*, p. 100.

4. See detailed planting plan in Jekyll, *Colour in the Flower Garden*, chapter 9.

5. An advertisement for George Bunyard and Company, Maidstone, recommended these borders 'for permanence, beauty and utility' (*The Garden*, 8 February 1919).

6. Jekyll, 'Edging to Roses', *The Garden*, 75 (8 April 1911), p. 162.

7. See earlier plan in 'Borders of Annuals', *Country Life*, 29 (11 March 1911), pp. 340–41. A modified planting is discussed in 'A July flower Border', *Country Life*, 40 (5 August 1916), pp. 161–62.

8. Jekyll, 'A July Flower Border', *The Garden*, 80 (11 November 1916), p. 548.

9. Russell Page, *The Education of a Gardener* (London, Collins, 1962), p. 204.

10. 'A Colour Scheme', *The Garden*, 67 (January 1905), p. 10 was the first article on the Grey Garden. A detailed planting plan appears in *The Garden*, 85 (26 March 1921), pp. 148–49, and a description of the borders in 'The Use of Grey Foliage with Border Plants', *Country Life*, 40 (7 October 1916), p. 401.

11. Jekyll, *Colour in the Flower Garden*, p. 74.

12. Jekyll and Weaver, *Gardens for Small Country Houses*, p. 36.

13. Frank Young, letter to Martin A. Wood, 15 November 1987.

14. Notation by Jekyll, first week of February, in *The Gardener's Calendar* for 1925 (Collection of Mrs V. Kenward). Frank Young recalled digging these borders in the orchard.

15. Jekyll, *Home and Garden*, p. 236.

16. Jekyll, 'Kitchen Garden Notes', *The Garden*, 81 (7 July 1917), p. 260.

17. Jekyll, *Home and Garden*, pp. 241, 245–46.

18. Young, letter to Wood. Details of the numbers of blooms for 1928 are found in Notebook 40, Godalming Museum.

19. Ibid.

20. Jekyll, 'Some Good Gooseberries', *The Garden*, 81 (11 August 1917), p. 321.

21. Young, letter to Wood. See *Wood and Garden*, p. 216, for a detailed description of the development of the strain. There were at least six named colour forms which were the backbone of the strain: 'Lemon Rose',

a pure primrose with six wide wavy-edged petals; 'Sultan', an intense gold yellow; 'Virginie', a large vivid white with a citron eye; and three whites with different eyes.

22. Young, letter to Wood.

23. Ibid. Vilmorin also bought seed of lamb's-lettuce from Munstead.

24. Jekyll, letter to Sir Amos Nelson, 3 December 1925, Folder 195, CED; also Jekyll, letter to Sidney Barnsley, 25 August 1925, Folder 185, CED.

25. Notebook 40, Godalming Museum.

26. Amy Barnes-Brand, letter to Jekyll, 22 February 1928, folder 208, CED.

27. Jekyll, letter to Amy Barnes-Brand, 29 October 1929, Lindley Library.

8. Professional Garden Designer

1. E.V. Lucas, 'A Beautifier of England', in *English Leaves* (London, Methuen and Co., 1933), p. 168.

2. Jekyll, *Wood and Garden*, p. 4.

3. F. Jekyll, *Gertrude Jekyll*, p. 167.

4. Capt. J.W. Greenhill, Fishers, Sussex, letter to Jekyll, November 1922, folder 167, CED.

5. Walter Brierley, letter to Mrs James Sykes, 1919, folder 135, CED.

6. Mrs Marjorie Goff, letter to the editor, *Gardening Illustrated*, 3 February 1928, folder 217, CED.

7. Jekyll, 'The Reconstruction of a Nottinghamshire Garden, Bulcote Manor', *Country Life*, 52 (23 September 1922), p. 385.

8. Jekyll, letter to Mrs McCreery, Stowell Hill, Somerset, April or May 1925, folder 190, CED.

9. Jekyll, letter to Mrs Temple-Richards, Wangford Hall, Suffolk, 9 May 1928, folder 223, CED.

10. Jekyll, letter to Mrs McCreery.

11. Albert Thomas, Lutyens office, letter to Jekyll, 24 November 1925, folder 195, CED.

12. Jekyll, letter to Mrs Temple-Richards, 13 February 1929, Folder 223, CED.

13. Jekyll, 'Planting a Carriage Drive', *Country Life*, 35 (7 February 1914), p.190.

14. Mrs Temple-Richards, letter to Jekyll, no date, folder 223, CED.

15. In the master-list for the final plans, the double borders required nearly 2000 plants, including 158 Monarda, 192

London Pride, 74 *Rudbeckia speciosa*, and no fewer than 230 Bergenia.

16. Jekyll and Weaver, *Gardens for Small Country Houses*, pp. 1–3.

17. Falkner, as cited in Massingham, *Miss Jekyll*, p. 101.

18. Ibid., p. 71.

19. Lutyens papers, cited in Jane Brown, *Gardens of a Golden Afternoon*, p. 153.

20. Henry Walter Molyneux Sarel (1873–1941) worked on seven projects with Jekyll, between 1895 and 1931. The first project was Banacle Copse in Witley; it was not carried out.

21. Sidney Barnsley, letter to Jekyll, 22 July 1925, folder 185, CED.

22. Jekyll, letter to Barnsley, 4 August 1925, folder 185, CED.

23. Jekyll, letter to Barnsley, 25 August 1925, folder 185, CED.

24. E.C. Macadam, interview with Martin A. Wood, January 1993.

25. Amy Barnes-Brand (1890–1974) came from a theatrical family; her father, Brandon Thomas, wrote *Charley's Aunt*.

26. Oliver Hill (1887–1968), 'An Architect's Debt to Country Life', *Country Life*, 141 (12 January 1967), p. 70.

27. Massingham, *Miss Jekyll*, p. 98.

28. Jekyll, letter to Amy Barnes-Brand, 20 September 1926, Barnes-Brand Papers, Lindley Library, London.

29. Jekyll, letter to Amy Barnes-Brand, 6 October 1926, Lindley Library.

30. Ibid.

31. Amy Barnes-Brand, letter to Jekyll, 5 November 1926, folder 208, CED.

32. Jekyll, letter to Amy Barnes-Brand, 6 October 1926.

33. Jekyll, letter to Amy Barnes-Brand, 27 August 1927, Lindley Library.

34. Edward Hudson, letter to Jekyll, 22 October 1928, folder 222, CED.

9. An Eloquent Pen

1. 'Old West Surrey', *The Studio*, 32 (15 July 1904), p. 174.

2. *Yearbook of the Massachusetts Horticultural Society*, 1930, pp. 58–9.

3. For a listing of articles, see Margaret A. Hastings and Michael J. Tooley, 'Bibliography of Gertrude Jekyll's published works', in Michael J. Tooley, ed., *Gertrude Jekyll: Artist Gardener Craftswoman* (Witton-le-Wear, 1984), pp. 135–51.

4. G.J., 'Notes from Garden and Woodland', *The Guardian*, 1 and 22 April, 20 May, 17 June, 15 July, 5 and 26 August, 30 September, 4 November, 16 December 1896; 20 January, 17 February, 3 March 1897.

5. *Country Life*, 7 (3 February 1900), p. 133.

6. 'Wood and Garden', *Country Life*, 5 (18 March 1899), p. 332; M.C.D., 'Miss Jekyll's Book', *The Garden*, 55 (8 April 1899), p. 245.

7. Jekyll, *Wood and Garden*, pp. 171, 197.

8. Harold Falkner, as cited in Massingham, *Miss Jekyll*, p. 165.

9. Herbert Cowley, as cited in ibid., p. 145.

10. It was also translated into German, appearing as *Wald und Garten* (Leipzig, Julius Baedeter) in 1906.

11. Jekyll, letter to Mrs Cooley, 15 July (no year), Judith B. Tankard collection.

12. J.E.V., 'Home and Garden', *The Garden*, 57 (10 February 1900), pp. 111–12.

13. *Country Life*, 7 (3 February 1900), pp. 133–35. Ernest Thomas Cook (1865–1915) edited *The Garden* between 1900 and 1911, prior to leaving Britain to take up landscape gardening in Canada; he formerly worked under Shirley Hibberd at *Gardeners' Magazine* and William Robinson at *Gardening Illustrated*.

14. Edward Hudson (1854–1936). See Judith B. Tankard, 'Gardening with *Country Life*', *Hortus* 30 (Summer 1994), pp. 72–86.

15. 'Munstead House and Its Mistress', *Country Life*, 8 (8 December 1900), pp. 730–39. Although the article is unsigned, it is undoubtedly by Cook rather than John Leyland, the editor who wrote about country houses for the magazine.

16. 'Rose Dundee Rambler', *Country Life*, 8 (1 December 1900), p. 686, is the first example.

17. 'Weasel Caught in Mole-Trap', *Country Life*, 7 (17 March 1900), p. 352. Jekyll may have written the feature on Crooksbury (15 October 1900) that was the first example of Lutyens's work to appear in *Country Life* (John Cornforth, 'Lutyens and Country Life: 81 Not Out', in *Lutyens*, Arts Council exh. cat, p. 26).

18. 'The Children's Play-House', *Country Life*, 9 (1 June 1901), pp. 707–8.

19. 'Wall and Water Gardens', *Country Life*, 9 (29 June 1901), p. 845.

20. 'The Book of the Lily by an Amateur', *Country Life*, 10 (23 November 1901), p. 665.

21. 'In the Garden', *Country Life*, 10 (7 December 1901), p. 731. Her requirements were for 'silver prints, glazed, and not less than half-plate size'.

22. Jekyll, 'Colour in the Flower Garden', *The Garden*, 22 (26 August 1882), p. 177, and (25 November 1882), pp. 470–71.

23. E.A. Bowles, 'Some Good Books for an Amateur Gardener's Library', *Journal of the International Garden Club*, 1 (August 1917), pp. 149–50.

24. Louisa Y. King, 'Colour in the Flower Garden', *Bulletin of The Garden Club of America*, January 1920, pp. 28–29. Mrs Francis King (1863–1948), who was a founder of The Garden Club of America, was the author or editor of nearly a dozen books on gardening, some of which have forewords or prefaces by Gertrude Jekyll.

25. Marion Cran, *I Know a Garden* (London, Herbert Jenkins, n.d.).

26. Louise Beebe Wilder, *Adventures in a Suburban Garden* (Garden City, N.Y., Doubleday, 1931), p. 53.

27. Julia H. Cummins, *My Garden Comes of Age* (New York, Macmillan Company, 1926), pp. 33, 39–40.

28. Louise Beebe Wilder, *Colour in My Garden* (Garden City, N.Y., Doubleday, Page and Company, 1918).

29. Following his visit to Munstead Wood in September 1909, Henry Francis du Pont (1880–1969) ordered hollyhock and primula seeds. On his return in June 1912 he brought along landscape architect Marian Cruger Coffin, who was just beginning her career. Notebooks, 1909–1912, Henry Francis du Pont Winterthur Museum, Winterthur Archives, Delaware.

30. It is the only one of Jekyll's books that has not been reprinted in recent years.

31. Eve Eckstein, *George Samuel Elgood* (London, Alpine Fine Arts Collection Ltd, 1995), p. 93.

32. Jekyll and Elgood, *Some English Gardens*, p. 122.

33. The all-prevading obelisks were, in fact, a play on the origin of the name, *mons acutus*, echoed in the three sharp peaks in the family coat of arms.

34. Jekyll and Weaver, preface to second edition, *Gardens for Small Country Houses* (January 1913).

35. Lockwood de Forest, Jr., *Bulletin of The Garden Club of America*, (September 1928), p. 67.

36. Jekyll, 'Historical Notes in Garden Ornament', *Country Life*, 30 (4 and 11 November 1911), pp. 662–64, 701–2.

37. *The Studio*, 15 July 1904, p. 174.

38. Jekyll presented the original manuscript, galley sheets, and a set of mounted silver photographic prints to the Surrey Local Studies Library, Guildford, in April 1908.

39. The original designs are included in the Design and Carvings Scrapbook, Lindley Library.

40. Notation on tearsheet, 'Indoor Gardening', *The Times: Woman's Supplement* (12 November 1910), p. 67. Courtesy of Melanie Aspey, Group Records Office, News International PLC, letter to Martin A. Wood, 11 June 1992.

41. Minutes, 27 August–10 September 1919, North Shore Garden Club, Hamilton, Mass., courtesy Hilary Creighton. The articles are 'Some Aims in Gardening' (November 1919), 'A Garden of Spring Flowers' (January 1920), 'The Flower Border' (March 1920), 'Wild Gardening' (May 1920), 'Ways and Means in the Garden' (September 1920), 'The Conservatory or Winter Garden' (January 1921), and 'Grey Foliage in the Flower Garden' (November 1926).

42. 'On a memorable day she asked me to Munstead Wood . . . and her twinkling eyes seemed to enjoy my enjoyment' as she admired the house. Kate Brewster, 'Gertrude Jekyll: The Patron Saint of all Gardens', *Home Acres*, 12 (February 1929), p. 117.

43. Edwin Lutyens, 'Old English Household Life: The Genius of Miss Jekyll', *English Life*, 5, no. 5 (1925), pp. 355–58.

10. The Legacy of Munstead Wood

1. Jekyll, letter to Mrs King, 21 April 1919, cited in F. Jekyll, *Gertrude Jekyll*, pp. 179–80.

2. Lutyens, letter to his wife, cited in Festing, *Gertrude Jekyll*, p. 228.

3. The *Daily Telegraph*, 'City Comment', 14 February 1996, p. 31.

4. Minutes of the North Shore Garden Club, Beverly, Mass., courtesy of Hilary Creighton, 27 August–10 September 1919; *The Garden Club of America History 1913–1938* (New York, 1938), p. 161.

5. Her Majesty's Probate Registry, Somerset House, Will of Gertrude Jekyll, 1933. The gross value of the estate was £20,091 8s. 8d., and the net value was £14,389 11s. 6d.

6. The income yield of the London Stock Exchange in December 1932 was 4.7 per cent. Assuming a capital investment of £15,000, this would have given a gross income of £705, which would have been subject to Income Tax and Surtax. BZW Research, telephone conversation with Martin A. Wood, 7 February 1995.

7. Frank Young, letter to Martin A. Wood, 15 November 1987.

8. Logan Pearsall Smith, *Reperusals and Re-Collections* (London, Constable, 1936), pp. 58–59, 64.

9. Ibid.

10. Ibid.

11. Jekyll, letter to Ellen Willmott, cited in F. Jekyll, *Gertrude Jekyll*, p. 203.

12. Jekyll, letter to Amy Barnes-Brand, 29 March 1932, RHS Lindley Library.

13. Lutyens, letter to his wife, 4 October 1932, cited in Percy and Ridley, *Letters of Edwin Lutyens*, p. 428.

14. Lutyens, foreword to F. Jekyll, *Gertrude Jekyll*, p. 9.

15. Nellie B. Allen, letter to Mrs King, 13 July 1938, private collection, courtesy of Virginia Lopez Begg. Nellie B. Allen (1869–1961) was a graduate of the Lowthorpe School of Landscape Architecture for Women (Groton, Massachusetts), where students routinely studied the colour border plans from *Colour in the Flower Garden*. She first offered the boots to The Garden Club of America, and when they refused them to the Tate Gallery for display next to William Nicholson's painting. After the Tate refused them, they were accepted by the Guildford Museum, in 1956.

16. Beatrix Jones Farrand (1872–1959) visited Munstead Wood on 3 July 1895 (Beatrix Jones's Journal for 1895, CED); Farrand, letter to Mildred Bliss, 21 May 1948, Dumbarton Oaks Garden Library, Washington, D.C.; the papers were purchased for 'a moderate sum' (*Report of Progress 1947–1948*, Reef Point Gardens Corporation, Bar Harbor, Maine, p. 4).

17. Master copy of catalogue, Lindley Library. Dr. William T. Stearn, librarian at the time of the sale, assisted Francis Jekyll with the donation (letter to Judith B. Tankard, 19 September 1991).

18. Mildred Bliss, telegram to Farrand, September 1955, Dumbarton Oaks Library, Washington, D.C.

19. M. Laurie, *Beatrix Jones Farrand* (Dumbarton Oaks, Washington D.C., 1982), p. 18.

20. Hussey, *The Life of Sir Edwin Lutyens*, p. 23.

21. Ibid., p. 25. See also *Nature and Tradition: Arts and Crafts Architecture and Gardens in and around Guildford* (Guildford, Guildford Borough Council, 1993), p. 9. Pugin considered the humanism of the eighteenth century and the Classical architecture with which it is associated as 'sacrilegious', and advocated Gothic architecture as the only Christian and truly national style.

22. Smith, *Reperusals and Re-Collections*, p. 55.

23. Lanning Roper, 'The Future of Great Gardens', *Country Life*, 141 (1 June 1967).

24. Jekyll, 'The Idea of a Garden', *Edinburgh Review* (July 1896), as cited in F. Jekyll and G.C. Taylor, *A Gardener's Testament*, p. 38.

Select Bibliography

MANUSCRIPT SOURCES

British Architectural Library, Royal Institute of British Architects, London (cited in notes as RIBA)
— Edwin Lutyens's Munstead Wood sketch-book, 1892–93, on loan from the Misses Jane, Jessica and Suzanna Ridley
— Architectural plans by Lutyens (see Richardson)
— Correspondence between Edwin and Emily Lutyens (see Percy and Ridley)
College of Environmental Design Documents Collection, University of California, Berkeley, California. Reef Point Gardens Collection
— Six photo-albums, 1885–1914. Catalogue available (see Tankard). Catalogue and microfilm on deposit at Godalming Museum, Surrey; National Monuments Record Centre, Swindon; Surrey County Council, Kingston upon Thames
— Garden plans and client correspondence arranged in 226 folders (cited in notes as Folder 1, CED). Catalogue available. Microfilm on deposit at National Monuments Record Centre, Swindon; Frances Loeb Library, Harvard University, Cambridge, Mass.; Neilson Library, Smith College, Northampton, Mass.
Garden Club of America, New York, N.Y. Original manuscripts for six articles and correspondence
Godalming Museum, Godalming, Surrey. Forty notebooks and two sketch-books (cited in notes by number)
Lindley Library, Royal Horticultural Society, London. Designs and Carvings Scrapbook, Amy Barnes-Brand Papers.
Surrey Local Studies Library, Guildford, Surrey. Original manuscript, photographs, and press cuttings for *Old West Surrey*

PRIMARY SOURCES

Gertrude Jekyll's books and contributions to books by other authors (unless otherwise noted, all citations are taken from first editions)

Annuals and Biennials, the Best Annual and Biennial Plants and Their Uses in the Garden, London, Country Life; New York, Charles Scribner's Sons, 1916.
Children and Gardens, London, Country Life; New York, Charles Scribner's Sons, 1908; second edition, with foreword by Bernard Darwin, 1933.
'Colour in the Flower Garden', in William Robinson, *The English Flower Garden*, London, John Murray, 1883.
Colour in the Flower Garden, London, Country Life; New York, Charles Scribner's Sons, 1908; *Colour Schemes for the Flower Garden*, third edition, 1914.
Flower Decoration in the House, London, Country Life; New York, Charles Scribner's Sons, 1907.
Foreword to Mrs Francis King, *The Flower Garden Day By Day*, New York, Frederick Stokes, 1927.
'The Garden', in A.C. Benson and Sir Lawrence Weaver (eds), *The Book of the Queen's Dolls' House*, London, Methuen, 1924.
Garden Ornament, London, Country Life; New York, Charles Scribner's Sons, 1918; second edition with Christopher Hussey, 1927.
'Garden Planning','The Water Garden', and other contributions to E.T. Ellis (ed.), *Black's Gardening Dictionary*, London, Black, 1921.

Gardens for Small Country Houses, with Lawrence Weaver, London, Country Life; New York, Charles Scribner's Sons, 1912.

Home and Garden, Notes and Thoughts, Practical and Critical, of a Worker in Both, London, Longmans, Green, 1900.

Introduction to G.F. Tinley, et al., *Colour Planning of the Garden*, London, T.C. and E.C. Jack, 1929.

Lilies for English Gardens, A Guide for Amateurs, London, Country Life; New York, Charles Scribner's Sons, 1901.

Old English Household Life, Some Account of Cottage Objects and Country Folk, London, B.T. Batsford, 1925.

Old West Surrey, Some Notes and Memories, London, Longmans, Green, 1904.

'On Garden Design Generally', in Lawrence Weaver, *The House and Its Equipment*, London, Country Life, 1912.

Preface to Wilhelm Miller, *The Charm of English Gardens*, London, Hodder and Stoughton, 1911.

Preface to E.T. Cook, *Gardening for Beginners, A Handbook to the Garden*, London, Country Life; New York, Charles Scribner's Sons, 1901.

Preface to Mrs Francis King, *The Well-Considered Garden*, New York, Charles Scribner's Sons, 1915.

Roses for English Gardens, with Edward Mawley, London, Country Life; New York, Charles Scribner's Sons, 1902.

Some English Gardens, with drawings by George S. Elgood, London, Longmans, Green, 1904.

Wall and Water Gardens, London, Country Life; New York, Charles Scribner's Sons, 1901; *Wall, Water and Woodland Gardens*, eighth edition, 1933.

Wood and Garden, Notes and Thoughts, Practical and Critical, of a Working Amateur, London, Longmans, Green, 1899.

A Selection of Gertrude Jekyll's Articles

'Annuals for Sunny and Shady Places', *The Garden*, 85 (29 January 1921), 54.

'An April Garden', *Country Life*, 31 (27 April 1912), 611–12.

'The Azalea Garden', *Country Life*, 54 (25 August 1923), 258–59.

'Borders of Annuals', *Country Life*, 29 (11 March 1911), 340–41.

'Borders of Spring Flowers', *The Garden*, 68 (21 October 1905), 257.

'Borders Round a House', *Gardening Illustrated*, 46 (2 February 1924), 68.

'Bulbous Plants in Grass and Woodland', *Country Life*, 36 (3 October 1914), 465.

'A Colour Border for August', *The Garden*, 84 (3 January 1920), 5–6.

'Colour Effects in the Late Summer Border', *The Garden*, 86 (9 September 1922), 452–53.

'Colour in the Flower Border', *The Garden*, 83 (20 September 1919), 450.

'Colour in the Flower Garden, I and II', *Country Life*, 45 (22 and 29 March 1919), 308–9, 348–49.

'The Court and Its Planting', *Gardening Illustrated*, 54 (29 October 1932), 633.

'A Cypress Hedge', *Gardening Illustrated*, 46 (21 June 1924), 375.

'Flowering Shrubs in the Flower Border', *Gardening Illustrated*, 54 (1 October 1932), 596.

'A Grey Border for Late Summer', *Country Life*, 52 (9 December 1922), 777.

'The Grey Garden', *Gardening Illustrated*, 49 (26 November 1927), 738–39.

'Hardy Azaleas', *The Garden*, 82 (28 December 1918), 478–79.

'How a Little August Garden Was Made Effective with Pink and Purple Flowers', *The Garden*, 85 (26 March 1921), 148–49.

'A July Flower Border', *Country Life*, 40 (5 August 1916), 161–62.

'A June Border of Irises and Lupines, *The Garden*, 76 (21 December 1912), 639.

'Lawn and Woodland', *Gardening Illustrated*, 48 (27 March 1926), 196–97.

'Michaelmas Daisies', *The Garden*, 79 (18 September 1915), 460–61.

'Munstead Bunch Primroses', *The Garden*, 82 (22 June 1918), 242.

'Native Ferns in the Garden, I–IV', *Gardening Illustrated*, 53 (January 1931), 11, 25, 37, 61.

'A Nut Walk', *The Garden*, 80 (11 March 1916), 128.

'Plants for Shrubbery Edges', *Country Life*, 42 (13 October 1917), 356.

'A Primrose Garden', *Country Life*, 53 (28 April 1923), 568–69.

'Pyrethrum uliginosum with Michaelmas Daisies', *Gardening Illustrated*, 48 (6 November 1926), 671.

'A Quiet Entrance', *Gardening Illustrated*, 46 (20 December 1924), 782.

'Regulating the Flower Border', *The Garden*, 86 (12 August 1922), 397–98.
'Rhododendrons', *Gardening Illustrated*, 46 (5 July 1924), 400.
'A River of Daffodils', *The Garden*, 84 (15 May 1920), 247.
'September Flowers', *Country Life*, 40 (11 November 1916), 580–81.
'Spring Flowers in a Surrey Garden', *Country Life*, 39 (3 June 1916), 706–7.
'A Self-Sown Wood', *Country Life*, 31 (18 May 1912), 735–36.
'Shrubbery Edges', *Country Life*, 40 (22 July 1916), 105.
'A Solace of Garden and Woodland', *Gardening Illustrated*, 48 (14 August 1926), 487.
'Spring Planting of Summer Flower Borders', *Gardening Illustrated*, 47 (14 March 1925), 166.
'Summer Flowers Carefully Arranged', *Country Life*, 40 (9 September 1916), 303.
'The Use of Grey Foliage with Border Plants', *Country Life*, 40 (7 October 1916), 101–2.
'A Young Heath Garden', *Country Life*, 38 (2 October 1915), 464.

SECONDARY SOURCES
Books, Catalogues and Reports

Arnander, Primrose, and Tooley, Michael, eds, *Gertrude Jekyll, Essays on the Life of a Working Amateur*, Witton-le-Wear, Michaelmas Books, 1995.
Bisgrove, Richard, *The Gardens of Gertrude Jekyll*, London, Frances Lincoln; Boston, Little, Brown, 1992.
Brown, Jane, *The English Garden in Our Time from Gertrude Jekyll to Geoffrey Jellicoe*, Woodbridge, Antique Collectors' Club, 1986.
— *Gardens of a Golden Afternoon, The Story of a Partnership: Edwin Lutyens and Gertrude Jekyll*, London, Allen Lane; New York, Viking/Penguin, 1982.
— *Miss Gertrude Jekyll, Gardener*, exh. cat., London, Architectural Association, 1981.
Davey, John, ed., *Nature and Tradition, Arts and Crafts Architecture and Gardens in and around Guildford*, Guildford, Guildford Borough Council, 1993.
Davison, T. Raffles, *Modern Homes, Selected Examples of Dwelling Houses*, London, George Bell and Sons, 1909.
Drummond, William, *Gertrude Jekyll, the Early Years, Watercolours and Drawings, 1859–1872*, exh. cat., Ticehurst, Pashley Manor, 1993.
Eckstein, Eve, *George Samuel Elgood*, London, Alpine Fine Arts Collection Ltd, 1995.
Edwards, Joan, *Gertrude Jekyll Before the Boots, the Gardens and the Portrait*, Dorking, Bayford Books, 1993.
— *Gertrude Jekyll Embroiderer, Gardener and Craftswoman*, Dorking, Bayford Books, 1981.
Festing, Sally, *Gertrude Jekyll*, London and New York, Viking, 1991.
Gloag, M. R., 'A Modern Garden, Surrey', in *A Book of English Gardens*, New York, Macmillan, 1906.
Gradidge, Roderick, *Dream Houses, the Edwardian Ideal*, London, Constable; New York, George Braziller, 1980.
— *The Surrey Style*, Kingston Upon Thames, Surrey Historic Buildings Trust, 1991.
Greenoak, Francesca, ed., *Gertrude Jekyll, 1843–1932, a Celebration*, exh. cat., London, Museum of Garden History, 1993.
Gunn, Fenja, *Lost Gardens of Gertrude Jekyll*, London, Letts; New York, Macmillan, 1991.
Hobhouse, Penelope, ed., *Gertrude Jekyll on Gardening*, London, William Collins Sons/The National Trust; Boston, David Godine, 1984.
Hobhouse, Penelope, and Wood, Christopher, *Painted Gardens: English Watercolours, 1850–1914*, London, Pavilion; Boston, Little, Brown, 1988.
Hussey, Christopher, 'Designs by Sir Edwin Lutyens for Munstead Wood', in Howard Colvin and John Harris (eds), *The Country Seat: Studies in the History of the British Country House Presented to Sir John Summerson*, London, Allen Lane/Penguin, 1970.
— *The Life of Sir Edwin Lutyens*, London, Country Life; New York, Charles Scribner's Sons, 1953.
Jekyll, Francis, *Gertrude Jekyll, A Memoir*, London, Jonathan Cape; Northampton, Mass., Roundtable Books, 1934.
— and Taylor, G. C., *A Gardener's Testament, a Selection of Articles and Notes by Gertrude Jekyll*, London, Country Life; New York, Charles Scribner's Sons, 1937.
King, Stephen, *Munstead Wood, Godalming, Surrey*, guidebook, 1994.
Lawrence, Elizabeth, Introduction to *Gertrude Jekyll on Gardening*, New York, Charles Scribner's

Sons, 1964; new edition, *The Gardener's Essential Gertrude Jekyll*, London, Robinson Publishing, 1991; Boston, David Godine, 1993.

Leyland, John (ed.), 'Munstead Wood, Godalming, the Residence of Miss Jekyll', in *Gardens Old and New*, vol. 2, London, Country Life; New York, Charles Scribner's Sons, *c.* 1903.

Lutyens, Robert, *Sir Edwin Lutyens, an Appreciation in Perspective*, London, Country Life, 1942.

Lutyens, The Work of the English Architect Sir Edwin Lutyens, 1869–1944, exh. cat., London, Arts Council of Great Britain/Hayward Gallery, 1981.

Massingham, Betty, *Catalog of Drawings by Gertrude Jekyll at University of California, Berkeley*, 1978.

— *Miss Jekyll, Portrait of a Great Gardener*, London, Country Life; North Pomfret, Vt., David & Charles, 1966.

Munstead Wood, Surrey, Client Report, London, Royal Commission on the Historical Monuments of England, 1994.

Ottewill, David, *The Edwardian Garden*, New Haven and London, Yale University Press, 1989.

Percy, Clayre, and Ridley, Jane. *The Letters of Edwin Lutyens to his Wife, Lady Emily*, London, Collins, 1985.

Richardson, Margaret. *Catalogue of the Drawings Collection of the Royal Institute of British Architect: Edwin Lutyens*, Farnborough, Gregg International, 1973.

— *Sketches by Edwin Lutyens*, exh. cat., London and New York, Academy Editions, 1995.

Robinson, William, *The English Flower Garden*, London, John Murray, 1883.

— *The Wild Garden*, London, John Murray, 1870.

Savage, Peter, *Lorimer and the Edinburgh Crafts Designers*, Edinburgh, Paul Harris, 1980.

Tankard, Judith B., *Annotated Catalog of Gertrude Jekyll's Six Photo-Albums at College of Environmental Design Documents Collection, University of California, Berkeley*, 1990.

— and Van Valkenburgh, Michael R., *Gertrude Jekyll, A Vision of Garden and Wood*, London, John Murray; New York, Harry Abrams/Sagapress, 1989.

Thomas, Graham Stuart. Foreword to Gertrude Jekyll, *Colour Schemes for the Flower Garden*, Salem, N.H., Ayer, 1983.

Tipping, H. Avray, 'Munstead Wood', in *English Gardens*, London, Country Life, 1925.

Tooley, Michael, and Tooley, Rosanna. *The Gardens of Gertrude Jekyll in Northern England*, Witton-le-Wear, Michaelmas Books, 1982.

Tooley, Michael J., ed., *Gertrude Jekyll, Artist, Gardener, Craftswoman, 1843–1932*, Witton–le–Wear, Michaelmas Books, 1984.

Weaver, Lawrence, *Houses and Gardens of E.L. Lutyens*, London, Country Life; New York, Charles Scribner's Sons, 1913.

Articles

Batey, Mavis, 'Landscape with Flowers: West Surrey, the Background to Gertrude Jekyll's Art', *Garden History*, 2 (Spring 1974), 13–21.

Brown, Jane, 'Memories of Munstead Wood', *The Garden*, 112 (April 1987), 162–63.

Festing, Sally, 'Gertrude Jekyll's Garden Note Books', *Hortus* 17 (Spring 1991), 86–89.

Gunn, Fenja, 'Gertrude Jekyll's Workbook', *The Garden*, 119 (June 1994), 250–51.

MacLeod, Dawn, 'Gertrude's Happy Families', *Hortus* 27 (Spring 1993), 31–36.

'Munstead House and Its Mistress', *Country Life*, 8 (8 December 1900), 730–39.

Schnare, Susan E., and Favretti, Rudy, 'Gertrude Jekyll's American Gardens', *Garden History*, 10 (Autumn 1982), 149–67.

Stageman, Peter, 'Always Ask Questions' [Jekyll/Barnes-Brand correspondence], *The Garden*, 100 (July 1975), 311–12.

Tankard, Judith B, 'The Garden Before Munstead Wood', *Hortus* 20 (Winter 1991), 17–26.

— 'Gertrude Jekyll's American Legacy', *Pacific Horticulture*, 50 (Winter 1989), 3–12.

— 'Gertrude Jekyll, Photographer', *Country Life*, 184 (4 January 1990), 40–41.

— 'A Perennial Favourite: [Robinson's] "The English Flower Garden" ', *Hortus* 17 (Spring 1991), 74–85.

— 'A Perfect Understanding', *Country Life*, 189 (2 March 1995), 48–49.

Thomas, Graham Stuart, 'The Influence of Gertrude Jekyll on the Use of Roses in Gardens and Garden Design', *Garden History*, 5, no. 1 (Spring 1977), 53–65.

Venison, Tony, 'Jekyll in the Garden', *Country Life*, 182 (7 January 1988), 52–53.

Wood, Martin A., 'Gertrude Jekyll Remembered', *The Hardy Plant*, 11, no. 1 (Spring 1989), 9–14.

Index

Illustrations are shown in italic

Achillea ptarmica 'The Pearl', 117
Aesculus parviflora, 19, *19*
Allen, Nellie B., 101, 160, *161*
Allingham, Helen, 14, 41, 61, 125
Amelanchier lamarckii, 7
American visitors, 2, 24, 96, *97*, 101–3, 106, 126, 142
Anchusa azurea 'Opal', 113
Annuals and Biennials, 147, *147*
Aquilegia vulgaris 'Nivea' ('Munstead White'), 123
Arkwright, Revd Edwyn and Alice, *105*
Arnebia pulchra, 33
Artemisia stelleriana, 17, 19
Arts and Crafts Movement, 2, 58, 75, 86, 125, 135, 150, 165
Aster 'Climax', 14
Aster 'Coombe Fishacre', 14
Azalea Garden, 8

Baker, Herbert, 1, 57, 109, 135
Barnes-Brand, Amy, 124, 136–9, 159
Barnsley, Sidney, 135–6
Bennett Poe, Revd John Thomas, 30, *36*
Bergenia cordifolia, 47
Bergenia crassifolia, 47
Berkeley Castle, Gloucs, 57
Berry, Arthur, 98, *99*
Blumenthal, Jacques and Léonie, 27, 41, 58, *60*, 97, 126
Bodichon, Barbara, 58, 78, 104, 107, 126
Bois des Moutiers (Le), France, 73
Border of early bulbs, 20
Bowles, E.A., 148
Bowler, Thomas, 61, *62*, 76

Boxall, Fred, 98, *99*
Brabazon, Hercules, 27, 104
Bramley Park, Surrey, 25–7, *26*, 57, 68
Brierley, Walter, 127, 135
Britten, James, 157
Bulcote Manor, Nottingham, 127
Burne-Jones, Edward, 58
Busbridge Hall, Surrey, 52, *54*

Calluna vulgaris, 9
Cameron, Julia Margaret, 41
Campanula latifolia, 15
Campanula pulla, 21, 33
Cannon, Mrs, *84*, 100, *118*
Cardiocrinum giganteum, 9, *11*
Carroll, Lewis, 41
Ceanothus 'Gloire de Versailles', 24
Cenotaph of Sigismunda, 12, 14, *16*
Centranthus ruber, 138
Chalet de Sonzier, Switzerland, 27, 57–8, 97, 107
Chance, Lady, 100, 107–8
Chapman, Arthur, 70–1
Chaenomeles speciosa, *12*
Chamaecyparis lawsoniana, 111
Charles Scribner's Sons (publishers), 146, 148
Children and Gardens, 25, 42, *43*, 49, 80, 144, *145*, 154
China Aster Garden, 117
China roses. *See Rosa × odorata* 'Pallida'
Choisya ternata, 124
Clematis 'Jackmanii', 24, 116
Clematis montana, 12, *13*
Colour in the Flower Garden, 11, 22, 54–5, 110, 117, *147*, 148–9

Combend Manor, Gloucs, 135–6
Cook, E. Thomas, 143–4
Corydalis solida, 15
Corylus avellana, 15
Country Life (magazine), 127, 142, 143–7, 150, 154, 163
Country Life Library (publishers), 56, 144–7, 149–50
Cowley, Herbert, 56, 101, 102, 110, *156*
Craftwork, 28, 29, 104
Crooksbury House, Surrey, 70, 72, *73*, 76, 127
Crowninshield, Louise duPont, 155
Cynosurus cristatus, 11
Cummins, Julia, 149

Dahlia 'Crimson Beauty', 24
Dahlia 'Fire King', 24
Danaë racemosa, 15
Davidson, Mrs K.L., *36*
Delphinium × belladonna, 116, *119*
Dodgson, Charles (Lewis Carroll), 41
DuPont, Henry Francis, 149

Earle, Alice Morse, 96, *103*
Earle, Theresa, 2, 44
East Runton Hall, Norfolk, 136
Echinops ritro, 116
Eden, Caroline, 25, 137
Edgeler, Mr and Mrs James, 49, *51*
Elgood, George S., 14, 149
Embroidery commissions, 27, 46, 58
English Flower Garden, The (Robinson), 35, 46, 47–8, *48*, 148
Erica cinerea, 9
Erica tetralix, 9
Erythronium dens-canis, 15
Euphorbia characias wulfenii, 22
Exochorda racemosa, 19, *20*

Falkner, Harold, 22, 88, 102, *102*, 107, 135
Fallopia baldschuanica, 131
Farrand, Beatrix, 2, 161–3, *162*
Fern Walk 8, *10*
Festuca ovina, 10
Fisher-Rowe, Edward Rowe, 41, 60
Flower Decoration in the House, 49
Folly Farm, Berks, 107, 131, *132*
Forsythia suspensa, 17
Francoa ramosa, 12, *12*

Garden, The, 30, 31, 32, 38, 46, 47, *47*, *49*, 50, *54*, 110, 120, 141, 142, 143, 144, 147–8, 154
Garden Club of America, The, 126, 148, 153, *154*, 155
    Bulletin of the Garden Club of America, 153, *154*
Garden design career, 125–40
Garden Ornament, 150
Garden of Summer Flowers, 22
Garden yard, 117–18, *120*, *121*
Gardener's cottage, 65, 79–80, *79*, *114*
Gardener's Testament, A, 154
Gardening Illustrated, 110, 127, 141, 149, 154
Gardens for Small Country Houses, 4, 68, 110, 132, 135, 149
Gentiana acaulis, 33
George Robert White Medal of Honor, 141
Gertrude Jekyll on Gardening (Lawrence), 163
Gibbins, Arthur, 97
Gledstone Hall, Yorks, 131–2, *133*, 135
Goldring, William, 31, 33, 36
Gravetye Manor, Sussex, *31*, 65, *68*, 126
Great Tangley Manor, Surrey, 68–9, *70*, *71*, 72–3, 74, 149
Green Wood Walk, 5, 10, 33, 90, 104, *158*
Greenways, Berks, 136
Grey Garden, 80, 110, 115, 116–17, *117*
Guardian (newspaper), 142

Haberlea rhodopensis, 33
Harshberger, Prof. John, 103, *104*
Hawkes, William, 98
Heath Garden, 9–10
Heracleum mantegazzianum, 20
Hestercombe, Somerset, 131, 135
Heuchera americana, 113
Hidden Garden, 20–21, *43*
High Barn, Surrey (Lorimer), 50, 87
Hill, Anna Gilman, 103
Hill, Oliver, 136–7
Hippophaë rhamnoides, 116
Hole, Reynolds (Dean of Rochester), 30, 127
Hollyhock 'Pink Beauty', *118*
Home and Garden, 57, 85, 86, 119, 120, 143, *153*
Hoo (The), Sussex, 73

Hudson, Edward, 107, 127, 139, 143–5, *143*
Hunn, Thomas, 112
Hursley Park, Hants, 127
Hussey, Christopher, 150, 163
Hut (The), 8, 19, 65, 76, 77–8, *77*, *78*, 87, 100, 122, 160

Interior design commissions, 27, *60*
Iris and lupin borders, 113, 115
Iris pallida pallida, 113
Iris pallida 'Queen of the May', 113
Iris unguicularis, 27

Jekyll, Lady Agnes, 108, 137
Jekyll, Barbara, *145*
Jekyll, Captain Edward, 26–7, 28
Jekyll, Francis, 41, 124, 126, 154, 160–62
Jekyll, Gertrude
    birth, 25
    boots, 1, 160
    childhood, 25–6
    correspondence, 95–6, *97*, 102, *103*, 106
    death and funeral, 159–60
    dress, 1
    education, 26
    finances, 155–6
    hospitality, 102–6. *See also* Visitors
    in old age, 156–9
    professional papers, 2, 126, 161–3
    travel, 26, 27, 58, 107, *108*
    vision problems, 46, 57
Jekyll, Herbert, 25, 27, 28, 33, 40, 42, 61, 71, 79, 159
Jekyll, Julia Hammersley, 26, 60, 79, 85
Jekyll, Walter, 25, 144
Jewellery designs, 28

King, Mrs Francis, 2, 103, 106–7, *106*, 141, 148, 155
Kitchen gardens, 76, 110, 111, *111*, 112, 113, 117, 119–20

Lavender 'Munstead', 122
Lawns, creation of, 10–11
Lawrence, Elizabeth, 163
Leighton, Frederic, 27
Leslie, George, 14, 27
Leucanthemella serotina, 14
Leucanthemum maximum, 115

Leycesteria formosa, 19
Liddell, Alice, 41
Liddell, Charles, 28, 41
Liddell, Lady Victoria, 41
Lilies for English Gardens, 146–7, *146*
Lilium auratum, frontis, 7, *23*
Lilium longiflorum, 117
Lily Walk, 9, *11*
Lindisfarne Castle, Northumberland, 107
Lingard, Asa, 136
Linnaea borealis, 21
Loft (The), 80, *81*, 116–17, *116*, *117*, *118*
Longmans, Green and Company (publishers), 142, 146, 150
Lorimer, Sir Robert S., 75, 80, 87, 89, 135
Loseley House, Surrey, 67, *69*, 135
Lucas, E.V., 52
Lupin 'Munstead White', 113
Lutyens, Sir Edwin Landseer, 68–74, *72*, 101, 106, 125, 127, 128, 144, 150, 154, 163
    design work with Jekyll, 130–35, 139
    entertains Jekyll, 107
    first commission, 70, *73*
    Jekyll's influence upon, 72
    last meeting with Jekyll, 159–60
    last visit to Munstead Wood, 98
    meets Jekyll, 1, 70
    tribute to, 160
Lutyens, Lady Emily 87, 98, 107–9
Lutyens, Elisabeth, 89

McKenna, Reginald, 156
Magnolia stellata, 17
Maianthemum bifolium, 9
Main hardy flower border, 22–4, *23*
Massachusetts Horticultural Society (The), 141, 161
Massingham, Betty, 163
Michaelmas daisy borders, 14, *17*, *105*, 149
Millmead, Surrey, 73, 132, *134*
Moon, Henry G., 30, 147
More-Molyneux family, 67, 135
Morris, William, 27, 58, 102
Morris and Company, 58
Mushroom House, 80, 82, *83*, 121
Munstead House, Surrey, 28, *28*, 49, 52, 58, 60, 126
    gardens, 31–9, *32*, *34*, *35*, *36*, *37*, *38*, *39*, *45*, 76, 141, 148
    workshop, 29, *29*, 30

Munstead Wood, Surrey
    acquisition of land, 58–60
    building of house, 75–94
    critical reaction to, 75
    development of gardens, 4–24, 35, 36,
        110–17
    gardeners, 97, 98, *98*, *99*, 100, 101, *112*,
        118, 123, 156
    indoor staff, 100
    interiors, 88–93, *91*, 95–6, *96*, 100, *101*,
        102–5
    Lutyens's designs for, 76, 85–94
    plans for gardens, 6–7, 111
    sale and auction, 160

Narcissus 'Horsfieldii', 8
Narcissus 'Princeps' (*N. gayi*), 8
Nelson, Sir Amos, 131–2
Newton, Charles and Mary, 26
North Court, 11–12, *13*, 92
Nursery catalogue, 123, *123*
Nursery gardens, 110–11, *111*, 121, 122–4,
    160
Nut Walk, 12, 15, 76, 94

*Old Cottages and Domestic Architecture of
    South West Surrey* (Nevill), 71
Old English Household Life, 154
Old Poorhouse (The), Cornwall, 107
Old Wall (The), *81*, 110, 111
Old West Surrey, 45, 57, 61, 76, 80, 104,
    150–51, *151*, 152, 153, 154, 157
Olearia × haastii, 19, *19*, 111
Onosma taurica, 34
Orchard gardens, 122
Orchards, Surrey, 100, 144, 148
Ourisia coccinea, 33

Page, Russell, 2, 116, 140, 163
Pansy border, 112–13
Papaver somniferum 'Munstead Cream
    Pink', 123
Park Hatch, Surrey, 74
Peony Garden, 22, 110
Pergola, 76
Perovskia atriplicifolia, 19
Phlomis fruticosa, 19, 113
Photography career, 40–56, 61–74, 164
    autochromes, 56, 113, 116
    building studies, 61–74

cottage gardens, *48*, 49, *51*, 65
E.F.G. series, 47–8, *49*
floral studies, 48–9, *50*
landscape studies, 50–52, *53*, *54*, *55*
paraphernalia, 42–3, *43*
photo-albums, 42, *44*, 46, 61, *62*, 73–4
Pleydell-Bouverie family, 50, *159*
Plumpton Place, Sussex, 139
Ponds, Berks, 127
Pot-pourri making, 121–2
Potting Shed, 82, *84*, 118
Primrose, Munstead bunch, 122
Primrose, Munstead Red strain, 122–3
Primrose Garden, 14–15, *18*
Primula 'Golden Plover', 122
Priory Farm, Isle of Wight, 58, *59*
Punica granatum, 24

Red House (The), 58
Reef Point Gardens, Bar Harbor, Maine,
    161–2
Rhododendron (Azalea) 'Nancy Waterer', 8
Rhododendron (Azalea) 'Narcissiflora', 8
Rhododendron 'Bianchii', 6
Rhododendron luteum, 8
Rhododendron 'Multimaculatum', *5*
Rhododendron ponticum, 8, 25
Ribes sanguineum, 113
Riddell, Lord, 25
River of Daffodils, 8, *9*
Robinson, William, 2, 30, 31, *31*, 33, 35,
    46, 47–8, 65, 67, *68*, 80, 87, 90,
    126–7, 141, 148, 159
Romneya coulteri, 47, *49*
Roper, Lanning, 163
Roses
    brier, 15
    Rosa arvensis, *38*
    Rose 'The Garland', 77, *119*
    Rosa × odorata 'Pallida', 11, 12, 113
    Rose 'Zéphirine Drouhin', 121
Roses for English Gardens, 146–7
Royal Horticultural Society, 2, 28, 120, 161
Royal School of Needlework, 27
Rudbeckia 'Golden Glow', 24
Ruskin, John, 26, 27, 60, 69, 142

Sackville, Lady, 106
Sackville-West, Vita, 106
Salvia sclarea, 116

Salvia × *superba*, 116
Sambucus nigra 'Aurea', 24
Sarel, Walter, 135
Scott, M.H. Baillie, 86, 135, 136
Sedum spectabile, 113
September borders, 113, *114*, *115*, 117, *164*
Shrub borders, 17, 19, *19*
Smith, Logan Pearsall, 156–7, 159, 163
Some English Gardens, 149
South Lawn, 4–5
Spiraea prunifolia, 17
Spring Garden, 2, 20–22, *21*, 76, 110, 156
Squirrell (The), Surrey, 49, *51*
Stable-yard, 63, 80, *81*
Stachys byzantina, 113
Stevenson, John James, 28
Summer borders, 115, *116*
Sunken Rose Garden, 21

Tank Garden, *frontis.*, 12, *14*, *15*, 27, *93*, 94
Taylor, G.C., 154
Temple-Richards, Mrs, 128–30
Three Corner Garden, 22
Thunder-house, 80, *81*, 117
Tigbourne Court, Surrey, 73
Topiary cat, 19
Turner, J.M.W., 22, 27

Underwood, Thomas and William, 87
University of California at Berkeley, 42, 126, 162
Unstead Farm, Surrey, 50, 61, 63, *63*, *64*, 80

Venice, 95, 136
Veratrum nigrum, 22

Veronica prostrata, 21
Viburnum opulus, 113
Viburnum tinus, 130
Victoria Medal of Honour, 2
Vinca minor 'Gertrude Jekyll', 122
Visitors, 2, 22, 23, 24, 96, 102–6, 110, 126, 142, 157
Vitis vinifera 'Purpurea', 24
Voysey, C.F.A., 86, 87, 135

Wall and Water Gardens, 146, 153
Wangford Hall, Suffolk, 128–9, *129*, *130*, 139
Wargrave Hill, Berks, 27, 28, 29
Warthin, Aldred Scott, 106
Waterhouse, Theodore, 46
Watts, George Frederick, 27, 41
Weaver, Sir Lawrence, 68, 149–50
Webb, Philip, 58, 69, 72–3, 74
Wharton, Edith, 106, 161
Wild Garden, The (Robinson), 33
Wilder, Louise Beebe, 148–9
Willmott, Ellen, 2, 127, 147, 159
Winkworth Farm, Surrey, 74, *74*, 87
Wood and Garden, 17, 34, 42, 44, 52, 95, 110, 126, 141–2, 151
Woodhouse Copse, Surrey, 136–9, *137*, *138*, *139*
Woodland gardens, 4–11, *5*, *7*, *8*, *9*
Workshop, 90, 101–2, *101*
Writing career, 30–31, 141–54

Young, Frank, 98, *98*, 100

Zumbach, Albert, 97, *112*

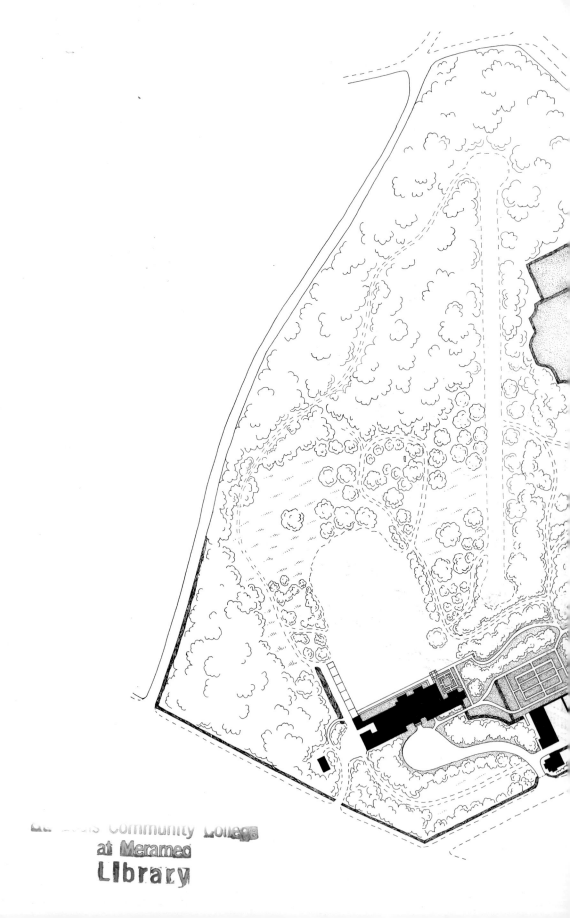